CHILTON'S
Off-Roading Guide

MICHAEL BARGO, JR.

Chilton Book Company
Radnor, Pennsylvania

Chilton's Off-Roading Guide
ISBN 0-8019-6727-9 pbk.

Library of Congress Catalog Card No. 78-7153

All photos not otherwise credited are by the author.

All opinions expressed in this book are the opinions of the author. The editors at Chilton Book Company have not tested, nor does Chilton Book Company endorse any of the products specifically mentioned. All products mentioned are typical of high quality products available from many reputable manufacturers of similar equipment, and the exclusion of any company or product is purely unintentional; it would be impossible to list them all.

SAFETY NOTICE

Proper service and repair procedures are vital to the safe, reliable operation of all motor vehicles, as well as the personal safety of those performing repairs. This book outlines procedures for servicing and repairing vehicles using safe, effective methods. The procedures contain many NOTES, CAUTIONS and WARNINGS which should be followed along with standard safety procedures to eliminate the possibility of personal injury or improper service which could damage the vehicle or compromise its safety.

It is important to note that repair procedures and techniques, tools and parts for servicing motor vehicles, as well as the skill and experience of the individual performing the work vary widely. It is not possible to anticipate all of the conceivable ways or conditions under which vehicles may be serviced, or to provide cautions as to all of the possible hazards that may result. Standard and accepted safety precautions and equipment should be used when handling toxic or flammable fluids, and safety goggles or other protection should be used during cutting, grinding, chiseling, prying, or any other process that can cause material removal or projectiles.

Some procedures require the use of tools specially designed for a specific purpose. Before substituting another tool or procedure, you must be completely satisfied that neither your personal safety, nor the performance of the vehicle will be endangered.

Contents

Acknowledgments

A great many people were responsible for giving me bits and pieces of information that went into this book. Others gave me suggestions and help in getting things done. Among the people who helped me at the very beginning were Tom Durante, a good friend who first gave me the idea of buying a military surplus four wheeler, and Jim and Helen Mattes of Little Rock, Arkansas who went to a great deal of trouble to help me buy my military Scout. Jim also helped by sharing his knowledge of auto mechanics and photography with me, and by lending me his Nikonos camera. A couple of the shots taken with that camera are in this book. Louis Hafencher and Greg Glassgen also shared their photographic knowledge and made the photos in this book better than they would have been.

The book would not have come into being without the help of my editor at Chilton, Peter Meyer, who saw an outdated, sketchy manuscript, and encouraged it to fruition.

Special thanks go to the manufacturers who supplied me with information and/or photos of their products. These are: Advance Adapters, Inc.; Avanti Research & Dev.; Blackstone Mfg. Co. Inc., RV Division; Dana Corp., Spicer Axle Division; Desert Dynamics; Detroit Automotive; Dodge Trucks; Eaton Corp., Fluid Power Div.; Helder Mfg. Inc.; Hickey Enterprises; HI-LIFT Jack Co.; Hoosier Machine Products; Husky Products Co.; International Harvester; K. C. Hilites; Koenig Iron Works, Inc.; L.O.W. Mfg. & Distr. Co.; Illumination, Inc.; Pioneer & Co.; President Electronics; Ramsey Winch; Rough Country, Inc.; Russell Industries, Inc.; Sun Electric Corp.; Superior Industries International, Inc.; Superwinch; Triple-D Ind.; Walker Mfg.; Warn Industries; and Western Products.

Many of these manufacturers also generously loaned me their products so I could test them and write about their performance in tough off-road conditions. These are: ACCEL; Advance Adapters, Inc.; Avanti Research & Dev.; Blackstone Mfg. Co. Inc., RV Div.; Burbank Spring; Cooper Industries; Duke's Wheels; Ever-Wear Products, Inc.; Gabriel shock absorbers; General Electric Co.; Goodyear Tire & Rubber; Gumout Div., Pennzoil Co.; Hickey Enterprises; HI-LIFT Jack Co.;

Husky Products Co.; K. J. Miller Corp.; Illumination, Inc.; Pioneer & Co.; President Electronics; Prestolite Battery Div., Russell Industries, Inc.; Superior/Ideal Inc.; Superwinch; Waldom Electronics; and Walker Mfg.

I would like to thank Gene Adelman of G.A.M.E. Sales in Skokie, Illinois for his advice and suggestions, his help in installing some of these products on my Scout, and for allowing me to take photos of some of the trucks outfitted for off roading by his off-road shop G.A.M.E. Sales. His opinions were always highly valued and appear throughout this book. Some of the best looking and toughest trucks in the Midwest come out of his shops at 9800 W. Greenfield Ave., West Allis, Wisconsin, and 3724 W. Oakton in Skokie, Illinois, 60076.

Thanks also go to John Teliszczak for posing for the cover, Frank Kania for allowing me to photograph his tools, Howard White, Glenbrook Ford, Inc., for allowing me to photograph Ford trucks, Michael Cook of British Leyland Motors for the information and quote on the Land Rover, and the publishers of *FOUR WHEELER* magazine and *PICKUP, VAN, & 4WD* for generously allowing me to reprint material and photos.

My greatest appreciation goes to my wife Candy. Her constant love, interest, encouragement, and support, more than anything else, made this book possible.

1

INTRODUCTION

Off-Road Driving

This book is a guide to the sport of off-road driving; taking your four wheeler out on a vacation to the mountains, woods, lakes, camping, or just for a weekend of mud running at the old strip mine. Have you ever wanted to see where that old railroad right of way leads? Drive down it and find out! Four wheeling involves elements of risk, equipment, and know-how. But what equipment do you really need? What spare parts, if any, are needed for a weekend in the woods? If you get stuck, how do you get out if you don't own a winch? Then again, when do you need a winch?

This book was written to answer all these questions and guide you through the demands of four wheeling with a minimum of risk and expense, and a maximum of fun and freedom.

If you're thinking of buying a four wheeler, you can learn about the advantages of four-wheel drive (4WD), how it improves traction and gives you greater control and off-road capability. You'll also find out if you really need a four wheeler for the kind of driving you expect to encounter. We'll discuss the various makes and body styles of available four wheelers. Picking the one you like will be easier after you read the sections on engines, transmissions, and differentials. Here you'll find the engine options available for the four wheeler of your choice with a discussion of what kind of performance you can expect to get out of each engine.

Which transmission works best off the road? You'll find a rundown of the transmissions and how they'll perform for you. Most four wheelers now use automatic and full-time 4WD. How does full time work? There is a discussion of the two kinds of full-time 4WD and the advantages and disadvantages of each kind. Next come the manual two-speed transfer case systems with locking hubs and the advantages and disadvantages they offer. You'll know what kind of axle ratio is best for you after reading about the available ratios and their pros and cons.

A discussion of the available four wheelers wouldn't be complete without mentioning the suspension packages available. You can find out what kind of suspension is best suited to your needs. Maybe you'll be better off buying an off-road suspension kit for the rig and type of driving you're considering.

This Jeep seems to stop and go in bursts as it flies through the mud

One of the most important decisions you will make in buying your vehicle is what size of tires and wheels you'll need. This can make an even bigger difference than the kind of engine and transmission you choose. You'll find out which tread patterns are best for an off-road tire and which to stay away from. The right tires will save you money and a lot of trouble by not getting stuck as often.

After you buy the four wheeler of your choice, you'll want to outfit it for your particular off-road needs. Even if you've owned your four wheeler for a long time you'll find the accessories chapter useful.

There are so many brands of major accessories and so many small items you can buy that you could spend thousands of dollars on accessories hoping to outfit your vehicle for the kind of job you want it to do, and end up with a lot of useless junk. You need to know what is good enough to do the job. This is particularly true of tires. Too many off-road enthusiasts buy huge tires only to regret it because they sometimes don't perform any better than a medium sized tire and cause all kinds of maintenance problems. Good advice on accessories is hard to find because the ads in off-road magazines want to sell big expensive items for a maximum profit and the car dealer wants to tack on his installation charge, which gives him a handsome profit. With everybody looking to make a buck, you really don't know where to turn. Many drivers end up relying on hearsay and buy what everybody else has. I don't pretend to know everything about all the possible accessories you can have, but I can tell you what has worked for me and others and I can tell you what you need and don't need for most kinds of off-road driving. You also need a fair idea of what's on the market. Your local off-road shop might not offer a handy accessory because he can't get a good price from the distributor. Then your best bet might be ordering through the mail. To top it all off, when you get a big item home you might find out that you don't have the tools or the know-how to install it. I'll forewarn you about the accessories that are very difficult to install yourself.

The first accessory is tires. All of my four wheeling has been in mud, sand, sandy hills, muddy hills, bogs, and riverbanks. Similar terrain can be found throughout the country, so we'll talk about the tires that work best on mud and sand. It seems that all the information we get on tires is from people who drive in Baja, California and nowhere else.

You'll get tips on jacking up the suspension and putting some armor under your rig's body to protect it from rocks and tree stumps. You'll also get the rundown on what lights work well and how much lighting you really need for off roading. If you want to get a little more power out of your engine without swapping, you can find out what works best with a minimum of expense and engine rebuilding. You'll get better gas mileage too. For those who want to get their hands into the gearbox, there are transmission and transfer case modifications that will give you a little more torque at the low speed range and stretch out the mileage at the high speed range.

Everybody gets stuck but nobody wants to put out $500.00 for a winch. You can put together an unstucking kit that'll cost much less, and get you out of almost every possible situation. There will always be situations where you will need a winch, and some where even a winch won't do the trick. We'll talk about these too.

Once you've bought your four wheeler you'll want to head for the nearest off-road trail, or possibly take off for a week or two on an extended trip. No matter how long you intend to stay out you'll find the chapter on off-road preparations extremely helpful. There's a checklist of things to look over before going on an outing; checking engine timing, U-joint tightness, oil in the transfer case, etc. For extensive winter driving, mountain climbing, or hunting you'll find the winter operations section essential.

Two Chevys, a Blazer and a pickup, duel it out at a drag race. A lot of 4WD clubs sponsor activities like this, open to all comers

A well-planned, off-road venture includes a good stock of spare parts. Breaking a simple item like a fan belt can be a real nightmare when it happens 50 miles from nowhere. Although you won't have to go so far as to carry spare leaf springs, other leaf spring components are a good idea, from center bolts to U-bolts, as you'll see. All spare parts, however, are useless without the tools needed to install them. In the tools section you'll find a complete list of necessary tools. That tool you wouldn't have thought of is listed there. For those situations when you get stuck you'll find a list of emergency equipment, from a jack to a fire extinguisher. Here again, a little forethought and planning can save a lot of grief and ten times the expense and trouble later.

Keeping you and your rig clean and comfortable during trips is the object of the section on household items. Here you'll be reminded of the little goodies that become dire necessities when you're away from civilization: mosquito repellent, no-pest strip, a raincoat, and of course the most essential item of all, an ice chest. These and the other little things listed make roughing it bearable.

One of the biggest problems four wheelers have is finding a place to go four wheeling. You want to be legal and not disturb anybody, so finding a vacant area that's large enough and a challenge is a real problem. Most four wheel clubs have their own favorite spots, and they're not anxious to tell everybody about them. These areas are so hard to find that you have to know where they are. We'll talk about some of the areas where off-road driving is legal, and about how to be careful when driving on private land when you're not sure if you're legal or not. After discussing navigation and how to use topographic maps, we can go through the various types of off-road hazards and how to drive through them. Mud, snow, sand, and deep water all present their own special problems. For example, a tire that's good on mud usually won't do well on sand. A tire that does well on sand will have to sacrifice something while performing in the mud. Similarly, snow and deep water present different problems. It's as important to keep your engine running in deep water as it is to pull yourself out.

Some 4WD club members on an outing, stopping to lock in the hubs before attempting the heavy stuff

This rig is used for pulling competition. A steel skid plate is bolted under the front like a sled. As the four wheeler pulls, the water-filled tank at the back advances toward the four front tanks, also water-filled. The friction increases and the sled becomes harder to pull. The four wheeler to pull it the farthest wins the competition

Having 4WD capability on your family station wagon makes for safer everyday driving. Here a Chevy Suburban drives through a heavy snowstorm

You can get stuck in many different ways. Some are more difficult to get out of than others, but the section on driving techniques will help you avoid trouble and get out of trouble, when you do get stuck. Just don't bury your rig up to the windows in a bog, the worst type of situation imaginable or get stuck so badly that you'll need a bulldozer to get out.

Four wheeling can be as exciting as competition hill climbing, or as serene as a sunset on a secluded lake. That's the great thing about off roading, you can do with it what you like. Go camping, hunting, mountain climbing, cave exploring, hiking, bicycle riding, or whatever, and have the rig that took you miles off the road and deep into the woods get you back out again to stop for a beer, a hot shower, and a comfortable bed in a motel. There's no need to make long arduous expeditions that take weeks. Instead of hiking to your favorite cliff to practice your climbing, drive there; your day will be longer and your climbing more enjoyable.

Whatever your recreation, automotive, or rough-country driving needs, your four wheeler can handle them. This book will tell you how.

2

Your Off-Road Vehicle

THE ADVANTAGES OF FOUR-WHEEL DRIVE

"What's so great about a four wheeler?" you might ask. "Why not just use my car or pickup or station wagon for off-road driving? Four wheelers don't look different to me." They may not look different but there are many reasons why four wheelers have the off-road capability they have.

First most four wheelers are light trucks. Like trucks, they have a stronger body, frame, and suspension. Most four wheelers have a leaf spring front suspension with the exception of the Ford Bronco, F-100 and F-150 and Subaru. These have front coil springs and Subaru has independent suspension. Coil springs produce a softer ride than the stiffer leaf spring setup, but the simplicity and stiffness of the leaf spring arrangement makes it more popular. The rear end is also sturdier and has a wide assortment of spring options, from heavy duty to trailer towing combinations. The body-to-frame mountings are larger and stronger due to the greater stress on these components in off-road situations.

Few people realize the pounding a vehicle takes going over a gravel or dirt road for extended periods of time. I once drove over 200 miles of gravel roads in Ontario, Canada at a speed of 40 miles an hour. Although well maintained, the road surface was a series of ridges crossing at right angles, giving the road a texture like corduroy. The front and rear wheels would hit a ridge, rebound and before they could recover, hit another ridge. The vehicle constantly vibrated like one of those hip-belt weight reducers. I didn't lose any weight, but my shocks were totalled, the leaf springs got a good workout, and one of the U-joints had to be replaced soon afterward. If an average car were taken out on this kind of road, the spot welds would loosen and the frame would split and fall apart after a few years. And there's nothing you can really do about it. The only non-truck vehicles that could survive this would be something like the Volkswagen Bus or Beetle, which because of their long travel suspensions would do quite well. That's why you sometimes travel for a hundred miles down a gravel road and see a Volkswagen Bus doing fine right next to you.

Another advantage four wheelers share with other trucks is that they have higher ground clearance. The differential housing is further from the ground—at least 8 inches. They also have less body overhang at the front and rear wheels to prevent jamming the front of the vehicle into a hill (this is called a high angle of approach), or scraping the rear end over bumps (angle of departure). The wheel wells are larger and give the tires more room. This allows you to put on much larger tires than you normally could fit on a car (for driving on soft mud, snow, and sand), and doesn't collect as much mud and road debris. At the rear the gas tank is tucked up out of the way of rocks and tree stumps, and skid plates protecting the tank are available on most makes. If necessary, an aftermarket skid plate can be bought to fit your vehicle. At the front end, you don't have headlights close to the sides where they'll get whacked by tree branches and flying rocks. The bumpers, front and rear, are more compact and not the fancy wraparound types that wouldn't last long off the road. Even the short bumpers found on four wheelers get bent back and torn off frequently. The only bumpers really suited for off roading are the kind found on military vehicles, which are made for function, not looks, and are too thick and short to get bent by tree branches.

Four wheelers have many showroom options specifically designed for off-road use that simply aren't available for other cars. Examples are such things as winches, snow plows, tires with off-road tread designs, swing-away spare tire and gas can carriers for the rear of the vehicle, roll bars and CB radios. Skid plates, tow hooks, auxiliary lights, auxiliary gas tanks, larger clutches and heavy-duty alternator and battery systems are some of the other options four wheelers offer. If you're handy at sheet metal fabricating and welding you can add many of these modifications yourself. The body and frame designs of 4WD vehicles allow room on the front and rear of the frame to add heavy bumpers, skid plates, and tow hooks.

Some of the best fun you can have in four wheeling is driving down old overgrown trails. Here's one I found in northern Minnesota

To round off the modification of your off roader, many suppliers offer custom-made off-road equipment. These aftermarket sources have well engineered accessories that are made for your vehicle to insure a perfect fit. These can, in some cases, be adapted to street cars with a lot of work, but are intended for use with the specific vehicle for which they were designed.

Better Traction

The most significant and obvious advantage that a four wheeler has in off-road situations, even above and beyond the characteristics they share with other trucks, is their four-wheel drive traction capability. With 4WD you can easily handle steep hills, heavy snow, deep mud and swampy areas with confidence. The reason is simple: you've got four wheels pushing and pulling, using all the torque of the engine to keep you moving. And with some of the full-time systems available now the transfer case even distributes engine torque to the axle with the best traction.

The easiest way to grasp the tremendous tractive advantage of 4WD is in mathematical terms. A helpful formula can be found in E. Christopher Cone's *Automotive Operation and Maintenance*, section 3.04. Cone explains that any surface over which a vehicle is traveling has a "rolling resistance." In other words, the surface of any road makes it hard for a vehicle to roll over it easily. He defines rolling resistance as "a measure of the retarding effect of a road surface to forward movement of a vehicle." To compute it he developed the following formula:

$$\frac{\text{(gross weight of vehicle, lb.)} \times \text{(road factor)}}{1,000} = \text{rolling resistance in lb.}$$

These values are used as the "road factor":

good concrete road	15
2 inches of snow	25
4 inches of snow	37
smooth dirt road	25
sandy dirt road	37
mud, varying with depth	35–150
soft sand	60–150

Here's what this formula means in actual practice. If your medium-sized car weighs 4,000 pounds (a good average although many cars weigh more), then on a concrete road with a road factor of 15 your car has to overcome

$$\frac{4,000 \times 15}{1,000},$$

or 60 pounds of road resistance. You know that with a little effort you can push your car to a trotting pace on a level, smooth, concrete road with this road factor. Now, if we go onto a sandy dirt road with a road factor of 37, the road resistance increases dramatically to 148 pounds. You wouldn't have any trouble going over this kind of road providing that it was dry and not too steep. This is the road factor and rolling resistance most people encounter when they drive to their summer cottage on the lake or favorite fishing spot on the river. This road factor is approaching the working limit of most cars.

Let's make things a little tougher and increase the road factor again. If you drive over medium-soft sand (the kind found on beaches) the road factor increases to 100 and the final road resistance will be 400 pounds. With wide tires you might be able to handle this sand, but it's not likely. And this is on level ground. You can imagine how the road resistance increases when going up a mud hill or a sand dune. It doubles with an angle of one-in-two, triples with one-in-three, and so on.

More pulling power on the wheels is needed to overcome increased rolling resistance. The wheels must turn with more torque, and this torque must not be wasted on slipping wheels—it must be applied with greater traction. Four-wheel drive, the unique attribute of four wheelers, accomplishes this. It does so in two ways: by distributing pulling power and contact with the road surface over all four wheels via two driveshafts, one for the rear and one for the front axle; and by giving you more gear reduction through a 2:1 transfer case gear ratio. The transfer case is connected to the transmission and transmits the rotational power of the engine to the driveshafts of the front and rear axles. In effect, the transfer case is a second transmission. It enables you to gear down to one half the wheel speed or twice the engine rpm, however you want to look at it. Increased engine rpm means increased torque, especially in off-road situations that demand slow speeds and high torque to the wheels to avoid slipping in the mud.

To see how this works, let's look at an average car's gear ratios and compare them to a four wheeler's. In an average car the first gear would be 3.0:1 and the rear axle ratio would be something like 3.5:1, resulting in a total gear reduction of 10.5:1. This means that every time the engine turns 10.5 revolutions the rear wheels turn once. If we put these same gear ratios on a four wheeler, the low range of the transfer case would give us an additional mechanical advantage of 2:1, for a net gear reduction of 21:1, twice that of a normal car. The actual ratios are even lower because first gear on four wheelers is usually lower than 3.00:1. Consequently, most four wheelers have gear reductions of between 25:1 and 30:1 in low gear. This means, of course, that the engine has to turn 25 to 30 times for the rear and front wheels to turn once. As you'll see later in the engine section, this enables the engine to develop its full torque potential, giving additional foot-pounds of torque for turning the wheels in demanding situations like hill climbing.

TWO DRIVESHAFTS ARE BETTER THAN ONE

Let's get back to the advantages of having two driveshafts. Even if the transfer case did not have an extra gear reduction of 2:1, the 4WD factor would make a great difference. In a normal car the front tires drag and skid on turns because they are being pushed against whatever road resistance the tires have to overcome. They are not rolling on their own. Consequently they pose an additional load on the rolling capability of the vehicle. This is particularly evident in the winter when you drive on snow. The front wheels are pushed against the snow and tend to plow it, creating a little mound in front of the tires. It is all the more difficult, then, for the rear wheels to get a grip and push the front tires over the obstacle. The drag factor is very real. Those who own front-wheel drive vehicles are amazed at how good the traction is in slippery or winter conditions. The front wheels are themselves pulling the vehicle along, not creating a drag. The net result is that the vehicle rolls more easily. The same effect occurs when you back up over snow.

Unlike a front-wheel drive vehicle, a four wheeler doesn't give you any feeling of being pulled forward by the front axle. If anything, you'll feel pushed along by all four wheels. This is because the front and rear axles are both pushing and pulling the vehicle forward; you don't have either one trying to take over the full load. All four wheels move as one synchronous unit. With some of the new full-time 4WD systems, each axle, as well as each wheel, is given torque when the other is slipping for an even smoother and more controlled ride. The net result of 4WD is rolling smoothly over rocks, through mud and up hills. It seems to crawl over steep hills and through ditches like a tank, because all four wheels have good traction and contact with the road surface. The extra gear reduction and two driving axles with turning power on all four wheels makes a four wheeler fully capable of handling steep grades, deep mud and heavy towing loads.

Even when traveling over rough off-road conditions you feel better because you know that the 4WD capability is operating. This is extremely important on slick roads in the rain or snow. The better grip of 4WD gives you better directional stability, particularly on turns. The greater feeling of security and control is not just a feeling, it's there, particularly on trips into strange territory when you don't know the funny turns and curves that can throw you off the pavement in the rain.

Once, while visiting some relatives in a rural area, I was run off the road by a drunk. This guy was weaving from shoulder to shoulder at 50 miles per hour. I slowed down and had to duck into a ditch or I would have been killed. I ended up front end down in a drainage ditch filled with 1½ feet of mud and water. The ditch was the kind that lies between the shoulder of the road and a cornfield, typical of those found where there are farms. Not a very hospitable situation, but better than being killed by a head-on collision. Sizing up the situation I knew that if I touched the gas too hard the rear wheels would spin and I'd dig myself into the mud. If I did that, I'd have to get out and jack the vehicle onto solid ground again; there were no trees or telephone poles around to tie a cable onto. Either that or I'd have to call a tow truck and be out 30 or 40 bucks. I put the transfer case in low 4WD and backed out as easily as if I backed out of a driveway. Then I put the transfer case in normal high and drove off as if nothing had happened. Only the mud on my front tires gave away the fact that I had been in a ditch.

My handling and evaluation of the situation I was in reflects another advantage of four wheeling; it gives you more road "savvy" than driving a regular car. In short, having been through everything off the road you're ready for any and every type of situation. Knowing your four wheeler can handle tricky situations also gives you more courage and confidence. I'd feel a little more confident going into a ditch or a muddy field with a light truck than with a small car.

DIFFERENT KINDS OF OFF ROADING

What do I mean by rough or rugged off roading? On the other hand, what does mild off roading or following an established trail mean? What may be tricky for one off roader might be easy for another. I've found this varies from club to club and even driver to driver. Some drivers beat their rigs, denting the rocker panels on tree stumps, fallen logs, and rocks. They occasionally bend a front driveshaft or break a leaf spring. This is what I call rugged off roading; if you get stuck it'll take you hours even with a winch to get out. You need a good roll bar and a seat belt or shoulder harness (racing type) to keep from conking your head on the roof (and even then you'll conk your head) and getting thrown out of your vehicle. You really push your vehicle and don't care. (Some people might call this attempted suicide.) You'll get a good idea of what I mean by roughing it from some of the photos.

On the other hand, some drivers use their four wheelers when 4WD really isn't necessary. They follow dirt roads and cut across grass or fields to get to a lake. This can be done with a 2WD pickup, Blazer, or Scout. No one can tell you how to drive or what kind of driving you should prefer. I just want you to get a perspective on what I mean when I talk about the different kinds of roughing it off the road. This will help you get an idea of what kind of off roading you intend to do and help you pick out the vehicle to suit your needs.

A LOOK AT THE FOUR WHEELERS ON THE MARKET

Choosing a four wheeler to suit your taste is a little different from choosing a car. Most cars function essentially the same way. The only real decision you have is what style, color and engine size you want. In these days of exorbitant gas and insurance costs more people are picking cars with smaller engines and less body weight, sacrificing luxury and appearance.

With a four wheeler, your decision to buy a particular model depends not so much on how it looks as on how you intend to use it. Four wheelers used to be pretty spartan in appearance; steel dashboards, vinyl seats in dull colors, little or no body chrome, no interior styling on the doors or roof. Now they are more in line with cars as far as luxury goes. You can get nice denim or fabric seats in many colors matching the exterior color of your choice. Radios, air conditioning, good interior ventilation, floor carpeting, and an attractively styled instrument panel are available. All these goodies were unheard of until about 1970, when the more stylish models came out and four wheeling started to become popular. The automakers have come a long way toward making four wheelers compatible with the other vehicles on the market. Your decision to buy a particular model now depends on the size of the vehicle, its performance in various off-road conditions, the availability of aftermarket accessories you may want, and the engine and transmission options available.

I've found, as I'm sure you have, that salesmen in the showroom know nothing about how their vehicles perform off the road. They're interested in selling the units in stock and that's all. Here you'll get the straight information based on how they actually perform, rather than a sales pitch.

There are five types of 4WD vehicles, based on their wheelbase length—short wheelbase 4x4s, longer wheelbase 4x4s, station wagons, mini-pickups, and pickups. Which one you pick depends on how you like the body style, if there's room in the vehicle for your use, and how it performs off the road. Last but not least is how the purchase fits your pocketbook. Let me tell you up front that four wheelers are not as cheap as they look. You'll have to spend at least $5,000 on a basic model, $7,000 to $8,000 if you want a V8 and air conditioning, and you could spend as much as $10,000 or $11,000 on a fully loaded Chevy Blazer or International Scout with a diesel engine. The only inexpensive models are the 2WD mini-pickups, and they are limited in rough off-road performance. The real off roaders are expensive.

Short Wheelbase 4x4s

Although the first production four wheel drive vehicle ever made was the FWD Scout Car, accepted by the United States Army in 1911, the most famous is the Jeep®. At the outset of World War II the army asked the automakers to submit designs and bids for a small 4WD vehicle that would be easy to drive, capable of carrying a good payload (500 lb.), run on gasoline, and be able to do just about anything in any terrain. It was to be used for just about everything from carrying stretchers to hauling supplies and towing. The army gave it the designation "general purpose" vehicle and in their usual way of doing things shortened the name to "G.P." Willys Overland submitted the most acceptable design and built most Jeeps used by the army in World War II, about 24,000, of which a few hundred still exist. The small vehicle soon acquired fame as a do-everything machine. Some clever G.I., his name forever lost to history, got tired of calling it the official designation G.P. and coined the word "Jeep" after his favorite cartoon character, the Jeep of Popeye fame. The name seemed to fit the small, odd-looking vehicle and has stuck ever since. Willys Overland sold out to Kaiser, which became Kaiser Jeep Corporation in the early fifties. Ford Motor Co. won contracts to build Jeeps for the army and still does. So do a lot of other people. Jeeps are now built under license in 27 countries and are extremely popular worldwide. For example, Mitsubishi of Japan builds an exact duplicate of the CJ-3B. Later, AMC bought out Kaiser Jeep and we now have the Jeep Corporation, a division of American Motors Corporation. Jeeps are now more popular than ever and will probably always be going strong.

The new AMC Jeeps® have a two-letter designation, "CJ." This means "Civilian Jeep" and distinguishes these from the army versions. Jeeps are still made for the army, but they differ from the old army Jeeps, the M38A1 model, and were designed by civilian designers. The ones used by the army now, the model M-151A(2), have independent suspension with coil springs on all four wheels. The M-151A was discontinued after it displayed a disturbing tendency to roll over at speeds of 50mph or more.

Army Jeeps, the vehicles that brought four-wheel drive into the popularity it enjoys today

The argument always pops up between ex-GIs and CJ-5 or CJ-7 owners over which is better, the civilian or the military version. The civilian Jeeps have more powerful engines, their Quadra-Trac® system is excellent, they have better heaters, ventilation, and weather protection (the army Jeeps leak rain), better upholstery, nicer paint jobs and interiors. The army Jeeps have four-bangers with less power, lower gearing for off-road use, tougher bodies of thicker gauge sheet metal, tougher instrument panel gauges, stiffer suspensions, and dull olive drab paint jobs and interiors. But I still like the military version better because of its toughness and simplicity. It won't accelerate as fast as the CJs, but with good tires it will go anywhere reliably. And if something does break down, it will be simpler to repair than taking off air conditioning, power steering, etc. My personal vehicle is a 1966 International Scout 800 military version. A new one would be nice but I would rather own both than get rid of the older Scout.

THE CJ-5 AND CJ-7

The Jeep has a lot to offer if you're interested in real off roading. It's small, lightweight, has all the off-road accessories available for it including a lot of adapters for different engines or transmissions, and performs well off the road with its short wheelbase (83½ inches). The CJ-5 has this short wheelbase, while the CJ-7 is somewhat longer (93½ inches) to accommodate the Jeep Quadra-Trac full-time 4WD system. The Jeep is the only short wheelbase four wheeler with full-time 4WD available. More about the Quadra-Trac full-time 4WD system later.

Here are the full specifications on the CJ-5 and CJ-7:

Jeep CJ-5

    Turning radius: 34.1 feet
    Engines: 232-6 1 bbl. (standard) electronic ignition
              258-6 1 bbl. (optional) electronic ignition
              304-8 2 bbl. (optional) electronic ignition
    Transmission: three-speed manual synchromesh (standard)
                    four-speed manual synchromesh (optional)
    Transfer case: two-speed Dana 20, 1:1 high range, 2:1 low

Jeep CJ-7

    Turning radius: 38 feet
    Engines: same as CJ-5
    Transmission: three-speed manual synchromesh (standard)
                    four-speed manual synchromesh (optional)
                    three-speed automatic with Quadra-Trac (optional)
    Transfer case: two-speed Dana 20 with manual
                  Quadra-Trac 1:1 high range, 2.57:1 low range

Other accessories: Skid plates are standard on both the CJ-5 and CJ-7. Both have power steering available, a big help especially with the full-time system; power front disc brakes, also a very good idea; and a CB radio. Snow plows and a Warn or Ramsey winch are also available. Both are good winches.

Good standard equipment for off-roading and a good heating and ventilating system characterize the 1978 Toyota Land Cruiser, the best buy in its price range

A 1978 CJ-7 set up by G.A.M.E. Sales of Skokie, IL. This will give you some idea of a few of the things you can add to your 4WD vehicle

The main difference between the CJ-5 and CJ-7 is that the CJ-7 has an automatic transmission with full-time 4WD available. It has more room inside, although both are small enough for tight off-roading situations. My opinion of the Jeep is that it is one of the best for rugged off-road performance.

TOYOTA LAND CRUISER

Along with the Jeep in the short wheelbase group is the Toyota Land Cruiser, a Japanese version of the Jeep. The Land Cruiser was probably developed for the Japanese World War II effort. Land Cruisers have been around since the early fifties and have been spotted in such improbable places as Japanese horror movies where scientists were using them to chase down the inevitable monster.

The Land Cruiser is a very intelligently designed off-road vehicle, built more for the person who lives out in the sticks and must have a 4WD, than for the weekend off roader who wants power and good looks. It is rugged inside and out, has a good rear heater (a fine idea), and is over all one of the best constructed four wheelers. It is a serious vehicle for the serious off roader who wants a dependable machine. They are very popular in the Middle East and Africa, but this is misleading because other four wheelers are on the Arab boycott list. It has a 90-inch wheelbase, which puts it in the short wheelbase group with the Jeeps and is 152.4 inches long.

The Land Cruiser has good off-road gearing. The 4.11 axle ratio takes care of this. Combined with a four-speed manual transmission, they are a tough, versatile pair, especially in heavy mud and up steep hills. The only drawback of a Land Cruiser is the engine size. It has a six-cylinder 258 available. That's it; no V8 options. This is a disappointment for the man who wants some power from his off roader. If you want the Land Cruiser's toughness and built-in off-road accessories, but a different engine, the next chapter will discuss how to put in the engine of your choice. This is done a great deal.

Here's the rest of the information on the Land Cruiser:

Transmission: four-speed synchromesh (close ratio, good setup)
Transfer case: two-speed (1:1 high range, 1.96:1 low)

Toyota builds steel skid plates and front towing hooks on as standard running gear. Top this off with a standard roll bar and you're getting a lot for your money. Toyota apparently is able to add on these goodies because of the money they save not having to cater to special orders for engines and transmissions. Remember, with the Land Cruiser you get one engine and one kind of transmission. No options. Even so, the Land Cruiser is one of the best buys on the market for the serious off-roading enthusiast.

INTERNATIONAL HARVESTER SCOUT

The International Harvester Scout was one of the first 4WD vehicles for civilian use. It was originally designed for the farmer, geologist, gas station, and the like where it would be used by working men who needed a small light truck with 4WD capability. It was an instant success when it first appeared in 1961 and has been successful ever since. Over the years its main shortcoming was that, although it was long on toughness and off-road performance, it was built by a company basically oriented to heavy trucks, farm machinery, and heavy earth-moving equipment. Consequently it was short on luxury accessories that would catch the consumer's eye. For example, paint colors would be conservative and interiors simple and functional.

International first made a concession to consumer tastes when it introduced the Scout II in 1971. This model was designed to appeal to the mass market with air conditioning, six and eight-cylinder engine options, and a choice of interior fabric and color combinations. International managed to handle this change well while keeping to a light truck philosophy. No concessions were made in the frame, engine, transmission, or drive train components, so the Scout II has changed very little since it was introduced. Here are the specifications of the Scout II as it looks today:

Wheelbase: 100 inches
Length: 166.2 inches
Turning radius: 36.33 feet
Engines: 196-4cyl. (standard) electronic ignition
         198 6cyl. diesel (optional)
         304-V8 (optional) electronic ignition
         345 V8 (optional) electronic ignition
Transmissions: three-speed manual (standard)
         four-speed wide or close ratio (optional)
         three-speed automatic (optional)
Transfer case: one-speed "silent drive" actuated by a knob on the dashboard
         two-speed gear drive Dana 20 (2.03:1 high, 1:1 low range)
Standard axle ratio: 3.07 with automatic transmission
         3.54 with manual transmission

INTERNATIONAL HARVESTER SS-II

International has recently gone all out and made an excellent off roader, the SS-II, that can take the toughest punishment right out of the showroom. The SS-II is essentially a Scout II with all the off-road refinements any demanding off roader could dream of. Its package includes a soft top, roll bar, grille guard, blackout grille, locking hubs, skid plates, steel spoke wheels with 10 x 15LT Goodyear Tracker A/T® tires and a heavy-duty suspension system. The only thing it doesn't have is a full-time 4WD system. It seems that International is still cautious about trying them out, although they have proven themselves capable. You can get an automatic transmission and a 345 V8 on an SS-II, but you still must take the manual two-speed Dana 20 transfer case with locking hubs. The other goodies on the SS-II more than make up for this slight shortcoming.

Early models were test-driven by a personal friend, the president of the Chicagoland Four-Wheel Drive Club, who liked it a great deal. The only shortcoming he found was that the suspension tended to bottom out going up very steep hills or over bad bumps. But the way he drives, almost any vehicle without a special off-road suspension system would bottom out.

The specifications of the SS-II are the same as those for the Scout II, with the additions I mentioned above. On the whole, the SS-II is an excellent off-road runner, and I would rank it as one of the best.

The other two vehicles that International makes, the Traveler and the Terra pickup, will be considered in later sections. The Traveler is really more of a station

The 1978 Scout SS-II is a good off-road runner, but can use an aftermarket suspension kit to cure a bottoming-out problem, give more tire clearance, and raise the body frame to avoid high-centering

The attractive GMC Jimmy, a close relative of the Blazer, is the choice of many city dwellers and suburbanites. It combines off-roading capability with passenger car comforts. You'll see a lot of families looking at this, one of the favorite wife-pleasers

wagon and the Terra can be considered a mini-pickup because of its short wheelbase.

Advantages of Short Wheelbase 4x4s

You may have noticed that I think highly of the short wheelbase four wheelers. I've said that the Jeep and the Scout SS-II are two of the best and that the Toyota Land Cruiser is the best buy. Why are these so good? The main reason is that they're small, relatively lightweight (under 4,000 lb. as against 5,700 or more for a Blazer or pickup), and can be purchased with powerful engines. When you get off the road these characteristics really pay off. The smallness provides excellent handling and turning characteristics, especially with power steering and power front disc brakes. They can also squeeze through narrow trails where a pickup couldn't fit through. Even if you don't mind getting your rig scratched on the sides, you still can't push trees over. This happens more often than you think. The narrowness also makes it easier to avoid bad holes or deep water on trails by driving along the sides on a ledge of more shallow mud.

Being lightweight makes a big difference. A Jeep with 11 x 15 Tru-Trac® tires, weighing a full ton less than a pickup with the same tires, has 500 fewer pounds on each tire. That means that the mud under each wheel has to support 500 fewer pounds; the Jeep won't sink as deep as the pickup. Different kinds of soil support varying amounts of pressure per square inch. Mud can only support about 20 pounds per square inch, so you have to pass over it quickly. Having to support 500 pounds less on each tire enables you to float on top of mud that other heavier rigs would sink into like a rock. I've seen pickups with Gumbo Monster Mudder® tires sink like the Titanic as soon as they stopped moving in soft deep mud.

Except for the Toyota Land Cruiser, these vehicles can be bought with a V8 powerplant for rough off roading. The SS-II, Scout II or Traveler can be bought with a 345V8 with excellent torque (290 ft. lb. at 2,000rpm), and you can get a 304 on the Jeep. This will give you as much muscle as the biggies, with less weight to pull and better flotation going over the soft stuff. No wonder the little ones do so well.

The Scout II is heavier than the Jeep. This extra weight has to be compensated for with bigger tires and engine, which are available. The lightest four wheeler you can get is an army surplus Jeep. If you care to go to the trouble, you can find out how to get one in chapter six, along with how to buy a Postal Service Jeep which is probably even lighter.

The Roomier, Medium Wheelbase 4x4s

The next class of four wheelers includes those with the longer wheelbase and larger body. These are the Chevy Blazer, Dodge Ramcharger, Plymouth Trail Duster, Ford Bronco and GMC Jimmy. These four wheelers are much larger in length and width then the short wheelbase models, providing more room inside for a rear seat and cargo. Five or six people can sit comfortably in one of these using the rear seat, just like a passenger car. These vehicles also have great ground clearance and wheel wells that will take the really huge tires. When you jack up the body of a Blazer and put on oversized tires, the body will stand over 30 inches off the ground. This gives it the off-roading ability of a pickup with a shorter wheelbase, so it will dip into an out of deep holes more quickly than a pickup will. You can get larger V8s with these rigs, and the Ramcharger even has a 440 engine available.

THE CHEVY BLAZER

The Blazer is a very popular vehicle, particularly with people who want a tough-looking four wheeler with a lot of luxury. The Blazer has a really nice interior and great looking upholstery and carpeting. Like the others in its class, it is the most luxurious type of four wheeler you can get. It performs very well off the road because it can be fully loaded with off-roading gear such as a good suspension, dual shocks on each wheel, large wheels and tires, roll bar, transfer case skid plate, rear differential skid plate, and loads of other goodies.

The problem with the Blazer though, is that although it looks like a really tough off roader, it isn't as tough as the Jeep, Land Cruiser, or Scout when it comes to really tough off-road driving over a long period of time. One reason is the suspension. In order to give the city driver a soft ride, it doesn't have the stiff leaf springs other four wheelers have. Consequently, the stock springs bottom out with off-road use. While all four wheelers have problems with stock springs that can't take the punishment, it's worse with the Blazer. If you're getting an off-road suspension kit, you shouldn't have any trouble. For serious off roading, where you really drive it hard, you must have a beefed-up suspension on a Blazer. Remember, a Blazer can weigh as much as 5,700 lbs.

Another problem often arises with overload of the front spindle bearings or driveshaft U-joints, caused by raising the suspension or by the excessive wheel offset necessary to install tires in the enormous class.

In short, the Blazer is a great vehicle, but as with all four wheelers, you'll have some maintenance problems when you run it hard off road. A common mistake is to put a 7½ or 8-foot snowplow on a Blazer with the standard two-leaf front springs, the weakest ones you can get. If you put a snow plow on your Blazer, do it a favor and get the heaviest suspension option. That plow adds an extra 500 pounds to the front end. And remember, really big tires will give you some problems with any four wheeler. Try to keep your tires down to a sensible size, about 11 x 15, and you'll avoid the problems with the suspension and drive train associated with running huge tires.

Here are the specs on the 1978 Blazer (K5 4WD):

A 1978 Chevy Blazer outfitted by G.A.M.E. Sales of Skokie, Illinois features a Burbank Safari suspension and body accessories by Hickey Enterprises

The 1978 Plymouth Trail Duster

Wheelbase: 106.5 inches
Length: 184.4 inches
Width: 76.6 inches
Turning radius: 37.1 feet
Engines: 250-6 electronic ignition
        305-2bbl V8 electronic ignition
        350-4bbl V8 electronic ignition
        400-4bbl V8 electronic ignition
Transmission: three-speed synchro (standard, but not available with 400 engine)
        four-speed synchro (optional)
        three-speed automatic (full-time 4WD) NP203
Transfer case: two-speed Dana 20 (standard)
        2:1 high range
        1:1 low range
        New Process 203 with full-time 4WD
Axle ratios: 2.76, 3.07, 3.73, 4.11

Skid plates for the gas tank and transfer case are available, as well as a snow plow. You can get a convertible top, and Goodyear Tracker A/T tires. If you do a lot of trailering, accessories are available. Power front disc brakes are standard and the option list is long-everything from cruise control to locking rear differential to high back bucket seats.

PLYMOUTH TRAIL DUSTER AND DODGE RAMCHARGER

Very similar to the Chevy Blazer is the Plymouth Trail Duster. I haven't heard of as many experiences with it as I have with the Blazer, mainly because I don't know enough people who own one to form a good opinion of it. I don't think it handles as well as the Blazer, but they're so close, the difference is a matter of personal preference rather than fact.

The Trail Duster has some nice options with it including a powerful battery, front disc brakes, CB radio, Goodyear Tracker A/T tires, a swing-away rear tire carrier, automatic speed control, snowplow, skid plates for the gas tank and transfer case, engine block heater for winter starts, increased engine cooling system for towing heavy trailers with a good trailering package, front bumper guards, a convertible roof, and a roll bar. It features the New Process Model 203 full-time 4WD system for good on and off-road control with an attractive Hurst shifter. Power steering is optional and a good idea. The only addition you should make is a winch. Like the Blazer, the Trail Duster is a good-looking vehicle suitable for rough off-road use.

Here are the specs on the 1978 Trail Duster (4WD only):

Wheelbase: 106 inches
Length: 184.5 inches
Width: 79.5 inches
Turning radius: 36.9 feet
Engines: 225 2 bbl 6 cyl. is standard (electronic ignition standard)
         318 V8 2bbl (optional)
         360 V8 2bbl (optional)
         400 V8 2bbl (optional)
         440 V8 4bbl (optional)
Transmissions: three-speed manual is standard
         four-speed manual wide ratio with full-time 4WD (optional)
         four-speed manual close ratio with full-time 4WD (optional)
         three-speed automatic with full-time 4WD (optional)
Transfer case: New Process Model 203, two-speed, full time
Axle ratios: 3.50 standard (good overall choice)
         3.2, 3.9 with all engines optional except 440, which has a 3.2 standard and a 3.5 optional

The Trail Duster has a bigger engine option than most; a 440 four-barrel is available. Unlike other four wheelers, the manual transmissions come with the NP 203 full-time 4WD system, instead of the two-speed manual part-time system. You can add the Rough Country conversion to part time if you like.

The Dodge Ramcharger is almost identical to the Plymouth Trail Duster. It does have a tougher appearance and has a good selection of paint schemes and custom paint jobs. If you want one of the nicest looking four wheelers available that can still take a pounding off the road, the Ramcharger or Trail Duster is worth looking at.

The Dodge Ramcharger and the Ramcharger Four by Four package for 1978 (Courtesy, Dodge Truck Public Relations)

The 1978 Ford Bronco, featuring an excellent suspension, larger size for more rugged off roading and better ground clearance, and a good off-road package

A Plymouth Trail Duster, temporarily bogged down in deep mud

THE FORD BRONCO

The final vehicle in the medium wheelbase class is the Ford Bronco. Due to the popularity of the medium-sized vehicles, Ford decided to redesign the Bronco in a larger version and came up with a winner. The 1978 Bronco is an excellent off roader, yet a good looking street machine. It has tight handling characteristics, and many subtle additions that the off roader would appreciate. These include a 25-gallon gas tank, a 32-gallon optional tank, long wide-leaf springs, optional double shocks on each front wheel, optional rear stabilizer bar, heavy-duty rear shocks, skid plates for gas tank and transfer case, light and heavy-duty trailer-towing packages, limited-slip rear differential, and the special Northland winter package including a 68 amp battery, 60 amp alternator, and a 600 watt engine heater, all as options. You can also get a roll bar that is foam padded, showing the extra touches Ford put into the Bronco. Front coil springs are used for a smoother response to bumpy trails.

It has a nice folding rear seat and offers a locking gas cap, spare tire lock, and inside hood release. Off roaders who live in the city will appreciate the spare tire lock. You can get Goodyear Tracker A/T tires on 8-inch rims, and front tow hooks. The spare tire can be put on a swing-away spare tire carrier, and a CB radio is available. The standard power plant is the Ford 351 V8, with an optional 400 V8. A 4-speed manual is standard with the Dana 20 transfer case and front hubs, while the Cruise-O-Matic automatic gives you a choice of part-time or full-time 4WD. In previous years, other manufacturers offered an automatic with the full-time system only.

The new Bronco is a little bit smaller than the Blazer, Trail Duster, or Ramcharger, which gives it better handling, especially with its low front overhang and good ground clearance. It is 180 inches long, has a 104-inch wheelbase, and is 79.3

inches wide—a good size. The Ford Bronco is a very capable off roader with a good suspension and a complete line of accessories.

The medium-sized four wheelers are very popular because they combine the comfort of an automobile with the toughness of a pickup truck and 4WD capability. They perform well off the road and can be dressed up to look really tough. As an example of their popularity, the Chevy Blazer, the most popular in this class, started out in 1969 with sales of 7,506. In 1976 71,242 were sold, ten times as many! And sales keep climbing. The reasons it's so popular are its luxurious interior and good off-road performance. When fully loaded, a Blazer can compete with any vehicle, and outperforms all but the best pickups—and even then they're evenly matched.

Since most people use their vehicles for off roading only a small part of the time, and use them to go to work or for other street uses about 97% of the time, the medium-sized four wheelers are a perfect combination. They look good, perform well and are a lot of fun.

Four-Wheel Drive Station Wagons

Four-wheel drive station wagons combine the versatility and ruggedness of the four wheeler with the body size of a large station wagon. While most station wagons are equipped with a heavy-duty suspension for carrying heavy loads, the 4WD versions have even heavier suspensions for handling the rough terrain found on off-road trails.

THE TOYOTA LAND CRUISER WAGON

One of the smallest wagons with 4WD is the Toyota Land Cruiser wagon. It has the same engine, transmission and transfer case as the Land Cruiser hardtop. The big difference is size: the station wagon has a longer wheelbase (106.3 inches versus 90 inches for the hardtop), is longer (184 inches versus 152 inches), and three inches wider. Like the hardtop, the station wagon is relatively light at 4,200 lbs. It also has bench seats front and rear, providing lots of room for the whole family. There is a cargo section in the back big enough to carry everybody's camping gear.

Like the hardtop, the station wagon Land Cruiser comes with many rugged extras that would be expensive to add on later. These include free-wheeling front locking hubs to go with the manual transfer case, a tool kit, power front disc and rear drum brakes, body undercoating and, reflecting its orientation to usefulness, front tow hooks. The front tow hooks really impress me because everybody needs them, but only with Toyota do you get them as standard equipment.

Other extra options available for the rough-going off roader are a PTO (power take-off) or electric winch, air conditioning, carpeting, and a cassette tape player for those lonely moments when the silence begins to get a little too heavy.

For having a sensible, tough construction, a good off-roading profile and ground clearance, fantastic standard equipment, and a cheap price (relatively, of course), I have to give Toyota the prize again for being the best bargain in its class at no loss of quality or off-road capability. The faults of the Land Cruiser station wagon are its somewhat small size, its medium-sized engine (six-cylinder 258), and its lack of full-time 4WD. These are not major drawbacks for the serious off roader who wants a rugged vehicle with off-road traveling uppermost in mind.

INTERNATIONAL'S TRAVELALL AND TRAVELER

International Harvester stopped making its classic station wagon, the Travelall, in 1975. It long had a reputation for ruggedness and dependability. I know people who still own 1961 models that are running perfectly—no body rust or problems. These huge beasts got too expensive to make, I imagine (they cost up to $9,000 when they were still available), and their heaviness didn't make them suited to the rugged type of off roading a lot of people like to do. They were, however, the best combination for those who wanted a large station wagon with 4WD and a chassis like a pickup truck.

The Travelall has been replaced by the Traveler, a stretched version of the Scout II, but not stretched too much. But because of the trend to smaller vehicles for better gas mileage it hasn't been stretched too far. It is only 22 inches longer than the Scout II, and its wheelbase is 18 inches longer. The Travelalls, when fully loaded with all the heavy options, got about five or six miles to the gallon in city driving. Not very good by any measure. All that weight would also sink the beast into the mud in any off-road situation, and would make hill climbing difficult. The new Traveler is more sensible in these respects, even though it has a GVWR of 6,200 pounds. It saves a little weight with a fiberglass top reinforced with steel similar to a roll bar.

The same engines are available for the Traveler as for the Scout II: the 196 four-cylinder, the 304 V8, and the 345 V8. The last engine, the 345, is great for off roading. It actually has more torque at 2,000rpm than the Chevy 400 V8 at 2,800rpm! You can get big Goodyear Tracker A/T tires for it, and a Warn winch; the 8,000 lb. or 3,000 lb. models are available. You can add quartz lights, front skid plates (the ones available are very good), and a snowplow if you live in the north. It's a good idea to add the heavy-duty step bumper with hitch ball, automatic locking hubs (which aren't standard), and heavy-duty front and rear springs. If you intend to do very rough off roading, I suggest you forget about the heavy-duty springs and buy an aftermarket spring kit. The ones you get from the factory, even the heavy-duty ones, aren't heavy duty enough. Power steering and the Trac-Loc® axle are also good additions with a vehicle this heavy. The swing-away mirrors are good for preventing mirror rip-off by tree branches on trails, and a gas tank skid plate is an obvious necessity.

The Traveler is a good family-sized vehicle with sensible options. The only thing you might not like is that full-time 4WD is not available. This turns some people off, but doesn't, in my opinion, make the vehicle less capable for off-road use. With the International Traveler, as with the Scout II and SS-II, you can be sure you're getting a vehicle made for years of hard off-road pounding, not just a street-oriented recreational vehicle.

JEEP WAGONEER AND CHEROKEE

Jeep Corporation makes two 4WD station wagons, the Wagoneer and the Cherokee. These are two truly classic four-wheeler station wagons, based on the Wagoneer design started in 1962, and still used today in a winning combination of highway comfort and off-road ruggedness.

If you're wondering if there's any difference between the Cherokee and the Wagoneer in size, there isn't. They're both 183.5 inches long, have a 108.7-inch

If you intend to use your vehicle for family shopping as well as off roading, here's the best 4WD station wagon, the 1978 Jeep Wagoneer

The attractive and tough Jeep Cherokee can be bought with the full-time Quadra-Trac 4WD option. It's a good looker for city driving but can be taken to the hills for off roading

wheelbase, and are 75.5 inches wide. The real difference between them lies in the power train and suspension. The Wagoneer has a standard 360 V8 with Quadra-Trac and automatic transmission, while the Cherokee has a three-speed manual transmission and the two-speed Dana 20 transfer case as standard. It is powered by a standard 258 six cylinder. The front springs on the Wagoneer are also heavier as standard equipment, but are available on the Cherokee as an option.

Basically, the Cherokee is an economical, stripped-down version of the Wagoneer. If you want the Wagoneer's smooth highway ride and rugged towing and roughing-it characteristics for less money, get the Cherokee. As an added benefit, the Cherokee does offer more flexibility in its power train capabilities. For example, you can get a 4-speed manual transmission with the 360 V8 two or four barrel and part-time Dana 20 transfer case, whereas on the Wagoneer you get only one transmission, the automatic, to complement the Quadra-Trac system. If you get the biggest V8, the 401, on the Cherokee, you have to go to the automatic transmission and Quadra-Trac full-time 4WD system.

Both models feature power front disc and rear drum brakes. Power steering is standard on the Wagoneer but optional on most Cherokees. Options available include a rear Trac-Loc differential, air conditioning, 3.54 and 4.09 axle ratios, flared wheel wells with the Goodyear Tracker A/T 10 x 15 tires (Cherokee only), CB radio, electric rear window defogger, engine block heater for cold winter starts, heavy-duty alternator and battery to go with it, a front stabilizer bar (a good idea), fuel tank skid plate (but you can't get front or transfer case skid plates), a snowplow, PTO or electric 8,000 lb. winch, and good towing and trailering packages.

I consider the Wagoneer and Cherokee to be two of the best 4WD station wagons, particularly because they handle like regular cars. Other station wagons handle more like trucks because they are built on larger chassis. The Jeep station wagons have just the right combination of smooth highway comfort and off-road toughness. The only shortcoming they have is that they can't go into very deep mud because they can fit no tires larger than 10 x 15. You can't put on larger flotation tires because the wheel wells won't handle them. You'd have to cut away the wheel wells in front of and behind the tires, and this would destroy the looks of the vehicle. The optional Goodyear Tracker A/T tires are versatile and a good choice, but you'd be wise to stay away from the really rough stuff unless you have a winch to pull yourself through when necessary. If you're a more conservative driver and won't be handling any vicious terrain, then the Cherokee or Wagoneer will suit your needs. It is a fine vehicle for highway and city driving and for towing your trailer down the dirt or gravel roads to your favorite fishing spot or boating area where the boat must be launched in the dirt or sand. It'll give you all the freedom you want for you and your family to strike out on your own to find a private spot on the lake.

THE CHEVY/GMC SUBURBAN

Chevy's 4WD station wagon is the Suburban. It is bulkier, heavier, longer, and harder to drive in tight spots than any other four-wheel station wagon I've mentioned, but its size is to its advantage if a large station wagon is what you're accustomed to and what you want in a four wheeler. It comes in two versions, the K-10 and the K-20, the K-20 being the stronger of the two. They both have an overall length of 218.7 inches, and a wheelbase of 129.5 inches. They're both 79.6 inches wide and carry the Chevy line of 305, 350, and 400 V8 engines; electronic ignition is standard. The K-20 has bigger standard tires, 8.75 x 16.5, as big as on a three-quarter ton pickup, while the K-10 has the smaller standard L78 x 15 tires.

The standard transmission is a three-speed manual, with a four-speed manual optional on both models. Four-wheel drive is accomplished through the New Process 205 transfer case. If you want the full-time system, it's the New Process Model 203. And of course you must take the three-speed automatic with the full-time system.

Off roading is made a lot easier with the standard power front disc brakes and rear drums and optional power steering. You can get optional gas tank and transfer case skid plates, a must for serious off roading, heavy-duty front springs and shocks to buttress the suspension system, heavy-duty rear springs, an extra-large capacity alternator, air conditioning, and a weight equalizing trailer hitch platform for distributing the weight of the trailer along the entire frame. All of these items are available on either model. For long trips into the boonies you can get a 31 or 40-gallon auxiliary gas tank. But the big difference between the two models is the GVWR. The K-20 has a maximum GVWR of 8,400 lb., while the K-10 can handle 7,300 lb. All together, the K-20 can move up to 11,500 lb., including itself, passengers, cargo, and trailer. This means it can carry a load of 3,100 lb., making it the biggest and most powerful station wagon in the 4WD station wagon group. If you need a heavy-hauling station wagon, this is it. In effect, it replaces the International Travelall as the muscle station wagon. With all this weight, don't expect great gas mileage or heavy mud-handling capability. With big tires, though, it'll do anything you want it to do with the whole family.

Switch the Chevy Suburban K-10 to the GMC K-15, and the K-20 to the GMC K-25, and all the specifications above are identical. The Chevy and GMC models of the Suburbans are the same.

Mini-Pickups

THE INTERNATIONAL SCOUT TERRA

Moving from the station wagon four wheelers to the mini-pickups, we come to the International Scout Terra. Since International ceased production of their pickups in 1975, the Terra has become International's entry in the 4WD pickup field. I refer to it as a mini-pickup because of its short length. It has the same length, wheelbase, and width as the Scout Traveler, making the cargo box 6 feet long and 54 inches wide. The same engines are available including the diesel, and it comes in standard, deluxe, and custom versions for more luxurious trim and interiors. It can carry a one-ton payload, pretty good for its size, although carrying this much would be stretching it to its limit. The only real difference between it and the Traveler is that the Terra has a cab for carrying two passengers and the Traveler has a rear bench seat and an enclosed rear area like any other station wagon. In ride, handling, and off-road performance the Terra is very good, identical with the other Scouts.

If you want a small pickup that is tougher than other mini-pickups, the Terra is your choice. It also has long had a reputation as a good working vehicle in its earlier form as the Scout 80 or 800. People who used the Scout as a 4WD light truck will find that the Terra suits their needs perfectly. Although it cannot carry large payloads like the big pickups, it has the advantage of being small and powered by a four-cylinder 196 for much better gas mileage.

Two-Wheel Drive Mini-Pickups

The other mini-pickups on the market are 2WD, except for the 4WD Chevy LUV. These can be converted to 4WD, bought as a converted unit, or driven as a conventional 2WD vehicle with better tires, a lifted body, and a winch. A winch is a sensible addition since you'll probably get stuck often in a 2WD mini.

The most popular converted mini-pickups are the Chevy LUV, Toyota, Ford Courier, and Datsun. Conversions can also be made for the Mazda, but these usually aren't available from dealerships. You can find converted units at some dealerships. For example, the Ford Courier can be fitted with a Dana 20 transfer case with an adapter and a Dana 30 front axle, making it into a 4WD unit. These conversions are expensive, though. The cost of the 4WD conversion itself is around $2,800 to $3,000, and since the converted units at dealerships are usually dressed up and painted for display, they can cost a lot. This defeats the purpose of buying a mini-pickup. For as much money you can get any four wheeler you want, capable of much tougher off-road running than a mini.

If you're thinking of getting a mini-pickup for 95% street use and light off-road use, don't be afraid to buy it. They're extremely lightweight at 2,500 lb., even lighter than the Jeep, so they can get by without a monstrous engine as long as they have good tires. Good tires will keep your neck out of the mud and you can literally roll over mud that heavy pickup trucks will have to power through. Gas mileage is another good reason for going with a mini-pickup for off-road use. Outfitted with front tow hooks and a winch; it'll go just about anywhere.

DATSUN'S KING CAB

Here are the specifications on the Datsun King Cab, one of the more popular mini-pickups:

Wheelbase: 110.7 inches
Length: 178.7 inches
Width: 62.5 inches
Turning diameter: 39.4 feet

Curb weight: 2,495 lb.
Engine: 119.1 cubic-inch four cylinder
Transmission: four-speed manual synchromesh (standard)
          five-speed (very good option)
          three-speed automatic (optional)
Suspension: Front independent coils with torsion bars and stabilizer bar
          Rear leaf springs

The Datsun also comes in a standard and stretched version, the only difference being the wheelbase and length. Options remain the same, as well as the basic four-cylinder engine—there is no other engine available. Other goodies you can get on a Datsun mini-pickup are air conditioning, rear step bumper, and tachometer. If you want to add a winch you'll have to do it yourself, as well as the other off-roading essentials like front tow hooks and skid plates. A snowplow on such a low-powered machine is out of the question. On the whole, it is a fine vehicle with good off-roading capability when matched with the right tires and a winch.

THE FORD COURIER

Another popular pickup in the mini-size is the Ford Courier. It is imported by Ford, to compete with the Japanese imports. Here's the specifications on the Ford Courier:

Wheelbase: 104.3 inches
Length: 171.5 inches
Width: 63 inches
Curb weight: 2,630 lb.
Engines: 110 cubic-inch four cylinder (standard)
        140 cubic-inch four cylinder (optional)
Transmission: four-speed manual (standard)
          five-speed (very good option)
          three-speed automatic (optional)
Suspension: independent coil spring in front, longitudinal semi-elliptical leaf
          springs in the rear.

Like the Datsun, the interior is rather spartan with only the essential in trim and instrumentation. Handling and mileage is good. Light weight makes it capable of some off-road use when properly outfitted with tires and a winch.

TOYOTA'S SR-5 LONG BED SPORT TRUCK

The Toyota mini-pickups are similarly equipped. The SR-5 Long Bed Sport Truck is one of four models available:

Wheelbase: 110 inches
Length: 184.6 inches
Width: 62.2 inches
Curb weight: 2,550 lb.
Engine: 2.2 liter four cylinder
Transmission: five-speed overdrive (standard)

The Toyota comes with standard power front disc and rear drum brakes, a good addition for off-road use. Otherwise it is very similar to the other models, gets good mileage, and handles well.

THE CHEVY LUV

The Chevy LUV fits in with the others with a 102.4-inch wheelbase, a length of 173.8 inches, and a width of 63 inches but it is the only mini-pickup with 4 WD (1979). It's powered by a 110.8 cubic-inch four cylinder and delivers 80 net horsepower. Two transmissions are available, a four-speed manual and a three-speed automatic. The suspension has front torsion bars and rear elliptical leaf springs for a smooth ride. The torsion bars can be cranked up a little with a wrench, as on the Datsun, to give it better ground clearance for off roading. It can carry a heavier load with more control than most minis, with a maximum GVWR of 5,326 lb., the best of any mini. It has a rather small gas tank, though, at 13 gallons. Only the Ford Courier's is smaller, at 12.5.

THE MAZDA SPORT TRUCK

The Mazda Sport Truck is the final entry in the mini-pickup line. Its engine produces 64 horses from 96.8 cubic inches, and only a 4-speed manual is available. It's one of the shorter minis in overall length at 171.5 inches with a 104.3-inch wheelbase. Front coils give it a soft ride. I haven't seen too many of them around and they aren't often converted to 4WD; at least I haven't seen any. It has a lower GVWR than most at 3,675 lb., and the declining popularity of the Mazda line has helped to make it scarce.

In general, your decision to buy a mini-pickup would be based on economy rather than off-road performance. But if you're looking for an inexpensive vehicle that will meet occasional off-roading needs, the minis will be your best choice. And remember, they can be converted into relatively good runners with the proper aftermarket tires and accessories.

Four-Wheel Drive Pickups

A lot of people today are going to pickup trucks when they buy their second four wheeler, and those who want a mean off-road runner and know the market usually buy a pickup first. Why? Because with a pickup you get more of an off roader for your money. And pickups aren't all that expensive when you compare them to the short wheelbase four wheelers or station wagons. In fact, they cost the same or less, depending, of course, on the model you buy and the kind of options you want.

The difference is that a pickup has a stronger frame, a better suspension because it's not made to second as a car, excellent body clearance, and wheel wells that are great for any size tire you desire. You usually don't have to worry about spending another $350 on an off-road suspension kit, you don't have to settle for smaller tires because the biggies won't fit, it won't be necessary to do a lot of body cutting to fit those big Gumbo Monster Mudders on, and best of all you can sneak around the EPA emission controls (catalytic converters) by ordering a heavy-duty pickup. The heavier pickups don't require much emission control equipment because they're not considered passenger cars. So, with a pickup you get a stronger rig with heavier driveline components, a stronger suspension, and more power under the hood without much power-robbing emission control equipment. No wonder pickups are getting to be so popular as off roaders.

The Chevy LUV can be dressed up to look really nice. Here it has pinstriping, Concorde Deserter tires, and a front-end guard with fog lights

Here's the 1978 Jeep Honcho pickup. Jeep is the only pickup you can buy with the Quadra-Trac full-time 4WD system

JEEP J-10 AND J-20 PICKUPS

If you like the Jeep Quadra-Trac full-time 4WD drive system and you want a pickup, Jeep offers two pickups to choose from, the J-10 and the J-20. The J-20 is bigger, has a longer wheelbase, heavier springs, and can carry a heavier payload. Here are the specifications on the two Jeep pickup models:

	J-10	J-20
Wheelbase:	118.7 inches	130.7 inches
Length:	192.5 inches	204.5 inches
Width:	78.9 inches	78.9 inches
Turning radius:	40.6 feet	44.5 feet
	41.2 inches (Honcho)	
Engines: 258 2bbl six	standard	N/A
360 V8 2bbl	optional	standard
360 V8 4bbl	optional	optional
401 V8 4bbl	optional	optional

Transmission: three-speed manual synchromesh, standard
three-speed Turbo Hydra-Matic, optional
four-speed manual synchromesh, optional
Transfer case: Dana 20 two-speed floor shift with manual
Jeep Quadra-Trac with three-speed automatic transmission (full time)

There is a wide variety of spring options available for light or heavy-duty use on both models. The pickups come with front power disc brakes and rear drums, a 19-gallon fuel tank, and bench seat. You can get air conditioning and the attractive and tough-looking "Honcho" package, including pickup box striping in gold, black, and white over a choice of five exterior colors, Goodyear Tracker A/T tires (10 x 15), aluminum wheels, and woodgrain instrument panel along with other little extras. A CB radio is available and a good idea for extensive off-road use. A tilting steering wheel, power steering, and rear step bumper are useful conveniences. You can get heavy-duty shocks, springs, cooling system, battery and alternator. For the northern states an engine block heater, heavy-duty battery and alternator are available. A rear Trac-Loc differential is available, as well as a snowplow, trailering accessories, and an electric or PTO winch.

The Jeep pickups are good off roaders, but haven't been very popular because they have a small cargo box, a somewhat cramped interior, and haven't been famous for quality workmanship. Jeep has been making improvements, though, and it is probably the best choice for someone who wants a good off roader and doesn't need a lot of cargo space. It's also the toughest looking pickup, in my opinion.

THE FORD F-150 AND F-250 4x4s

The word "Ford" has long been synonymous with pickups from the days of the wooden-spoked wheels. They still make a tough pickup, and their four wheelers are some of the finest. Two models are available, the F-150 and the F-250.

A 300 six cylinder is standard on the F-150, with a 351 or 400 V8 option. The standard transmission is a four-speed because of the extra weight. A two-speed transfer case is standard, or you can get a Cruise-O-Matic with the full-time 4WD system. The V8s with Cruise-O-Matic also have a part-time system available. It has a very good suspension, with heavy-duty gas quad shocks and heavy-duty springs optional, as on the Bronco. Aluminum wheels, blackout grille and bumpers, and a GT roll bar are available. Other niceties include a CB radio and air conditioning. The F-150 has an overall length of 194.8 inches, and a wheelbase of 117 inches. It is 79.1 inches wide. It has a maximum GVWR of 6,500 lb., so it can burn regular gas except in California. New for 1978 is the SuperCab with a back seat to seat a family of six.

The F-250 is a tremendously capable off roader, and in my opinion is the best available. It has a lower profile than previous models, which seemed to stand on stilts. The transfer case has been lifted more out of harm's way. It has standard power steering and heavy-duty power brakes. It also is available in the SuperCab version for more passenger space, as well as the familiar CrewCab. The same engines are available as with the F-150, and it has a four-speed standard with optional Cruise-O-Matic. Full-time or part-time 4WD can be had with the Cruise-O-Matic, a good option. The 1977 model had an automatic available only with the full-time system. A rear axle ratio of 4.10:1 is optional, but necessary when you take the hefty 8,500 lb. GVWR. In the suspension department, you can't get quad front

The Ford F-250, shown here with Gumbo Monster Mudders, is one of the most capable off-road vehicles

With an aftermarket suspension, tires, and wheels, the 1978 Ford F-250 pickup is one of the best off-road vehicles

shocks, but you can get heavy-duty shocks and springs, including a strong 4,500 lb. front axle for pushing a big plow with its extra 600 lb. The F-250 is longer than its little brother, having a wheelbase of 150.3 inches, and a length of 228.3 inches. It is just as wide at 79.1 inches. The Ford pickup has a nice trim package and doesn't look as large as it really is.

Put some giant mud tires on your F-250, and you'll appreciate its size. The wheel wells take these tires with ease. Its suspension and power plants will get you through the toughest trails reliably, but I'd bring along a winch just in case.

THE DODGE POWER WAGONS

The Dodge Power Wagons are another class of tough 4WD pickups. Chrysler started making four wheelers for the military in 1934 and introduced its first civilian model of the Power Wagon in 1945. New Process Gear, a division of Chrysler, now makes the NP 203 full-time transfer case used on all four wheelers except Jeeps, so Dodge has a lot of experience with 4WD. In 1978 three basic models of the Dodge Power Wagon were available: the W150, W200, and W300. Here are the specifications on the W150:

Wheelbase: 131 inches
Length: 210 inches
Width: 79.5 inches
Turning radius: 44.4 feet
Engines: 225, six cylinder, standard
   318 V8, optional
   360 V8, optional
   400 V8, optional
   440 V8, optional
   243 diesel, optional
Transmissions: three-speed synchro, standard
     four-speed close ratio, optional
     four-speed wide ratio, optional
     three-speed automatic, optional
Transfer case: NP 203 full time
Rear axle ratios: 3.55 standard, 3.2, 3.9 optional (on all engines except 440. The
     440 has a standard ratio of 3.2, with a 3.55 option.

The diesel engine is a new offering by Dodge. It is made by Mitsubishi Motors Corporation of Japan. Maximum horsepower is 103 at 3,700rpm, and maximum torque is 168 ft. lbs. at 2,200rpm. With this engine you have a choice of a four-speed manual gearbox or the three-speed automatic; the other transmissions are not available. The diesel option has power steering and power brakes as standard equipment. Dodge has found that the diesel engine has 50 percent better fuel economy than a comparably-sized gasoline engine, so the diesel is a good economy option as well as a powerful and durable engine for off-road use. Diesel fuel is also a little cheaper than regular gas.

Dodge is offering a tilting steering column and a choice of six radios, including two 40-channel CBs, one with AM and the other with AM/FM. They've also added a two-barrel carburetor to the 225 six, for an increase of 10 horsepower. Power disc brakes are standard on all pickups. Some of the other extras are air conditioning, custom paint and striping, and nice interiors.

The W200 looks identical to the W150, but the axle ratio is 4.10 in order to handle the heavier GVWR and payload. The GVWR is 8,000 lb. for the W200 compared to 6,100 lb. for the W150. It can also carry a heavier payload, 3,560 lb. versus

The 1978 Dodge Utiline Power Wagon. A good off-road runner, it's also popular in off-road racing. (Courtesy, Dodge Truck Public Relations)

1,865 lb. for the W150. Engine options, including the diesel, are the same, and transmission options are identical. If you intend to use the pickup as a four wheeler, I would get the W150; it's lighter and would run a little better off the road. The W200 is made for construction or farm work, but could still be used as an off roader. The 400 or 440 would give you plenty of power.

Two of the more rugged looking Dodge trucks. Macho Power Wagon top, Warlock bottom. They're popular for their sporty appearance, good performance, and price (Courtesy, Dodge Truck public relations)

The W300 is the largest Power Wagon. It's very similar to the others, but doesn't offer the three-speed manual; the four-speed (wide or close ratio), and the three-speed automatic are your only choices. It comes with a higher standard gear ratio, 4.88, because it's expected to lug around heavy loads with a GVWR of 10,000 lb., the heaviest of any pickup. It'll carry a payload up to 5,445 lb., making it a heavy-duty working truck. I wouldn't use this for off-roading fun because it's so long and heavy. You'd need dual rear tires, and would get terrible gas mileage and bog down in the mud. It has a 135-inch wheelbase and is 215.9 inches long, so you'd get high-centered easily on big bumps and have poor ground clearance on uneven terrain.

New, starting with 1978 Dodge Power Wagons have better trailering options, including hitches. You can also buy a roll bar, skid plates, and step bumpers. The 10 x 15LT tires would work well in most situations, and would run quietly on the highway. For tough off-road mud you should go with larger tires for the W150 and W200. Power Wagons are a little more difficult to handle than most pickups due to the large turning radius, but this doesn't interfere with their off-road capability. If you like the styling and engine options of the Power Wagons, they're one of the best combinations of great street looks, comfort, and tough off-road capability.

INTERNATIONAL PICKUPS

It used to be that any discussion of four wheel drive pickups wouldn't be complete without mentioning the excellent and rugged International Harvester pickup trucks. But the pickups have gone the way of the Travelall. International discontinued them in 1975 due to rising production costs. Many of these are still around and in good running condition—they were built well. International decided to make the Scout II into a pickup style, and came up with the Terra. With a diesel engine it's a tough worker, and is more than a mini-pickup. Perhaps International is right about the trend to smaller trucks, but for now the big pickups are very popular and are dominating the ever-growing 4WD pickup market. I'm sure the Terra will be waiting patiently for the mid-1980s when the big pickups become scarce and the little ones move in on the market.

CHEVY AND GMC PICKUPS

Chevy has three excellent 4WD pickups on the market: the K10, K20, and K30, going up in GVWR. The K10 is the smallest pickup with a GVWR of 6,200 lb. No heavier payload option is available. Here are the other specs on it:

Wheelbase: 117.5 inches, 131.5 inches with longer bed
Length: 192.2 inches, 212.1 inches
Width: 79.6 inches
Engines: 250 six (standard), 350 V8 (optional), 400 V8 (optional)
Transmissions: three-speed manual, four-speed manual, three-speed automatic
Transfer case: New Process 205 (with manual)
               New Process 203 full time with automatic transmission
Rear axle ratios: 2.76, 3.07, 3.73, 4.11

The K10 is an excellent example of a pickup that doubles as a street machine, rather than a street machine that does a poor job of doubling as an off roader. It runs smoothly and comfortably with its available V8 and automatic transmission. It has a gas tank skid plate, front tow hooks, AM/FM radio, power steering, glide-out

Creative paint schemes and nice interiors mark the GMC short bed pickup for 1978

A 1978 Chevy pickup outfitted for rugged off roading by G.A.M.E. sales of Skokie, Illinois. It features Gumbo Monster Mudders, Burbank springs, and Hickey accessories including super tube bumpers and roll bar

spare tire, heavy-duty shocks and springs, cargo box side rails, below eye-level mirrors, rally wheels with 10x15B tires, and chrome bumpers available. The springs work well off the road, and the truck won't bottom out coming out of the deepest hole. The suspension is a drawback on the street, though; it tends to be stiff and responds to every bump and crack in the pavement. If this annoys you, get softer tires and shocks, but this is the price you pay for a tough off-road suspension. A soft luxurious suspension hasn't been invented that won't bottom out on rough trails. Because of its relatively short wheelbase, it drives and handles well, on and off the highway. It's a good idea to have plenty of gas, even when not venturing far from home, and the 16-gallon auxiliary fuel tank is a worthwhile option.

The K20 is Chevy's medium-sized pickup. With a GVWR of 6,800 lb. to 8,400 lb., it should be bought with heavy hauling in mind, unless you want an extremely stiff ride. If you're not going to drive with a camper, then get the 6,800 lb. GVWR. Only a lot of weight in the cargo bed would give you a smooth ride if you go any higher. It has a wheelbase of 131.5 inches, is 212.1 inches long and 79.6 inches wide. A 292 six cylinder is standard, with the same V8 options as the K10 available. The same transmissions and transfer cases are available, but the standard axle ratio is 4.10, with one option of 4.56. This is better for off road use, but doesn't help mileage, especially when going over 50 mph.

The standard tires on this rig are 8.75x16.5D; you could use better flotation tires for mud-running. You can get power brakes and steering, heavy-duty battery and alternator, side mirrors, electric windows, sliding cab window, bed-mounted spare tire, and a complete instrument panel for a nice-looking four wheeler. Chevy has done a good job in dressing up its tough trucks. On the whole, this is a very durable and nicely laid out and decorated four wheeler—a good combination for comfortable highway riding and tough off-road use, with a tough suspension and decent tires.

The K30 is Chevy's largest entry in the 4WD pickup class. Like the K20, it comes with a standard 292 six, with a 350 and 400 V8 available. No three-speed transmission is available only a four-speed manual with the New Process 205 transfer case. The three-speed automatic is standard for the New Process 203 full-time 4WD system. Also standard on the K30 is the 4.10 axle ratio, with an optional 4.56. It comes with slightly larger standard tires, 9.50x16.5D to accommodate the larger GVWRs of 8,600 lb. and 10,000 lb. The wheelbases are 131.5 and 164 inches, and it's just as wide as the others at 79.6 inches. Being the biggest, it's also the longest—212.1 inches and 245 inches.

The same options are available for the K30 as with the K20, but the suspension components are heavier. Air conditioning, power steering, front tow hooks, gas tank skid plate, and auxiliary tank to hold 18 extra gallons are available. The K30 does not offer a snowplow or winch. Larger tires, wheels, lights and other off-road goodies must be added later for a rugged off-road performance. Be sure to add a roll bar and semi-flotation tires—you'll need them.

The GMC pickups are similar to the Chevy pickups. The K15 is the same size as Chevy's K10, and offers the same engine and transmission options. The GMC K25 is similar to the Chevy K20, and the GMC K35 is similar to the Chevy K30. The GMC options are almost identical to Chevy's. Small wonder the GMCs are so similar to the Chevy pickups, they're both made by General Motors Corporation.

Summing up this pickup section, I would have to say that the best overall four wheeler in the pickup class is the Ford F-250. It has a nice look, good workmanship, handsome paint options, and best of all performs very well off the road. It also seems to be well balanced for mud running. The F-250 is the biggest selling four wheeler of any kind. On the other hand, the best bargain is probably the Dodge W-150, being about the cheapest pickup with four wheel drive.

Any pickup I've mentioned here is a good choice. They're all similar in engine, transmission, and configuration. Your choice is a matter of the style and brand you happen to prefer. Off-road performance depends upon how you outfit your truck (whether or not you put decent tires on it), and most of all how you drive it. A lousy driver will make the best four wheeler look bad.

Two-Wheel Drive Pickups

Although 4WD is superior on all counts to 2WD in off-road traction, a 2WD will often perform well off the road with good tires and an experienced driver. This is not because four wheelers aren't better, but because most of the time we don't push our four wheelers to their traction limit. I've seen some clubs drive through muck so deep that no 2WD pickup could go a foot in it. On the other hand, I've driven up some steep trails I've thought only a four wheeler could handle, only to find a 2WD pickup already there. Pickups are good off-road vehicles, with 4WD or 2WD, so if you think you'll hardly ever need four-wheel traction, don't spend your money on it. You will get slightly better mileage without a 4WD system, but you'll also have a harder time in the really demanding off-road situations. Use your own judgment.

If you already have a 2WD pickup with good tires, and are fed up with getting stuck all the time, then make your next vehicle a four wheeler. If your pickup has taken you up and down your favorite trails and you're not going to be more ambitious, then stick to 2WD. The only one that has to be satisfied with your vehicle's performance is you. Two-wheel drive pickups come in the same sizes as the four wheelers, so you can still use the wheelbase and lengths I've given here as a rough guide. If you own a Chevy or GMC 2WD pickup you can get suspension kits and other accessories from aftermarket accessory companies.

ENGINES

After you pick out the rig you want, the first thing you'll want to decide is the size and type of engine you'll need. Your choice will be based on two things: the engines available, and the kind of off-road driving you expect to do. Since you can easily look up the available engines in the previous section, we'll discuss the kind of performance and gas mileage you can expect to get from the engine of your choice.

Once upon a time the only engines available on a four wheeler were a four-banger for the short wheelbase models such as the Jeep, and a six cylinder on Dodge Power Wagons. Now, the only model offering a four-cylinder engine is the International Harvester Scout II. It's a good engine, has high torque and is very durable. It's made to take a beating off the road. The only problem is that it doesn't offer much in the power department. My 1966 Scout has great gearing and can climb like a goat, but in acceleration and quick hill climbing it is very poor. My Scout weighs in at 3200 lb.; the Scout IIs weigh more, but even its slightly larger 196 isn't powerful enough to get you moving through the heavy stuff.

The only thing a four is really good for is gas mileage. But because the Scout II four is a slant four (really half a V8) and has good torque, it doesn't get mileage anywhere near what you'd get with a mini-pickup. So the four cylinder is a good idea if you plan to go camping or medium-duty four wheeling, but it simply doesn't have the power to pull you through the heavy mud and sand.

Six-cylinder engines, on the other hand, have enough power for the short wheelbase vehicles to get you through the tough stuff. Jeeps with the 6-cylinder do well as long as they have good semi-flotation tires and a good driver; the reason is that the Jeep weighs a ton less than a pickup or Blazer and can walk over mud the heavier rigs would have to power through. On the Toyota Land Cruiser, the six is the only engine you can get. It will get you through some pretty thick stuff as long as you have decent tires. You can swap the Toyota six for a bigger engine; this is done often by people who like the Toyota but want more power.

Sixes are available on most four wheelers, even on the pickups. I wouldn't recommend them unless you don't intend to do much off-road driving, at least not through heavy mud. The big rigs need more torque to pull their heavier weight. They must also pull those big Gumbo Monster Mudders through the slosh, and need a lot of power to overcome the increased rolling resistance big tires create. You need big tires to float heavy trucks over mud and you need a big engine to turn them.

The Jeep CJs will get by with the 258 six, or sneak by with the 232, if you don't plan to do very rough off roading. The 258 will turn 10 x 15LT tires on 8-inch rims with no trouble, and these will provide you with all the flotation you need. For the Wagoneer and Cherokee, the 360 four barrel is adequate for most needs. You don't really need the 401 unless you're going to carry big loads or tow heavy trailers. You can't use bigger tires anyway, since the wheel wells won't accommodate them.

For most off-road use the Blazer can use the well-tried and proven 350 V8, four barrel. The 250 six won't do the trick, and the 400 is a bit large and fuel-consuming for all but the roughest off-roading situations. I've seen Blazers with the 350 go anywhere with no problem as long as they had decent tires. The same goes for the GMC Jimmy, which has the same engine.

The Plymouth Trail Duster and Dodge Ramcharger work well with the Chrysler

360 V8. You can opt for up to a 440 cubic inch engine, but this isn't really necessary unless you want to blow everybody else off the hill. I'd reserve the 440 for the biggest pickup and most demanding off roading. With better carburetion and headers, the 350 and 360 engines will give you all the power and torque you need.

Torque vs. Horsepower

Unless you do off road racing the name of the game in off-road performance is torque, not horsepower. Torque is a measure of rotational force, the brute strength needed to turn big tires through situations with heavy rolling resistance. Racing cars are light and ride over hard, level, smooth pavement on tracks. Four wheelers, on the other hand, are heavier, have bigger tires with greater road contact and friction, and must climb steep hills and roll through thick mud. This places an entirely different demand on the engine.

The V8 that gets the prize for having the best torque for its size is the International Harvester 345. It has 292 ft. lb. of torque at 2,000rpm, an engine speed commonly used off roading. Compare it to the Chevy 350, which has only 255 ft. lb. of torque at 2,800rpm. You'd have to go the biggest engine Chevy offers, the 400, to compare with the International engine, and the 400 has only 290 ft. lb. of torque at 2,800rpm. You have to run the 400 at 800rpm higher to get roughly the same amount of torque as the International 345.

In the horsepower department, the Chevy beats the International. The Chevy has 165 horsepower at 2,800rpm, while the International has to wind out to 3,600rpm to reach 163 horsepower. Okay, which is better for off roading? Higher horsepower you say? Wrong! Higher torque at a lower rpm range is what you need for off-roading running.

At increased engine rpm the front and rear tires (with 4WD) turn more rapidly. Fine, you want the wheels to turn as fast as possible so you can accelerate up hills, right? Only partly right. If you accelerate too fast your wheels will spin, especially on a muddy hill, and you'll stand still. Even worse, you'll get part-way up the hill, your tires will become loaded with mud, and you'll start to slide backward. Remember, gravity is there to pull you down any hill you go up.

What you want is a compromise between horsepower and low-end torque, with something extra in the torque department. The Dodge or Chrysler 360 V8 is a good combination. It has 285 ft. lb. of torque at 2,400rpm, and 175 horsepower at 4,000rpm. You'd have to lower your wheel spin with a high axle ratio to keep from slipping too much. Take the 3.90 axle option on the Trail Duster and on the Ramcharger as well. You want the highest torque and horsepower possible at the lowest rpm possible; this means gearing down. The standard 4.09 axle ratio on the International Scout II, Terra, and Traveler is meant to accomplish this. The lower gear ratios contribute to poor gas mileage, and the only way to improve efficiency is to get an overdrive and drive with mileage in mind.

The Chevy 350 is a good choice for the Chevy Suburban, the GMC Suburban, the Chevy K10 and K20 pickups as well as their GMC counterparts, the K-15 and K-25, but I would take the 400 cubic-inch engine with the Chevy K30 or the GMC K-35.

The same goes for the Dodge pickups. The 360 is adequate for the W-150 or the W-200, but for the W-300 it might be weak. The 400 or 440 can be used in the W-300, depending on how much power you prefer. The Ford F-150 can take the

300 six cylinder if you're mileage conscious and won't be doing anything but camping or hitting trails. Rough running requires the 351 V8 or 400 V8. The F-250 needs at least the 351, and could use the 351 with some modification, or the 400 for heavy off-road running.

The economical 258 six cylinder is adequate for the Jeep J-10 pickup if most of its running will be on the street. It would also be good for camping, traveling down established trails, and even some rougher going if you have a winch on hand to pull you through bogs. Get the standard 360 V8 with the J-20; it'll be good enough for medium-rough going and even rugged off roading with good tires. The 401 is a necessity for extended heavy trailer pulling, load hauling or rough off roading through heavy mud with oversized tires.

Selecting Engine Accessories

All the engines I've mentioned here have electronic ignition as standard equipment. This gives the spark a little more zap and avoids the replacement and adjustment of points and condenser. Some drivers don't like it because it's not as simple as the old contact point system. When it goes wrong it's not as easy to diagnose the problem. I haven't heard of anybody having trouble with them yet, and they seem to be very reliable.

Before choosing an engine, you should also be familiar with the carburetor, battery, alternator, engine block heater, and cooling system. When a four-barrel carburetor is available, take the option. It will give you more power, acceleration, and engine breathing because of the improved air-fuel mixture and the secondaries. Four barrels improve off-road performance when you really need it, like charging through a mud hole or up a steep hill. They are available on all the engines mentioned here except the Scout four, the sixes, and the smallest V8 for any model. The intermediate and big V8s all have four-barrel carburetors available. You may want to get the stock carburetor and put on your own four barrel, in which case you should refer to the next chapter on aftermarket accessories and modifications.

Engine block heaters are very useful for cold weather starts, and with the winters we've been having lately, a necessity. The trouble is, they're electric, and if you go camping you may as well not have it. You don't usually find electrical outlets in the middle of nowhere. You can make things easier on yourself by going to a campground with an outlet, but these are usually closed in the winter. See more winter tips in the winter operations section.

A heavy-duty (increased capacity) cooling system is a must for trailer towing, camper carrying, and heavy hauling. These chores will also be made easier with a heavy-duty battery, alternator, or generator. They're available on all models because four wheelers are made for more serious work.

It's a good idea to replace the paper air filter on your engine with a foam element. You have to have a good filter to catch the dust from rigs ahead of you on trails and the dust you generate yourself while driving dry trails. If the truck you want has a dry foam cover option for the paper element, get it. Only Ford and Dodge offer the old-fashioned oil bath air filter, a good off-road choice.

TRANSMISSIONS

While you're thinking of the body and engine you'll be needing, you'll have to direct your attention to the transmission. Not many people give the transmission much thought until they have torque and rpm problems in tough off-road situations like hill climbing and mud running.

Four wheeling sensitizes the driver to the transmission because the capabilities of the transmission are as severely tested off the road as the capabilities of the engine. This is because the transmission is what translates the rotary force (torque), power (horsepower), and speed (rpm) of the engine into motion. A transmission is a necessity on a vehicle with a gas engine because peak horsepower and torque are attained at relatively high rpm and lie within a small rpm range. On some engines the torque peak might be at 1600 to 2,800rpm, while peak horsepower requires higher rpm of 2,800, 3,600, or 4,000.

You have to try to keep your engine running as close as you can to the peak rpm for the work you're doing. If you run at too low an engine rpm, the truck will lurch forward in jerks and conk out because it doesn't have the power to overcome the rolling resistance and turn the wheels. This happens a lot on hills, when you try to take the hill in third gear or even second if it's very steep; you quickly slow down, lurch, and stop. You have to hold your foot on the brake and restart the engine, then try to quickly move your left foot off the brake and onto the clutch, engaging first gear fast enough to keep from rolling backwards excessively. Had you started up the hill in first or second gear, you could run at an engine rpm high enough to attain the necessary torque and horsepower to run up the hill. If you have an automatic, as most do, you have to give it enough gas to keep pushing up that hill.

An engine rpm that is too high is just as bad. Very high engine rpm, 3,000rpm or over, will usually cause the wheels to spin, especially in mud, snow, or wet leaves and grass. This can be dangerous on a hill where you can easily slide sideways, topple over, and roll down the hill. In situations like mud or snow, you'll just dig yourself in and get stuck.

Gearing Down to Keep Moving

The transmission, when used correctly, will keep you from going at too low or too high an engine rpm, so you have just enough power and torque to move, but not slip. It does this by allowing the engine to run at high rpm while the wheels are geared down to turn much more slowly. For example, on most cars the first gear is about 3.5:1, and the rear axle is about 3.75:1. This produces a final gear ratio of 3.5 x 3.75, or 13:1. The engine makes 13 revolutions for every one revolution of the rear wheels. Shifting into second and third allows you to maintain a high engine rpm while increasing wheel speed. The result is that the vehicle moves faster and faster. The same thing happens in an automatic, only it isn't as noticeable. To sum up: higher gears are actually lower (numerical) gear ratios and allow the wheels to turn faster than the lower gears (first and second), which are numerically higher gear ratios.

What does this mean for the off roader? Well, you want high ratios for the first two speeds, and low ratios for the third and fourth. This setup will enable you to get high engine rpm for the tough torque situations at lower speeds, and higher speeds on the highway with lower engine rpm. Much less torque is needed to keep a vehicle moving at high speed than is needed to overcome steep obstacles. The result is great off-road performance and good gas mileage on the highway.

Hey that sounds great! The only problem is that this ideal is impossible to attain in actual practice. Gears must be spaced closely together so you can shift smoothly and efficiently without requiring the engine to make quick jumps between rpm and torque outputs.

Different Transmissions For Different Needs

The transmissions available now are compromises in gearing that are meant to give the best overall performance in a wide variety of situations (off roading and street use). Basically, the three speeds that are standard on most four wheelers are relatively close-ratio transmissions with about a 3.0:1 first gear, going down to 1.0:1 in third, with a second gear spaced in the middle, usually closer to first with a 1.83:1 or 1.75:1. These ratios permit smooth shifting from first to second and a good highway clip at 1.0:1. The high gear on any transmission is always 1:1 unless the transmission has an overdrive, in which case the high gear would be under 1.0. The Chrysler overdrive four speed, for example, has a fourth gear ratio of 0.71:1. This allows the rear wheels to turn once for every 0.71 revolution of the engine. A fourth gear is needed because the jump would be too great from second to third, and any demanding off-road situation would cause the engine to stall.

The three speeds are all pretty much the same, evenly spaced with a relatively close ratio for easy shifting and torque transfer. There are three other kinds of transmissions: wide ratio four speeds with a granny low first gear; close ratio four speeds; and automatic three speeds.

The wide ratio four speeds are the most common. These are usually offered as an alternative to the three speed. They have a "granny" low or "creeper" first gear with a ratio of 6.0:1 or more. The New Process 435 offered as an option on the Dodge Ramcharger and Plymouth Trail Duster has a first gear of 6.68:1. This gives you really high engine rpm at very low running speeds (3–5mph) for those really demanding torque situations, like tree-stump pulling or yanking a trailer out of the mud. Couple this with a low rear end and the low range of the transfer case, and you won't go anywhere, but you'll have tremendous pull. Jeep once changed their granny low to 4.0:1 and had so many complaints that they went back to 6.32:1 in 1977.

The second kind, and a good choice for extensive off-road use, is the close ratio four speed. This has a first gear of 4.0 or 4.5, a second of around 2.5, a third of about 1.4, and a fourth of 1.0. It's very useful for off roading because the gears are so close together that there is little rpm drop (and torque drop) between gears. You can shift quickly and easily going up hills and through deep mud and not lose engine power. These are the least common, though. They're only offered on Dodge, Plymouth, International and Toyota four wheelers.

To give you an idea of the gear ratios on the vehicle you're thinking about buying or already own, I've listed them here. You can check the models listed earlier in this chapter to see what's available with the rig of your choice. Most of them are available on all the models; the exceptions are the bigger pickups that have a standard four-speed manual instead of the three-speed manual, and the Jeep Wagoneer which comes with the automatic only.

AMC JEEP

	1st	2nd	3rd	4th
Three-speed manual: Warner T-15A	3.00	1.83	1.00	
Four-speed manual: Warner T-18	6.32*	3.09	1.69	1.00
Three-speed automatic: Turbo Hydra-Matic	2.48	1.48	1.00	

Available on all Jeep CJs, wagons, and pickups. Exceptions are no automatic on the CJ-5, and Wagoneer comes with an automatic only.

CHEVY/GMC

	1st	2nd	3rd	4th
Three-speed Heavy-Duty Muncie	3.03	1.75	1.00	
Four-speed: CH 465 Muncie	6.56*	3.58	1.70	1.00
Three-speed automatic: Turbo Hydra-Matic	2.52	1.52	1.00	

Available on all Chevy and GMC four wheelers, including Suburban and Blazer. No three-speed on the big pickups, the Chevy K-30 and the GMC K-35.

FORD

	1st	2nd	3rd	4th
Four-speed overdrive	3.29	1.84	1.00	.80
Four-speed manual: Warner T-18	6.32*	3.09	1.69	1.00
Three-speed automatic: Ford three-speed	2.46	1.46	1.00	

The overdrive is not offered with 4WD.

DODGE

	1st	2nd	3rd	4th
Three-speed manual: New Process A-230	3.02	1.76	1.00	
Four-speed manual: New Process 435 (wide ratio)	6.68*	3.34	1.66	1.00
Four-speed manual: New Process 445 (close ratio)	4.56	2.28	1.31	1.00
Three-speed automatic: Dodge A-727 Load Flite	2.45	1.45	1.00	
Four-speed overdrive: Chrysler A-833	3.09	1.67	1.00	.73

The four-speed overdrive is available only on the D100. The three-speed manual is not available on the W300, which has the 435 standard. The three-speed manual is standard on the W150 and W200.

*Indicates granny low first gear.

INTERNATIONAL HARVESTER

	1st	2nd	3rd	4th
Three-speed manual: Warner T-15D	2.997	1.55	1.00	
Four-speed manual: Warner T-19A (close ratio)	4.02	2.41	1.41	1.00
Four-speed manual: Warner T-19 (wide ratio)	6.32*	3.09	1.68	1.00
Three-speed automatic: New Process T-407	2.45	1.45	1.00	

Available on all 4WD models, except diesel 4 x 4 which comes with T-19A standard.

TOYOTA LAND CRUISERS, HARDTOP AND STATION WAGON

	1st	2nd	3rd	4th
Four-speed manual: Toyota (close ratio)	3.55	2.29	1.41	1.00

The Toyota transmission is a good close ratio off-road runner, but don't be disappointed when it doesn't accelerate up the hill as fast as you want it to.

As far as mini-pickups go, the standard four-speed is a good off-road choice. The five-speed overdrive gives better gas mileage, but doesn't give any benefit off the road. If you're only going off road occasionally and want the economy, the five-speed is okay.

Guidelines for Selecting a Manual Transmission

1) On short wheelbase models such as the Scout and Jeep, the three speed is best. With the Scout, I would get the close ratio four speed. The wide ratio four speeds on the short wheelbase models are okay with the larger V8 engines. The same goes for pickups: get a three speed with a six or small V8, a four speed with a large V8.

2) For heavy hauling, such as carrying a camper, towing a big trailer, or heavy cargo carrying, get the closest ratio four speed available and a lower rear end (higher number, such as 4.10) for maximum control and pulling power.

3) Automatics come with full-time 4WD, except on the International Scout, which doesn't have full time available, and Ford, which gives you a choice of full time or part time.

What About Automatics?

The old hats are suspicious of automatics; they like to hear the gears whine and feel them mesh. I personally prefer the touch of a manual, but realistically eight out of ten new four wheelers are bought with automatics. They work well with the full-time 4WD systems, and out-perform the old part-time manual systems, especially in tough situations like hills, slick mud and snow. Off roading is nothing but tough driving situations, and we old hats just don't like to admit that automatics work better. Another advantage is that other family members can drive your four wheeler

---

*Indicates granny low first gear.

quite easily and benefit from 4WD safety in the snow or rain. I'm just waiting to see how the full-time systems hold up after years of hard use. They seem to weather pretty well, judging by the trucks I've seen. The point is, don't be afraid to get an automatic if you prefer it; they work well.

Don't worry too much about the effects of the transmission gear ratios on off roading. You'll do a lot better to get a good set of tires and a winch, and to improve your driving skills. You only notice a transmission when it's not made for the work you intend to do. If you buy an old pickup that wasn't geared for off roading, you may have problems. For the most part, the transmissions offered now are good gearboxes with years of use and experience behind them. If you do get stuck with a transmission that isn't suited to your driving needs, you can change the gears, get a new transmission, or buy a new truck.

DIFFERENTIALS: DO THEY MAKE A DIFFERENCE?

The purpose of a 4WD vehicle is to have traction, pulling power, on all four wheels. Yet the truth is that you don't always have traction on all four wheels; the traction is distributed by the differentials. When you make a turn or go over uneven terrain, the wheels do not turn at the same speed. In fact, in a turn all four wheels turn at different speeds. If the wheels were locked to the driveshaft, the ring or pinion gear teeth would break from the strain caused by the difference in turning speeds of the two axle shafts.

Automotive engineers have devised gear units that differentiate between the speeds of the two wheels on the axle. These units are differentials, those round bulges you see in the middle of each axle. The most common differential is the "open" type. When a vehicle turns, it allows the inner wheel to slow down while the outer wheel speeds up an equal amount.

Since this differential is designed for turns, it causes problems off the road when the wheels spin at different speeds for reasons other than turns, as in climbing over a rock with one wheel and slipping in the mud with another. The open differential, the kind found on every standard car and four wheeler, doesn't know that it should give more torque to the wheel with better traction. When a rear wheel slips, the open differential gives it virtually all the torque, sensing that it is making a turn. The slower wheel could get better traction because it isn't slipping, but the differential can't sense this.

Normally the standard or open differential divides the torque to both wheels, not just one as myth has it. It's a common mistake to believe that only the right rear and left front wheels of a four wheeler have torque because you can see those wheels spinning often. They're not spinning because they have all the torque, they're spinning because the rotational torque of the driveshafts acting on the axles tends to reduce the load on those wheels a little. With less load, they spin more easily. The standard differential, following normal turning procedure, then gives them all the torque.

The limited slip or Positraction® differential, called "posi" by many drivers, handles turns by letting the faster wheel slip, and giving more torque to the slower wheel. This setup works well on turns, in mud, climbing over rocks, and in other slipping situations. When one wheel slips in the mud, the slower wheel, which in actual situations is the one on drier ground, has more torque, better traction, and will pull you out.

The limited slip differential has its share of drawbacks. Since most limited slips are designed with clutch discs, they wear out because of the heat generated by the friction buildup. The Trac-Lok®, made by Spicer and available on International Scouts and Jeep four wheelers, has this drawback. The Trac-Lok uses regular gear oil, while other units need special lubricant additives to keep the differential from chattering and clunking after several years of wear. The Ford Traction-Lok also has a clutch arrangement, needing frequent oil changes as with the Spicer unit. The least common limited slip in use is the Chrysler Sure-Grip®, or antispin differential. It uses clutches like the Trac-Lok and has similar wear problems. Chrysler suggests that if you have noise problems, you should use their special hypoid lubricant. If the noise doesn't disappear, get the unit replaced.

With all limited slip units you have a maintenance problem. Part of it is due to the friction caused by the slipping clutches, and part is due to the fact that they were originally designed for use with a lubricant derived from whale oil, which has remarkable lubricating properties. This whale-oil derivative is no longer available. Whales are threatened with extinction and the federal government has banned use of the lubricant. Automakers have been trying substitutes for years, but none work as well. Consequently, these units need periodic rebuilding and frequent gear oil changes. Another problem is fishtailing at highway speeds on slippery surfaces; one wheel can slip slightly, causing the differential to grab and swing the rear end out. Limited slip units are even sensitive to differences in tire height; a mismatched spare or a difference in air pressure between two tires on the same axle may cause fishtailing. If you want to put up with the maintenance and the handling problems, fine. But there is another alternative—the locking differential.

There are three currently popular models: the Detroit Locker®, the Eaton®, and the Triple-D Dual Drive®. Locking differentials use gears instead of frictional clutches. On turns, the slower inside wheel gets all the torque, while the outside wheel freewheels. If either wheel reaches an excessive speed, both wheels lock together. Locking differentials overcome the problem the limited slip differentials have of wearing out quickly, and the handling problem when one wheel is larger than the other or has lower tire pressure. They're not as sensitive to changes in rpm between the two axle shafts, so they don't fishtail easily on slippery highways. In short, they overcome the problems of the standard "open" differential while avoiding the maintenance problems and most of the handling problems of the limited slips. The only major handling problem associated with the Detroit Locker is a tendency to lock in suddenly and hard. This can be tricky on turns. They all have a locking ratchet that can make noise, especially the Detroit Locker. Sometimes you have to hit the gas just right for the axle to lock up. It seems that the Detroit Locker is the most troublesome in this respect.

The Eaton locking differential is available on GMC and Chevy trucks. It doesn't lock up like a limited slip when there's a difference in tire pressure or height, only in bad slipping situations. Best of all, it can only lock up while the vehicle is moving 20mph or less, avoiding the dangers of unwanted highway lock-up. Eaton also uses a clutching system to engage the lock, avoiding the shock of lock-up experienced with the Detroit Locker. It requires no special lubricants, doesn't need frequent gear oil changes, and doesn't have to be rebuilt periodically. Unfortunately, as far as I know the Eaton can't be purchased for installation by the consumer. It has to be bought as an option with Chevy and GMC trucks.

What kind of differential should you get? If you get a full-time system, don't worry about the differential setup. You'll get enough traction with the full-time system to more than make up for it. You'd be better off getting a good set of tires. As a matter of fact, Jeep doesn't recommend a limited slip or locker with its Quadra-Trac system. It probably puts too much stress on the limited slip differential built into the transfer case. On Dodge and Plymouth four wheelers, you can order the Sure-Grip differential with the full-time system. I don't feel it's worth the bother, but if you like a limited slip and find it useful, its available. It will improve off-road traction somewhat, but good tires will make a bigger difference.

I would only recommend a limited slip with a part-time system. Limited slips and lockers make a bigger difference on the rear end of part-time systems, and aren't recommended for the front axle. In fact, they are no longer available from the factory for front axles on any models covered in this book. The reason is that they can cause dangerous handling on slippery surfaces.

FOUR-WHEEL DRIVE: PART TIME OR FULL TIME?

With nearly all of the 4WD models listed in this chapter, you have a choice between a two-speed manual transfer case and a full-time system. Toyota Land Cruiser and International Scout, however, do not offer the full-time 4WD system. These models only come with a manual two-speed transfer case. The other models have the full-time 4WD system as an option or as standard equipment with an automatic transmission. On Ramcharger and Trail Duster, only full time is offered.

Part-Time 4WD

Four-wheel drive requires a front driving axle and a front driveshaft as well as a rear driving axle and driveshaft. This is accomplished through a transfer case, an accessory gearbox located behind the transmission. From the transfer case the two driveshafts deliver power to the front and rear axles. The transfer case is the essential component of any 4WD system. Without it, the vehicle would have no four-wheeling capability.

Well that's very simple, you might think. All you need is an extra driveshaft up front and you can have 4WD on any vehicle. Unfortunately, it is not that simple. Remember that when you make a turn all four wheels turn at different speeds, each making its own arc of a different length. Consequently, each axle as well as each wheel moves at a different rate. So you have three problems now: you have to account for the difference between rolling speeds on each rear wheel; you have to account for the rolling difference between each axle; and you have to account for the rolling difference between the two front wheels. The front and rear wheels are easy to deal with, because the differential in each axle solves the problem.

The axles, however, require a different solution. If you lock them together, they will turn at different speeds and mash the gears in the transfer case and the splines on the axles. The driveshafts will literally wind up with torsional stress and quickly give. The two axles move at different speeds, and something has got to give to allow that movement.

Until 1973, the driveline was relieved of these "wind-up" stresses by allowing the front driveshaft to be disconnected from the transfer case. The front driveshaft would only be used in off-road situations, where the mud, sand, dirt, or water would allow the rear wheels to slip and skid while they followed the front wheels with no danger of torsional stresses building up. The part-time system is nothing but a way of dealing with the difference between the rolling speeds of the front and rear wheels in turns. It's like making a differential that drives only one wheel and lets the other roll freely, and is the easiest way out.

LOCKING HUBS

The front wheels are allowed to roll more freely by a clever invention, the locking hub. The locking hub can be used to disconnect the wheel from the splines of the drive axle when not in 4WD. The wheels then roll freely and won't force the driveshaft to turn. When not in 4WD, the front driveshaft just sits there. An even more ingenious invention is the automatic locking hub. This hub engages the front wheels automatically whenever there is torque applied to the front driveshaft. Shifting into 4WD automatically locks in the front wheels—you don't have to get out and lock them in. The only drawback to this setup is that the hubs are torque-activated. They won't engage when there is no torque on the front driveshaft, such as when rolling down a hill or coasting through a curve. In these situations you want the front driveshaft working so you can use the front wheels to get better control. So it's wise to lock in the hubs, even if they're automatic.

Hubs are used almost universally on part-time systems, but they aren't actually a

The locking hub enables you to lock the front wheel to the front axle shaft in the LOCK position, and lets you save gas by disengaging in the FREE position

Here's how the shifter looks on the Dodge NP 203 transfer case. HI LOCK or LO LOCK positions lock the transfer case differential for tough off/road situations (Courtesy, Dodge Truck Public Relations)

necessary component. Military vehicles never use them, since their function is to be combat ready at all times. Uncle Sam doesn't fret about gas mileage too much.

The best known hubs are made by Warn. They invented the locking hub to reduce wear on the front driveshaft and differential and to allow the vehicle to get better gas mileage. Warn also invented the Lock-O-Matic ® automatic hub. If these hubs are available with the four wheeler you want, get them; you'll never have to worry about maintaining them. Some of the other hubs on the market are Husky ®, Selectro ®, Easylok ®, and Dana/Spicer ®. All makes are good, having overcome the old problem of difficult engagement. The Warn hubs on my Scout are eleven years old and still work perfectly.

TRANSFER CASES

Transfer cases almost always come with two speeds to allow for a double reduction of all gear speeds. There are only a few exceptions; the Subaru and the bottom-of-the-line International Scout II. All other current four wheelers with the part-time system have a two-speed transfer case.

The two-speed transfer case doubles the number of speeds you have by doubling the reduction in low range. The Dana 20 transfer case has a high range of 1.0:1. This means it retains the gearing of all transmission speeds just as they are. For increased torque and engine rpm in tough traction conditions, a low range is provided. This reduces by 2.03 the gear ratios in the transmission. For example, a first gear ratio of 4.56 becomes a first gear ratio of 9.12, giving about twice the engine rpm at the same vehicle speed. The Dana 20 is used on most part-time 4WD models made by Ford, International Harvester, and AMC Jeep.

Another very common transfer case is the New Process Gear Model 205. It is a heavy-duty unit with higher torque ratings, and is used on Chevrolet and GMC four wheelers and the Ford F-150 and F-250 with the standard four-speed transmission. It has a high gear ratio of 1.01:1 and a low of 1.96:1, yielding about the same gear reduction as the Dana 20.

HOW TO USE PART-TIME 4WD

Having a part-time 4WD transfer case shift is like having another stick shift. With the transfer case shifter you can place the vehicle in 2WD high for normal driving, 4WD high for normal off-road driving, 4WD low for tough off roading when the going is slow, and neutral, where the transfer case is disengaged and no power is transmitted to the driveshafts at all. This is used while powering a PTO winch, or when towing the vehicle.

If you have locking hubs on your four wheeler, they should be locked in before you come to an off-road situation. Simply turn the dial on the hub into the "lock" position; to unlock, turn the dial the other way, usually counterclockwise, into the "free" position. You may have read (probably in an advertisement) some criticism of the locking hub because you have to get out and lock the hubs manually. Full-time systems overcome this annoyance by being engaged all the time, so they tell you. This is one of the most petty criticisms I have ever heard. Locking hubs are so simple and easy that anybody who considers it a chore shouldn't be driving off the road. If getting out and locking the hubs is work, imagine digging out a pickup while up to your knees in mud.

Some four wheelers don't have locking hubs with their part-time system. Instead, the front axle is engaged all the time. These are becoming rare, however. It just doesn't make sense to keep your front driveshaft and differential spinning with no torque on them. You'll also have poorer gas mileage.

Remember, lock the hubs *before* you shift the transfer case into 4WD and disengage 4WD at the transfer case before you unlock the hubs. If there is any tension on the driveshaft, the hubs might stick. Disconnecting the transfer case first helps eliminate any tension. If the hubs still stick in the locked position, try rocking the vehicle or backing up about a foot. They will come out, just keep trying. Automatic hubs don't have to be unlocked unless you locked them manually. Simply put the transfer case back into 2WD. The absence of torque on the front axle will disengage the hubs.

Locking hubs and transfer cases are very tough and will last a long time. Use a little sense and caution and you'll never have any trouble with your part-time 4WD system. If you follow some sensible precautions, your locking hubs will last forever:

1) Never lock one side and not the other. This could damage the differential. Occasionally check your hubs in your driveway to make sure one isn't locked. A curious kid might lock one by accident.

2) Never drive in 4WD low on a hard, level surface. This really makes things tough on the drivetrain. You'll soon hear it groaning and snapping as torsional stresses build up.

3) Don't drive in 4WD high for extended periods of time on the highway. It's all right if it starts to snow or rain, but otherwise, try to avoid the practice. Keep it in 2WD on the highway and 4WD off.

Full-Time 4WD

In 1973, a new engineering concept in 4WD appeared—the full-time system. With this system the front and rear driveshafts operate all the time, keeping the vehicle in 4WD constantly. There is no way to disengage the front driveshaft, hence the term "full-time 4WD."

How do such systems avoid the drivetrain windup characteristic of part-time systems? A differential between the axles is built into the transfer case. Just as a regular differential allows different turning speeds of two wheels on the same axle, the differential built into the transfer case allows varying speeds of the two axles. It's called the inter-axle differential, and here's how it works: when turning on a hard surface the differential allows the rear driveshaft to turn more slowly than the front, just like a regular axle differential.

There are two models of full-time 4WD available, the New Process Model 203 and the Jeep Quadra-Trac system. The Quadra-Trac system is not made by AMC, but by Borg-Warner. As of now, AMC Jeep is the only manufacturer that Borg-Warner sells the unit to. Every other four wheeler uses the NP 203 unit, made by New Process Gear, a division of Chrysler Corporation. If you've got full time and your four wheeler is not a Jeep you've got an NP 203 unit.

THE NEW PROCESS 203 FULL-TIME SYSTEM

This unit was first offered on Chevrolet and GMC four wheelers in 1973. The central feature of this unit is the inter-axle differential. It distributes torque to the two axles and allows slower movement of the rear axle in turns. The inter-axle differential is built into the transfer case, but can be manually locked to deliver equal torque to both the front and rear axles. This can only be done, of course, on soft or slippery terrain, not on hard pavement. If it were locked on hard pavement, the drivetrain windup problem would occur.

The crucial fact to remember about the NP 203 is that the inter-axle differential is an open differential. If the front axle begins to slip, most of the torque will be given to the front axle, causing it to slip more. The same thing would happen to the rear if it began to slip. Since the differentials in the axles are usually the open type, just *one* wheel slipping would be enough to start the whole thing slipping. When one front or rear wheel slips, the open differential on that axle gives most of the torque to that wheel. The whole axle would then begin slipping. Since the inter-axle differential is also the open type, it would deliver most of the driveshaft torque to the axle that's slipping. In a matter of seconds all traction and torque would be lost because of just one wheel slipping—you'd be stuck.

There is only one way to control this problem. You must lock the differential into HI or LO LOC. This can be done with a simple shift of the transfer case lever. The GM shifting configuration looks like this.

LO LOC

LO

N

HI

HI LOC

The high range has a gear ratio of 1.0:1 and the low range has a gear ratio of 2.01:1, about the same as the Dana 20 part-time transfer case. LO range would be used in rough off-road situations, like climbing a very steep hill, or when towing a heavy trailer or moving a very heavy payload. HI range could be used for normal off roading, driving down trails, through mud and the like. Since the inter-axle differential is an open differential, the HI loc position would be used a great deal off the road. Another way of improving off-road performance with the NP 203 would be to get the limited slip or locking differential option for the rear end. Because of the slipping problem in full time, automakers have made a rear limited slip available with the NP 203 full-time system.

A warning light on the dash of most models reminds you that you're in LOC, so that you will shift out before going back to hard pavement. If you forget to take it out of LOC you may have some difficulty getting it back into HI because of drivetrain windup. If so, handle this the same way you would handle it with the part-time system: put the transmission into reverse and back up a few feet. This should relieve the drivetrain of windup enough for you to put it into HI. If it doesn't, just back up again and move the lever until it slips into place. The shift into and out of LOC is spring activated and could get stuck.

Could you put locking hubs on the front axle of your four wheeler with a NP 203 system? Yes, but you gain no advantage. The axle on your front end is probably the same as the axle on most other four wheelers, a Dana 44. You could put freewheeling hubs on it, but it wouldn't make any sense and will lead to weird consequences. The differential would interpret the freewheeling front hubs as slippage. It would then deliver all the torque to the front driveshaft, and you would stand still. The same thing would happen if you disconnected the front driveshaft. The differential would interpret this as slippage and your front output shaft of the transfer case would spin wildly, getting you nowhere fast. You could disconnect the front driveshaft as an emergency procedure if the front driveshaft or differential were damaged, put the transfer case in HI LOC and drive home. This would cause some strain on the transfer case, but it would get you home. If you're in the middle of nowhere, wrecking the transfer case is worth saving the whole vehicle. Don't do this as normal practice, or you will ruin the transfer case fast.

Would this help your gas mileage? Not really. Unlike conventional transfer cases such as the Dana 20, the NP 203 uses engine oil and drives the front driveshaft with a big drive chain about 3 inches wide. The chain works smoothly and efficiently on needle bearings, cutting down on wear and friction. You would get little better mileage by disconnecting the front driveshaft, mainly because you'd still be carrying all that four-wheeler weight with its lower gear ratios.

Old-timers who feel uncomfortable with the full time idea can rest at ease; the full-time system avoids the problems of the old manual transfer cases. The really great advantage of the NP 203 is that you're in 4WD all the time, even on hard pavement, you can drive with more control and better handling.

JEEP QUADRA-TRAC

The Jeep Quadra-Trac system is similar to the NP 203 in that it is designed to deliver torque to both driveshafts in all driving situations, while compensating for the difference between the speeds of the front and rear axles. This gives you full-time 4WD on and off the road without stopping to lock in hubs or shift the transfer case. Unlike the NP 203 unit's open differential in the transfer case, the Quadra-Trac has a limited slip differential so that the transfer case will not deliver all the torque to the spinning axle. In spinning situations the Quadra-Trac will not get you stuck. Instead, it will provide torque to both axles giving more to the axle that has traction. However, limited slip differentials are not available on the axles. When one wheel on an axle loses traction, the torque on that axle will go to that wheel. More torque will go to the other axle, though, to pull you out. What happens when one wheel on each axle slips? Then you're stuck. Torque will be distributed equally between the two axles, and since they're both slipping, you'll stay where you are. The locked NP 203 system with a limited slip on the rear axle would work better in this case.

The Quadra-Trac system is not designed to be locked in as frequently as the NP 203 unit. Lockout, as it is called, is done by operating a vacuum control switch located in the back of the glove compartment. The switch deactivates the limited slip differential, resulting in both axles being locked together as with part-time 4WD. It is inconveniently located in the glove box so it won't be used frequently. Jeep cautions that it be used only for emergencies, such as when high-centered or when one driveshaft has to be disconnected due to damage. Lockout puts great strain on the transfer case.

Can locking hubs be put on the Quadra-Trac? Again, the answer is definitely no.

The limited slip unit of the inter-axle differential would have constant pressure applied to it to deliver all the torque to the rear axle with the front freewheeling. This would result in premature transfer case failure. The biasing unit of the limited slip would quickly wear out.

The Quadra-Trac unit also has only one speed on the standard unit. The low range unit of the transfer case, having a gear ratio of 2.57:1, is optional and can also be added on by the dealer. It is activated by a lever under the driver's seat. This is an excellent gear ratio for a low range, and is a good idea if you expect to do a lot of rough slow-going or heavy trailer towing.

The Quadra-Trac uses a special Jeep lubricant—do not use other oil. The limited slip differential requires certain additives in the lubricant and use of oil without the additives will damage the unit.

DIFFERENCES BETWEEN THE TWO FULL-TIME SYSTEMS

The main difference between the two units is that the Quadra-Trac system has a limited slip differential built into the transfer case. This cripples it, though, when one wheel on each axle is losing traction. However, a NP 203 without a limited slip on one axle can be crippled with only one slipping wheel, whereas the Quadra-Trac works well in this situation. Also, the NP 203 can be locked in easily, while locking in is not recommended for regular off roading with the Quadra-Trac. So all in all, the NP 203 with rear limited slip will outperform the Quadra-Trac in ultimate traction situations. In actual use, both systems work pretty well. You just have to pick the one that does what you want to do best.

Another advantage of the NP 203 is that on the Dodge and Plymouth four wheelers you can get a standard transmission with the full-time unit. On Jeeps the full-time unit only comes with an automatic transmission. The same is true for Ford, Chevy, and GMC full-time four wheelers—they must be purchased with automatics. The NP 203 also provides for a PTO winch, the Quadra-Trac does not. Most people don't use a PTO because they're more expensive and complicated than the electric units, so this doesn't really make any difference. The Quadra-Trac also uses special lubricant and the NP 203 uses the 10W 30 or 10W 40 engine oil.

Comparing Part-Time and Full-Time 4WD

Okay, now that you've taken in all the technical stuff, what is the compelling reason to buy a full-time four wheeler?

With the part-time system, you always drive in 2WD with the front axle shafts idly spinning or disconnected by locking hubs. Reaching a trail, you get out and lock the hubs, move the transfer case lever into 4WD HI, and you're off. Both axles are now locked in. If one wheel loses traction, the other driveshaft is locked in to give you traction. If the second axle also has a wheel that starts to slip and you have open differentials on both axles, then you're stuck. The best way to use part-time is with a limited slip on the rear. Limited slips are not a good idea on the front since they cause handling problems on turns and in tricky off-road situations. With a part-time system, you're either in 2WD or have both axles locked in. You don't have an inter-axle differential that can play with the torque between axles. Also, you gain extra gas mileage and reduced wear as a result of having locking hubs.

With a full-time system, you're in 4WD all of the time. When you reach an off-road trail, you can do one of two things depending on the system you have. If you have the NP 203 unit, shift it into HI LOC, locking in the two axles, and take off. Now you have the same system you would have with a part time; both axles are locked in. If you don't lock in the inter-axle differential, your full-time NP 203 will get you into more trouble than a part-time system. The open differential in the transfer case will give torque to the axle that's losing traction.

If you have a Quadra-Trac 4WD full-time system, you can drive right onto the trail. Since it has open differentials, as soon as one wheel on one axle slips, the transfer case shifts the torque to the other axle. If a wheel on that axle slips the torque is shifted to both axles, and both axles will slip. Remember, you can't get a limited slip with Quadra-Trac.

What is the advantage then, of full-time 4WD? An automatic transmission, making accelerating up hills and through mud easier, and full-time 4WD handling on the highway are the advantages. Four-wheel drive on the highway is the only thing you get with a full-time system that you cannot get with a part-time system. Since part time is cheaper, you can go with a four-speed transmission and rear limited slip, and perform as well as a full-time system off the road. The full-time system is easier, that's all. For the money I'd take the part-time system, but you should decide for yourself. The fact is that 80 percent of all new 4WD vehicles are purchased with automatic and full-time 4WD.

3

ACCESSORIES

Outfitting Your Vehicle for Off Roading

INTRODUCTION

Today you can drive out of the showroom with practically a fully loaded off roader, equipped with skid plates, auxiliary gas tank, wide footprint tires, winch, tow hooks, trailer ball, and even a CB radio. Some models even offer roll bars and front end guards. Detroit has been doing an excellent job of responding to consumer needs in the four wheeling market.

For those of us who don't have new four wheelers, and who want to add the accessories that make a difference in appearance and performance, a wide range of off-roading accessories is available. Even those with new trucks aren't completely satisfied with the stock setup. They usually add bigger tires, nicer wheels, a roll bar, lights, headers, dual exhausts, a good stereo and speaker system, etc. And the emergency items like fire extinguishers, as well as unstucking necessities like extra cable, nylon straps, snatch blocks, and jacks aren't available on new rigs. You can't go off roading without putting out some cash for some of these items.

The nagging question with accessories, though, is what do I really need? How much should I shell out for items I may not use very much? What's essential and what's a waste of money? Since most of us do not belong to four wheeling clubs we are pretty much on our own in regard to off-roading knowledge. Most of our information comes from books, magazine articles and advertisements. The best alternative, however, is a knowledgeable friend who may not know or have experienced everything, but knows most of what you'll run into. You can avoid the mistakes I've made by heeding my warnings. Other mistakes you'll make in spite of what I say, like not bringing along a winch.

Ultimately you'll have to decide for yourself. I have my own preferences and driving habits, and so do you. On some points you'll say I'm all wet and on others that I'm right on. And you'll be right, because your needs are different than mine.

The best of the old and the new. Here is the author's 1966 military Scout 800. The galvanized body, built for the Navy, is virtually rustproof. The dents and scratches attest to years of off-road use. With a Burbank spring kit, Goodyear Wrangler R/T tires on Duke's wheels, Hickey Sidewinder III winch, Marchal lights, ACCEL ignition, and Advanced Adaptor headers it can outperform many new trucks, especially on the soft stuff. The right accessories can make any four wheel drive truck, new or old, an excellent off-road vehicle. See the text for details on how to set up yours

TIRES

Driving a four wheeler is different from driving the family car. Driving your car involves watching the traffic, stopping at signs and lights when needed, getting on the expressway at the right entrance and knowing when to exit, keeping out of accidents, and trying to get where you're going as safely and quickly as you can.

The four wheeler, on the other hand, is a very different ball game. Off the road, your main concerns are not to get stuck and to get where you're going. There's no sense worrying about getting to your favorite fishing spot on the lake if you get stuck after leaving the road. When you go off-roading you have to gear your head to think: "How can I get the best traction and not get stuck?" One of your first considerations will be tires. There are three things to look for in an off-roading tire. In order of importance these are: 1) flotation, 2) traction, and 3) appearance.

Flotation

When you think of floating you think of sitting on a raft in the ocean or of a beer can floating in water. Floating means staying *on* the surface, not sinking into it. This is a great word to use to describe tires because that's what an off-roading tire should do—keep you floating above the mud, silt, snow and soft sand. You can't get any traction if your tires sink so deeply into the soft stuff that the axles, frame, and skid plates bog down. This is the worst way to get stuck. It takes a tremendous amount of pull to yank a pickup out of a bog when it's up to the wheel wells in mud.

You can't make your four wheeler light enough to float on mud, so you must

Here you can see how an H78x15 tire digs into heavy gravel. A semi-flotation tire with round shoulders, such as the Armstrong Tru-Trac, would correct this problem

Compare the H78x15 tire on the left to the Goodyear Tracker A/T on the right. The Tracker is wider, gives more support over soft surfaces like mud and sand, and has an unbroken center design for quiet highway running

spread the weight of the rig over a wider surface area. This is where the flotation tire comes in. By using a tire with a larger footprint you can cover a larger surface area with the tire and decrease the weight of the rig per square inch of road surface. This is very important, since any road surface can only support a set number of pounds per square inch. When you get into soft surfaces such as mud, snow, silt and sand, the amount of weight that can be supported per square inch decreases to 20 pounds or less. Of course the tires themselves will not provide enough flotation to keep you out of trouble; if you stopped your off roader in mud or sand you would begin to sink. Only by maintaining a steady speed of at least 10–15mph can you keep your neck out of the mud. And the faster you go, the better are your chances of not getting stuck.

Most of the tires popular now are not true flotation tires, they're of the semi-flotation type. The true flotation tire is extremely wide, like the Goodyear Terra® tire for swamp and tundra conditions. Armstrong Tru-Tracs or Formula Desert Dogs® are really semi-flotation tires. They provide a wide footprint for soft running, but can still hold together under highway speeds. The true flotation tires can't.

An important characteristic of semi-flotation tires is the shoulder design. On some tires, such as the Desert Dog and Tru-Trac, the sidewall bulges out when it's inflated. The sidewalls become more vulnerable to rocks, but they provide much smoother movement through sand, silt and mud because the rounded shoulder adds to the footprint area. The round-shouldered tire is more vulnerable to sidewall damage when running over sharp rocks, but this isn't a major problem in most parts of the country.

Traction

Traction means grip on the slippery stuff, such as mud and snow. Picking an off-road tire with good flotation and grip would be easy except for one snag: sand and mud require opposite tread designs. It's like the problem with transmissions: tall gears are good for the highway, short ones for off the road. The best practical transmission is a compromise. So it is with tread designs and traction. Sand requires a smooth tread design, no lugs or center zig-zags, and mud requires center zig-zags

One of the best mud tires is the Gumbo Monster Mudder®, while the best sand tires are the Armstrong Hi-Way® or Gates (National) Dune Command®. Another great sand tire, particularly for uphill competition, is the Dick Cepek Multi-Paddlë®. The problem with the Multi-Paddle, though, is that it can't be used on the highway or street. It's strictly an off-road tire, while the Gates Command and the Armstrong Hi-Way can be driven on the highway as well as off the road. Incredibly, the Multi-Paddle is also good on mud, very good from what I hear. However, it tends to slip on dry dirt. So while it isn't the perfect all-purpose tire, it is the exception to the mud vs. sand rule. It can be used with great success in any extreme condition. You might consider getting a set and putting them on your rig if you're going to do a lot of running in mud or sand and don't mind switching them or towing your four wheeler on a trailer. For most of us, some sort of combination mud-sand-street tire will have to do. The best combination is a semi-flotation, semi-smooth tire with no lugs or zig-zags, but with some biting tread for mud.

If you do a lot of sand running, a good sand-highway combination might be the best for you. Sand tires run smoothly and quietly on the highway, unlike aggressive mud tires. Most off roaders I know have aggressive mud tires like the Tru-Trac. As a rule, these tires make more noise on the highway, sing loudly at high speeds, and cause excessive vibration. If you like to drive with your window open like I do, the sound will drive you crazy. The Monster Mudders have dozens of lugs as deep as $^{19}/_{32}$ inch and really make a lot of racket. They wear down more quickly on the street too. Owners of Gumbo Monster Mudders have told me that they expect about 25,000 miles of use from their tire. This is mainly because they do 97 percent of their driving on pavement, as most off-roaders do.

Appearance

The third and least important characteristic of tires for off-road performance is appearance. Once your tires get caked with mud, it won't matter how nice they looked, and even when clean their looks won't keep you from getting stuck. It's nice to have good-looking tires, though. Plain old tires can make an otherwise beautiful machine look bad.

Some tires have a tougher appearance than others. Gumbo Monster Mudders, with their huge lugs and treads, look massive and rugged, especially on a big pickup like the F-250. Other tires don't look as impressive, but their appearance can be improved with raised white lettering and a nice wheel. White spoked wheels are the most popular, with chrome wheels coming in second. White spoked wheels are popular because they wear well, are easy to clean, and are strong enough to hold up to tough off-road use. Chrome wheels scratch, are harder to keep clean, look bad when they're dusty or dirty, and are much more expensive. What kind of wheels you like is, of course, a matter of personal preference.

Popular Brands of Off-Road Tires

The following opinions are based on experience and the performance of the tires in actual use. Scientific studies are necessary for the design of new tread patterns, but when it comes to judging a tire the best measurement is how it holds up in actual use. I avoid evaluating new tires, because a tire performs differently after it has

20,000 miles on it. The tires I evaluated worked well on the street and off the road under much the same conditions you'll be using them.

ARMSTRONG TRU-TRAC

In its most popular size, 11 x 15, the Tru-Trac can fit all but the smallest four wheelers. It's a favorite in the Midwest where it is used for its aggressive tread design and round-shouldered semi-flotation characteristics. It performs well in mud, snow and silt (the soft stuff on the banks of sandy rivers), and does well in sand. It will dig into sand if you come to a dead stop and gun the engine. Some drivers find Tru-Tracs too noisy, others aren't bothered by them. They cost about $60 each, a good price, and fit on 8-inch rims. Overall, it is an excellent tire—one of the best—and will last about 30–35,000 miles under 90 percent street use.

ARMSTRONG NORSEMAN®

These are very good general-use tires, and are quieter on the highway than the Tru-Tracs. They aren't too popular but have good potential, especially for those like myself who like to use an H78 x 15 tire. They are the best in this size for off-road use. They are cheaper than Tru-Tracs by about $20, and run well in mud, snow and sand. They don't have as much flotation as Tru-Tracs, but on a smaller vehicle such as a Scout, Land Cruiser, or Jeep they could be perfect. Not too many people know about them, so check them out if you needs will be met by what I have described. On a smaller four wheeler they should last over 40,000 miles easily.

GUMBO MONSTER MUDDER

These have become popular for use in thick mud, and are without qualification the best tires for the deepest mud. They have very thick lugs and center treads, $^{19}/_{32}$ inch, and are wide for good flotation in the soft stuff. I have seen Ford pickups with the biggest Monster Mudders, the 14/35 x 16.5 size, dig trenches as they plowed through 2½ feet of mud. With these tires on your Blazer or pickup you won't get stuck in any but the worst mud. They're unbelievable. They're also noisy and have a short life, about 25,000 miles. This is because they only fit on the biggest rigs which wear them down faster with their weight, and they have massive lugs which get chewed down quickly.

You can get them in smaller sizes, down to G78 x 14. Make sure that your gears are low enough (high numerically) to handle the large diameter of these tires, and that your engine has the guts to pull them. If you can fit them and pull them, and you do a lot of driving through heavy mud, then these are for you. In snow they are excellent, although the unbroken center zig-zags can slip on icy roads. Chains would take care of this problem. On sand, keep moving because they will dig in. They're so large though, that it isn't easy to get stuck in even the softest sand.

FORMULA DESERT DOGS

All three Formula Desert Dogs, the Desert Dog, the Desert Dog PCV, and the Desert Dog Xtra, are excellent tires. They are very similar to the Tru-Trac in that they use an aggressive zig-zag tread with a round-shouldered shape for good flotation in the mud. They are very noisy on the street, and will last approximately 15–18,000 miles. The Desert Dog PCV is quieter and will last over 20,000 miles.

King of the mudders is the Gumbo Monster Mudder, here mounted on a Blazer. If this tire won't get you through the mud, nothing but a winch will

The Formula Desert Dogs are one of the best overall traction tires, particularly good in sand. They give good flotation and can be let down to low pressure for the really soft stuff

The Dogs give excellent traction on sand, dirt, and powdery snow. They are also good on slippery surfaces such as wet mud and snow, but don't perform as well as tires with more aggressive lugs.

The tires mentioned so far have aggressive treads, good for mud and snow but not so hot for sand. There are several good middle-of-the-road tires, compromises made for the street-driver who still wants a capable off-road tire when he leaves the pavement. They are characterized by a square rather than a rounded shoulder, closer packed treads for unbroken contact with the street so they will run quieter, and less accentuated treads so they won't dig your grave on the beach. Detroit has been responsive enough to offer these on new models.

GOODYEAR TRACKER A/T®

Available on almost all new four wheelers, these 10x15LT tires are an excellent choice for street and occasional off-road use. They have smaller treads, no large lugs, and a square side profile for solid street contact, reducing road resistance (thereby increasing gas mileage) and noise. They are the quietest tires you can get, but be warned that they will not grab as well in snow and thick mud. They will get you through occasional slippery stuff that isn't too bad, but you can't expect to do a lot of heavy mud running with them. I test drove them for a weekend on a 1978 Scout SS-II and did not get stuck. I went through steep rocky hills, dirt, and occasional mud holes and they did grip fairly well. Even though they do not have an aggressive tread, they will grip in moderate situations and are very good on dirt. I would say they are the perfect tire for someone who does occasional off-roading to the cabin or campsite and does not go in for rigorous off roading. With these tires you can drive out of the showroom and handle most moderate traction situations with no problem. Their flotation is good and they look nice.

GOODYEAR WRANGLER R/T®

This is Goodyear's more aggressive tire. It is a very wide tire, available in 11.50 and 13.50 widths, and has lugs on the sides. I chose them for my own use because

The Goodyear Tracker A/T has good flotation and runs quietly on the highway. It is a good choice for mainly highway use with only occasional off roading in mud and sand

The author's choice for the best all-around on/off-road tire, the Goodyear Wrangler R/T. Shown here is the 11.50x15 size. The Wrangler has fantastic flotation, excellent traction on all sorts of terrain, and is the quietest aggressive tread tire available

they are remarkably quiet and have tremendous traction and flotation. I have 11.50 x 15 Wranglers on my Scout and they will tiptoe through a soft bog and not even break the surface. Larger trucks should use the wider 13.50 size for more flotation because of their extra weight. They come closest to being the ideal tire: they have excellent flotation, excellent traction in all type of terrain, and are almost perfectly quiet on the street, quieter than any other aggressive tread tire you can buy. This is due to the unbroken center rib. They are also very good on sand because the center rib will not dig in.

They have another unique feature: their normal inflation pressure is a low 20psi. When you go into really soft stuff, they can be deflated to 10psi with no trouble, giving you great flotation. You won't often need to do this, since there is a full 10½ inches of tread contacting the ground. In the slippery stuff, the wide-spaced lugs at the sides provide great grip and clean themselves quickly. Goodyear has broken all the rules with this tire: that aggressive tires are noisy, that aggressive tires won't grip on sand, and that a tire can't be good on all types of terrain. The Wrangler is the best overall tire for off-roading in my opinion, and you won't find a better looking tire. It will enhance the appearance of any off-roader. They cost about $120 apiece with raised white lettering.

UNIROYAL LAND-TRAC®

Another good 10 x 15LT tire for mainly street use, the Land-Trac shares many features with other tires in its class. It has unbroken treads around the circumference of the tire, so it won't make a lot of noise. The edge has a rugged biting pattern, fairly good for slippery surfaces, but a digger in sand. It's quiet on the high-

The Uniroyal Land-Trac is a good mud and sand runner and a quiet ride on the highway

The B. F. Goodrich Radial T/A is a quiet runner and leaves a wide track. It's a good choice for a machine used mainly on the street. (Courtesy, Hickey Enterprises)

way and leaves a wide footprint, about 9 inches, for good flotation. The Land-Trac costs about $65, and will last about 30,000 miles or more, depending upon your truck size, driving habits, and how often you take it into gravel or other abrasive conditions.

GOODRICH RADIAL ALL-TERRAIN T/A®

This tire has one of those mosaic patterns, with the rubber forming zig-zag chunks all over the tire. This breaks up the noise somewhat and provides rather even contact with the road surface to make the ride quieter and smoother. They are good overall traction tires, having a very wide footprint due to their 12R x 15LT size. They are only fair to good on slippery surfaces like mud and snow. They should be mounted on 8-inch rims. The main things that stand out about this tire are the wide size, the price ($140 each) and the long tire life. Being radials, they should last 60,000 miles or more.

SEARS CROSS COUNTRY®

This is a fairly wide tire with good flotation. The 10x15LT is good for mainly highway driving and occasional sand and mud running. The grooves running around the circumference of the tire keep it very quiet on the highway and allow it to move smoothly through the sand without digging itself in. It will slip in heavy mud though; the grooves can't clean themselves as well as lugs can. The main advantages of buying this tire are that it is widely available, it has wheels readily available from Sears to go with it, and it's backed with a Sears warranty. At $63 each and a life of about 40,000 miles, it's a pretty good buy.

CONCORDE DESERTER®

This tire uses an unusual ribbed tread design around the whole tire, mainly for sand use. The ribs won't clean themselves of mud and snow readily, but they won't dig into the sand either. They run quietly on the highway and have a good life of

40,000 miles or so. I'd recommend them for mini-pickups or the smaller four wheelers. They're good lookers and will do well in the kind of terrain you'd take a mini-pickup into.

The Concorde Deserter, a quiet runner with good flotation, and an excellent choice for this Chevy LUV

WHAT TIRE SIZE IS BEST?

For most uses, don't agonize over tread design. The only time you have to be really picky with your tires is if you have some highly specialized use in mind, like dune racing, mud racing, drag racing, pulling, etc. The proper tire size is far more important. As I said before, the 10 x 15LT size is about the best for general off-roading. It will give you the flotation and traction you need for most situations, and has the added advantage of being available with wheels as a package deal in the showroom.

You can go to a larger tire size, but be careful. Just as a wider tire gives you more ground contact, it also reverses the process and gives the ground more contact with the vehicle. The suspension takes more punishment and must be beefed up to handle the load. The engine also has to give more and should be ordered larger if you intend to use really big tires. Double shocks on all four wheels and heavy-duty leaf springs, as well as riser blocks will be necessary.

Another important consideration with large tires is the rear and front axle differential ratios. For bigger tires, a higher (numerical) gear ratio is needed. At least 3.7, and 4.10 on a pickup with 14/35 x 26.5 Gumbo Monster Mudders won't hurt. A larger tire (a tire with a larger diameter) takes longer before it makes one complete revolution. This lowers engine rpm for the same speed. This is fine if you want lower engine rpm at 55mph for better gas mileage, but off the road it can be disastrous if taken too far. An engine usually gets its best torque midway through its rpm range. As you lower engine rpm with larger tires, you lose vital torque at the low rpm end. If you're driving off the road and come to a steep hill, you won't have the engine rpm or the torque to make it. The engine will conk out and you'll roll down backwards, or slide sideways and roll over.

So, be careful and choose an axle ratio high enough to insure good engine rpm at off-road speeds. Here's a table you can use to get a good idea of how tire sizes affect your rpm:

AXLE RATIO, TIRE SIZE AND ENGINE RPM*

AXLE	TIRE SIZE (OUTSIDE DIAMETER IN INCHES)												
RATIO	27.0	27.5	28.0	28.5	29.0	29.5	30.0	30.5	31.0	31.5	32.0	32.5	33.0
2.73	1870	1830	1800	1770	1740	1710	1680	1650	1630	1600	1580	1550	1530
3.08	2110	2070	2030	2000	1960	1930	1900	1870	1840	1810	1780	1750	1730
3.23	2210	2170	2130	2100	2060	2020	1990	1960	1930	1900	1870	1840	1810
3.31	2270	2220	2180	2150	2110	2070	2040	2010	1980	1940	1910	1880	1850
3.42	2340	2300	2260	2220	2180	2140	2110	2070	2040	2010	1980	1950	1920
3.78	2590	2540	2500	2450	2410	2370	2330	2290	2250	2220	2180	2150	2120
3.90	2670	2620	2580	2530	2490	2440	2400	2360	2330	2290	2250	2220	2180
4.10	2810	2750	2710	2660	2610	2570	2530	2480	2440	2410	2370	2330	2300
4.56	3120	3070	3010	2960	2910	2850	2810	2760	2720	2680	2630	2590	2550
4.88	3340	3280	3220	3170	3110	3060	3010	2960	2910	2860	2820	2770	2730
5.12	3510	3440	3380	3320	3260	3210	3150	3100	3050	3010	2960	2910	2870

NOTE: Engine rpm is at 55 mph.
Reprinted with permission of Hickey Enterprises

Here's an example of how to use this table. My H78x15 tires have a diameter of 28.5 inches, and my axle ratio is 4.10. (Front and rear axles have the same ratio, of course.) The table shows that my engine rpm at 55 mph is 2660. If I want to buy a larger tire, I call the tire dealer and get the diameter. In this example, the tire I want to buy is the 12 x 15 Gumbo Monster Mudder with a diameter of 32 inches. Looking across the table along the 4.10 line, I see that my engine rpm would drop 300rpm, from 2660 to 2370. To find out if 300rpm will affect my off-road performance, I can test my engine power at the lower rpm. A 300rpm drop would also occur at speeds lower than 55mph. If I drive up a hill at 1,500rpm and then back off the acclerator until the engine slows to 1,200rpm, the engine will respond as if I were using the larger tires. If I still get good power, then it would be safe to go to the Mudders.

If you've got a good-sized V8 in a big truck, or a large six in a Jeep or Land Cruiser, then you can handle the bigger tires. The Land Cruiser's 258 can handle it, but don't expect to gun it up hills. Another factor to consider is the transmission. Do you have a close ratio trans? This would balance the rpm in your favor. The best bet is to make sure you get axle ratios over 3.5 with your new rig, at least 3.6. A higher number such as 3.9 or 4.1 would be safer if your dream machine includes huge tires.

If your axle ratio doesn't exactly fit in with the numbers on the table, you can estimate. If the difference is a jump of 150 rpm and your axle ratio lies midway between two numbers in the table, the way 4.27 lies between 4.10 and 4.56, then go up proportionately, adding about 100 rpm. You can also check with owners of similar vehicles to see if they have any trouble with the bigger tires. If you're a novice making plans to equip your off roader, the help of fellow four wheelers is indispensable. Check the back pages of the popular off-road magazines for the address of the nearest 4WD shop and club. A few words exchanged with these people will be a great help. I've found off-roaders to be friendly and willing to give suggestions and advice.

What About Ply Ratings?

A "B" tire has a four-ply rating, a "C" tire six, and so on down the alphabet. A ply is the layer of material under the rubber that serves to reinforce the sidewalls and provides an even base for the surface treads. Going to a higher ply rating is only necessary if the tire has to carry extra weight, such as a large camper on a pickup. If you get a lower ply rating than you need, you'll have bursting sidewalls and swaying tires at high speeds. The sidewalls will also be more vulnerable to damage from curbs and rocks. If your ply rating is too high, on the other hand, you'll have a stiff ride and feel the bumps more. You'll think you have solid rubber tires and wonder if the suspension and shocks are up to par.

Plies only make the sidewalls stronger so they can support more weight. They do not improve off-road performance. Tires usually list the weight they can carry on the side. The best way to see if your ply rating is adequate is to find out the weight of your truck, add the gear you carry, your camper, the passengers you will be carrying, and add about 300 pounds. Divide this by four and the answer is how much weight each tire must be able to support. When you buy tires ask the salesman for the number of pounds the tire can support or read it off the tire yourself.

Are chains or studs a good idea? If studs are legal in your state they will help in icy surfaces, but will be quickly torn off on heavy gravel or rocks. Chains work far better and cost less in the long run. You can switch them from vehicle to vehicle, provided that the tires are roughly the same size, and they will last for years. A good pair cost about $50, but are worth it for the slippery situations.

Wheels

Be sure you get a good set of wheels to go with those expensive tires. The typical 10x15LT tire fits on a rim 8 inches wide, the 15 x 8 size. A great variety of wheels is available at a wide range of costs. As with other off-road equipment, the better wheels will cost more, about $30 to $40 each.

I prefer steel wheels; they are a little easier to take care of than aluminum, much easier than chrome, and don't bend or show knicks as easily as aluminum. Aluminum wheels, on the other hand, are lighter and actually stronger, although they will bend. Chrome wheels are the nicest looking, but are the most difficult to keep looking nice. They require constant cleaning and polishing and look bad when they get grimy. The choice is really up to you. If you have a heavily chromed rig and want the chrome wheels to top off your accessories, fine. While you are polishing all your other chrome parts such as bumpers you won't mind spiffing up the wheels. If you like the appearance of aluminum wheels, the lighter weight will be a bonus. Don't let anybody tell you one type wheel is better than another. It may be better for a particular reason, but overall it's your choice.

With a 4WD vehicle you must always buy all tires at once. Having front tires that are different from the rear tires does bad things to the transfer case and U-joints. Match a good set of tires, carefully chosen for how you are going to use them, with a good set of wheels. Remember that you will save money by ordering tires with your new truck. Nobody wants a set of slightly used tires, and you will only get about $20 each for your stock tires and wheels in trade-in for a new off-road set.

For quick reference I've compiled the following tire and wheel troubleshooting guide. It'll give you a general idea of how to cure most tire ills.

TIRE AND WHEEL TROUBLESHOOTING GUIDE

PROBLEM	SOLUTION
Tires slip in mud	Get tires with deeper, wider-spaced lugs such as Mudders or Tru-Tracs.
Tires drag in sand	Get wider tire with better flotation. Engine could be underpowered.
Tires dig in on mud	Get better flotation tire such as Goodyear Wrangler R/T.
Tires dig in on sand	You need less aggressive tread; better flotation would help.
Tire bulges out of wheel excessively	Mount tires on wider rim.
Tire slips off rim when deflated	Mount tires on narrower rim, if it's a good off-road tire. Otherwise get one of the brands mentioned.
Tires slip badly on snow and ice	Get more aggressive tread or add chains.

See how your tires run in the conditions around your area. If they do well and get stuck only occasionally, keep them. No tire is perfect. If they perform badly, if you get stuck repeatedly when you go off roading, then you either don't know how to drive off the road or have made a bad tire choice, or both. Unless you have plenty of money, you'll have to put up with bad tires until they wear out.

SUSPENSION KITS

Although you can get by on a stock heavy-duty suspension, an aftermarket kit is probably the best and cheapest accessory you can get for improving the off-road performance of your four wheeler.

An aftermarket suspension kit will completely change the ride and handling of your truck. The tires will no longer bounce up into the wheel wells, you will have more clearance between the body and frame and the ground, and the handling on turns as well as off the road will improve. It will get rid of the porpoising character-istic of some vehicles such as the Blazer, and will control swaying and bouncing on the springs.

I have a Burbank spring kit on my Scout. After the springs were installed with compatible Gabriel Strider shocks, the ride became much stiffer. The front end was lifted about 5 inches (the old front springs sagged), and the rear end lifted about 2½ inches. This made it possible to put on Goodyear Wrangler R/T tires, the 11.50 x 15 size. They are available in a wider size, 13.50, but that would be so wide that the front wheels would not turn properly.

Even with the Gabriel Striders adjusted on "regular," the ride is very stiff com-

Notice how the right rear tire is hitting the top of the wheel well and the frame just clears the sand. An aftermarket suspension kit will raise the body, avoiding the bottoming-out problem and giving better ground clearance

pared to what I was used to. The springs are engineered to handle the heavy wheels and tires that are so popular. They improve handling off the road, and since the body is raised much higher you won't get hung up on the frame as often. Using larger tires will also increase the height of the body another 1 to 2 inches. I raised my front end even further by using Advance Adapters heavy-duty shackles. These gave me about another 1½ inches of lift. The main reason I used them was not so much for the lift as for their strength. They are made very sturdily, with a square piece of steel welded to the center. This gets rid of the sideways movement of the looser independent shackles.

You can install a completely new spring kit on your new vehicle, or, if you don't want to throw out your new springs, you can add a lift block set to the rear and some extra leaves to the front. Many people do this because it is cheaper and still does a good job of lifting the vehicle. Burbank has extra leaf springs for most vehicles. A friend of mine bought a leaf and block set for his new Chevy pickup. This set included cast iron rear blocks, the best and safest type, two extra leaves for each front spring, front and rear U-bolts, front center bolts and clips, rear shock studs and adapter sleeves, and front shock adapter sleeves. He then added longer Gabriel Adjustable E shocks to cover the extra 3 inches of lift the blocks and leaves gave him. The cost without shocks was about $150 and he didn't have to throw out his new leaf springs.

You can do this with many other vehicles, such as Ford pickups, Scouts, etc. The

To the left of the Gabriel Adjustable E shock absorber you can see the extra long U-bolts and riser blocks used to give this Blazer extra clearance for the Gumbo Monster Mudder tires

The J-2 Burbank spring kit installed on the author's Scout. Advance Adapters heavy duty shackles and Gabriel Striders shocks are also used

extra leaf set for the Scout II costs only $100 without shocks. This price can't be beat for the improvement in off-road performance and tire clearance it gives you. One thing you should note, though , is that the extra leaves are intended to give better handling and ground clearance, not to carry extra weight. They are not the extra load type you can get to carry an extra 1,500 lb. of payload. These springs are for extra performance only.

Off-road performance and highway handling can also be improved by adding a set of off-road shocks. I am most familiar with the Gabriel shocks, the Striders and Adjustable E. Striders are for smaller vehicles such as Chevy LUVs or Scouts, and the Adjustable E shocks are for larger vehicles or the rear axle of Scouts and Jeeps. These shocks improve the handling of your vehicle off the road by dampening the movement of the springs and controlling sway and excessive bouncing. Particularly the Adjustable Es, which have a massive 1⅝-inch bore. Both shocks can be set for

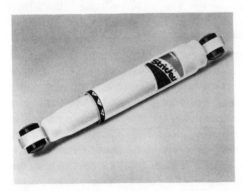

A good shock for off-road use is the Gabriel Strider. Having adjustments for "Regular", "Firm", and "Extra Firm", it works with both stock and aftermarket suspensions (Courtesy, Maremont Corp.)

A steering stabilizer will give you better front-end control and reduce shimmy and wear on front-end parts (Courtesy, Husky Products Co.)

one of three settings: regular, firm, and extra firm. Firm or extra firm is best for improving off-road performance. I used two Striders (45722) on the front of a 1978 Scout SS-II and Adjustable Es (63383) on the rear. This improved the ride both on the highway and off the road. The shocks helped to stiffen the suspension, improved the handling, and controlled bouncing. Owners of SS-IIs should note the numbers I used, since they are not given in Gabriel application charts.

After you install new springs, shocks and bigger tires, you will need a steering stabilizer for the front end. You may have noticed your steering wheel moving from side to side at higher speeds, particularly if you hit a hole with only one front wheel. It may even start to vibrate violently if the shocks are badly worn. You can correct this by dampening the lateral movement of the wheels with a steering stabilizer. A stabilizer is basically a shock absorber mounted laterally between a tie rod and the front axle. The movement of the tie rod, which connects your steering wheel to the wheels, is dampened and brought under control. The result is much smoother steering, particularly on rough roads, and more lateral control on streets and highways. The steering stabilizer is a necessity if you have large tires because their greater unsprung weight only compounds tie rod movement. Your vehicle will be easier to drive, there will be less wear and tear on the tie rod ends and joints, and less jumping of the wheel out of your hands when you hit bumps while off roading. I have tested the Husky steering stabilizer and found it to be easy to install and very effective in controlling front wheel movement. Since my Scout doesn't have power steering it really made a big difference. It should be used on any vehicle with or without power steering and is particularly effective with large tires.

BODY PROTECTION

One of the most important things that has made four wheelers as popular as they are is the body style and paint job on a new four wheeler. People who see my military olive-drab paint job immediately say, "When are you going to paint it?" I tell them I'm not going to because if I painted it it would look like any other old Scout. With the military paint job it keeps the looks and value of a military vehicle.

In the post-military days of four wheelers, every four wheeler looked like a construction vehicle or a piece of farm equipment. Now they have interior and exteriors like cars, and it's really all for the better. The only problem is that some work has to be done to protect the vehicle against the tree branches, brush, rocks, and sand mounds it will encounter off the road. This is where my Scout excels. It came with an excellent front brush guard, full width: a great slanting front skid plate, the best I've ever seen; and a four-foot-long, two-foot-wide skid plate that bolts under the bell housing, transmission, and transfer case for excellent protection. The plate is so heavy (about 50 lb.) that I get better gas mileage on my four banger without it, so I leave it off for local four wheeling. Only on longer trips do I bolt it back on. I wondered if the extra weight was worth it until I felt a sharp rock scrape all the way down from the bell housing to the end of the skid plate. Who knows what that rock would have done to the drivetrain. Now I always remember to put that skid plate back on. If it's used only once on a trip it's earned its weight.

A real skid plate. This plate protects everything from the bellhousing to the transfer case, with no loss in ground clearance. It weighs about 50 pounds

Here you can see how a roll bar mounts. The mounting plates will be bolted through the bed of the pickup

Roll Bars

Starting from the top, the useful accessories you can get begin with the roll bar. For most drivers a roll bar is a necessity, and most four-wheel clubs require that their members have a roll bar. While a roll bar won't keep your truck's body from getting dented up and scratched if you flip over, it may save your life.

In recent years the roll bar has been improved greatly in design and strength. Now they're made of wider diameter and thicker-walled tubing, and sometimes even feature a flotation plate welded across a double roll bar. This will give you a better chance of staying above the soft stuff. Four-wheel enthusiasts who are handy at welding sometimes make their own roll bars. Homemade jobs can work as well or better than the manufactured roll bars; it's up to you if you think the effort is worth it or not.

Many manufacturers now offer roll bars on four wheelers as an option. Before ordering one, look at it closely to see how well it's welded together and how well the base plates are bolted to the floor or bed of the vehicle. Some models have poorly-made roll bars that aren't worth the money. Most are good enough for general off roading and are cheaper than the aftermarket roll bars. Also, it's usually less painful to pay for it along with your truck than to add it on. Some of the vehicle and accessory manufacturers offer non-functional decorative bars that look like a roll bar, but are really designed only to support a pair of lights. Obviously, these should be avoided.

If you do choose to make your own, be sure you bolt it to the bed of your pickup or the inside steel floor if the back is enclosed like a Jeep, Scout, or Toyota Land Cruiser. You might think that the frame would make a stronger base and provide more protection. This is partially true, but the frame twists and flexes as the vehicle moves over unequal ground, especially if you're carrying a heavy load. It's made to flex in order to avoid structural stresses. However, roll bars are smaller stock and can't flex, so they bend and come apart at the seams.

The ultimate in roll bar protection is the cage. This is popular among off-road racers because they expect to roll often and want to minimize damage to their

This double hoop sand bar is designed to offer flotation in case of a rollover on soft surfaces. The trend in roll bars is to stronger, doubled-up types (Courtesy, Hickey Enterprises)

Following the trend to more extensive roll bar protection is this front cage assembly that bolts on, shown in a Toyota Land Cruiser (Courtesy, Hickey Enterprises)

vehicle. Also, they use their truck only for racing and can remove the doors without any problem. A cage isn't really necessary on a rig that will double for street use.

More protection can be added with a heavy-duty seat belt or competition harness. The harness will keep you firmly in your seat through rough off-road trails, and the seat belts are superior to the stock belts in your truck.

You can buy foam pads to cover your roll bar so you won't knock yourself out when you hit hard bumps. Makeshift pads can be made from dense foam rubber or the thick black kind used to insulate cold water pipes, but they don't match the appearance of the store-bought item.

Front-End Protection

The next thing you'll want is some sort of front-end protection. Front-end guards and brush guards bolt onto the front of the frame. These vary in size from little winch guards that probably wouldn't do much good in a collision, to full-width boonie-running brush guards, complete with wire mesh for warding off threatening branches and rocks. Rocks can fly up and smash headlights and dent the front end, especially if you're following another big rig.

When you buy a winch you'll get an extended bumper and some sort of small front-end guard attached to it. The extended bumper is necessary since the winch must protrude enough to make the controls workable. Manufacturers of winches usually have these bumpers and front-end guards available as either part of the winch kit or an accessory. Often, however, they're so small they don't offer much protection. I'm in favor of the full-width, complete protection brush guard. It usually spoils the appearance of the whole front end, but I've used mine many times to shove away branches that would have poked out a headlight or scratched the paint.

Most people find these small front-end guards adequate, though, and they are necessary for attaching the all-important front tow hooks to the frame. You can compromise function and appearance, and go with medium-sized front-end and brush guard, such as those available from House of Steel or Hickey Enterprises. For the rear end, too, House of Steel offers big pipe bumpers with provisions for tow hook installation. These bolt to the frame and offer an instant trailer ball or tow

You can protect the top of your tailgate with this tailgate protector. It is chrome plated for looks and rust protection (Courtesy, Superior/Ideal, Inc.)

This front-end guard is a great idea. It gives protection for the grille, looks good, and mounts the tow hooks (Courtesy, Hickey Enterprises)

hook connection, plus a heavy-duty bumper to replace that plated thin gauge metal job standard on vehicles today.

Spare Tire and Gas Can Carriers

Another popular accessory is the rear swing-away tire and gas can carrier. These are available from several companies, and can be adapted to a wide variety of vehicle sizes and body styles. They serve the double function of carrying gas and a spare tire on the outside to leave more room on the inside, swinging away so you can get into your vehicle when you want to. For vehicles with cramped interiors, such as Jeeps and Toyota Land Cruisers, this is a great idea. If you're going to carry gas, a gas can cover is a good idea. You'd be amazed at the amount of dust and road dirt that gets into the gas can, no matter how tightly you close it, and whatever is in the gas will find its way into the carburetor.

Should you carry gas all the time in your can? This is up to you. If you like the looks of your gas can hanging on the back, then keep it empty and covered, and fill it only if you're going to use the gas that same day or within a few days. Not only will the can keep cleaner inside, but you'll avoid a dangerous explosion and fire if somebody slides into your rear end. I would recommend carrying that extra five gallons of gas even on afternoon outings with the four-wheel drive club. You'd be surprised at the amount of gas you eat up while off roading. I've seen off-roaders go one mile off the road into a really muddy area, get stuck with the exhaust pipe

A rear spare tire carrier can carry a gas can, too. I'd back off

Even on a Blazer there's barely room for a Monster Mudder and two gas cans

under water and have to keep the engine running for hours. Nobody carried along a gas can but fortunately someone with a winch came along before he ran out of gas and filled his engine with muddy water. In the right situation, that five gallons will be worth its weight in gold.

Rocker Panel Skid Plates, Fender Extensions, and Running Boards

Really rough going will damage the paint and body metal of your rocker panels. To protect them, you can get diamond plate rocker panel skid plates from companies such as Hickey Enterprises or Edgewood National, Inc. These are attached with sheet-metal screws to the rocker panels and protect against flying rocks, scrapes, and scratches from brush. The sides of the vehicle may also be protected from rocks flying from the front tires by attaching rubber fender extensions. Fist-sized rocks and gravel can be thrown by the wheels into the quarter panels, chipping away the paint and denting the metal.

Because of the high lift many pickups have with aftermarket suspension kits, running boards are coming back to make stepping into your truck easier. One of the best is made from rustproof aluminum by Superior/Ideal. It is called the EZ Sider®. It is made from one piece of bumper-type aluminum, bright dipped and anodized. The surface has ridges so your shoes won't slip, and they come with matching splash guards. Installation is easy; the brackets are made to fit existing bolt holes, making it unnecessary to drill holes in the frame. It is very sturdy when installed, and doesn't wobble. Best of all, it gives excellent body protection from gravel, mud, and water. Rocks that would normally bounce off the rocker panels and chip body paint hit the splash guards and the undersides of the running boards and bounce off. Chevy pickups used to have a problem with water spray entering through the crack around the front of the door. These running boards will keep the doors completely dry inside. They keep the body free from road grime all the way back to the rear wheels. Running boards are a great idea not only to improve the looks of your truck, but to increase the resale value of your van or pickup by protecting the body paint.

This chrome plated swing-away step will provide entry and exit convenience when your vehicle is raised with a suspension kit. It bolts to the frame (Courtesy, Superior/Ideal, Inc.)

The EZ Sider running board, shown here on a pickup, protects body metal as well as providing a step. It can be had for medium and large size off roaders. (Courtesy, Superior/Ideal, Inc.)

The front skid plate on the author's Scout is the lowest point of the vehicle and protects the front steering components and differential housing

If your transfer case hangs low, protect it with a skid plate like this one (Courtesy, Hickey Enterprises)

Skid Plates for the Transfer Case and Differential

Hickey Enterprises has transfer case skid plates for most four wheelers. Even though the transfer case may look like it's well above the ground, you will hardly ever be going over level ground. The transfer case will often be scraping against rocks, sand, and mud. If you don't have a skid plate, you can be sure one of those big rocks will have your name on it. The skid plate lets you ride over the obstacle rather than bash into it. The same goes for the differential case. Unless protected, your expensive differential and axle can be badly damaged. It could cost you over $1000 to replace an axle and differential. You can also get a combination rear axle guard and truss support from Off-Road Performance, Inc. that will protect the differential and axle as well as give the axle extra support.

Some drivers don't get rear differential skid plates, figuring the front will encounter an obstacle first so it needs more protection. I don't have any rear differential protection; the only time I needed it was when I became high-centered on some tree branches in a swamp. I was pulled out by a pickup, and ripped through the branches with my differential case. Fortunately the case is built with a sloping design that helps it to slide over obstacles rather than meet them head on. There was no damage to the differential although the tree branches were badly chewed up. Again, it's your choice; you may want to get a rear differential skid plate, although one on the front is more of a necessity.

LIGHTS

Although you can get by without auxiliary lights, it is a good idea to use lights that will make things easier for the kind of driving you do. Stock vehicles come with regular driving lights. These cast a medium width and depth beam in front of the vehicle and a little to the sides. They're fine for driving in traffic where the street lights and lights of other cars help you find your way. But going into the boonies where it really gets dark requires some extra lighting, but check your state laws before installing auxiliary lights.

Here's the kind of illumination you get with Marchal 950 long range driving lights (center spot) and 950 fog lights (on left and right sides). This combination is great for trail driving and night driving in the country

Spot Lamps, and Driving Lamps, and Replacement Headlamps

Spot lamps cast a long straight beam, narrowly focused, for a great distance in front of the vehicle. These are useful for driving down highways at high speeds in total darkness, but the illumination is so narrowly focused that I would suggest using a pair of long-range driving lamps instead. Marchal makes long-range driving lamps in two rectangular sizes, the 850 and the larger 950 series. I use two 950 long-range driving lamps mounted on my roof. They light up the road for about 1,500 feet ahead, and have a total reach of 6,000 feet. These are really all you need for night driving. They are really a cross between spot lamps and driving lamps. Their beams are two spots that gradually dissipate farther ahead. Another good driving lamp is the KC Hilites Daylighter #1752, but these use up more amperes than the Marchal 950s.

I use a pair of Marchal H-4 headlamps in place of my regular headlamps and I would recommend these lights to everybody, off roader or not. These lamps, as the other lamps by Marchal, use quartz-halogen bulbs which give off a steady white light. I say "steady" because regular filament headlamps lose their power somewhat and become dimmer as they age. They also have a yellowish cast to them, whereas the quartz-halogen lamps are white. The H-4 lamps are about four times brighter than regular headlamps and are a pleasure to drive with. One interesting feature of these lights is that the lenses are fluted so they aim the beams at a slant, rising on the right side. This is to keep them from shining into the eyes of oncoming traffic. People used to flash their brights at me with my old headlamps since my truck is so much higher than a car. Now, even though the Marchal headlamps are brighter, no one flashes their brights at me. The bonus on these lights is that when you go to the high beam you have an excellent off-road driving lamp. They will light up everything for about a quarter of a mile. Unlike ordinary lights which are discarded when they burn out, the Marchal headlamps use a replaceable bulb.

Fog Lights and Floodlamps

The other major light for low visibility conditions in bad weather is the fog light. I use two Marchal 950 fog lights. These have an extremely wide-angle beam pattern of 116 degrees. Owners of 35mm cameras can appreciate how wide this beam pattern is. It is equivalent to a 13mm wide angle lens. These fog lights light up everything in the front and to the sides of the vehicle. The vertical beam is only 10 degrees, so the beam doesn't rise more than 5 feet above the ground 50 feet in front of the vehicle. The net effect is to produce a very wide beam that lights up everything to the sides and hugs the ground enabling you to see under bad weather. I use these on foggy or misty mornings as my only lights. They are legal and don't annoy other drivers.

Another lamp you might find useful is a floodlamp. This is a very powerful light for illuminating a wide area with strong light. It's great for nighttime camping and for lighting up a vehicle that is stuck while you work on getting it out. Of course the fog lights are good for this too, but the floodlamp has a swivel base and can be mounted in the rear of the vehicle. You often have to pull someone out with your truck and need good lighting behind your vehicle as well as up front. I use a Marchal 850 fog light as a backup light.

Wiring, Relays, and Mounting

The crucial component of a good lighting system is the wiring. Many times I have seen drivers turn on their lights and burn out the wiring. This is caused by two errors: having lights that are too powerful and not having a relay. I have four big 950 lamps (about 9½ inches wide and 6 inches high), but they are only 55 watts each. I can turn on both long-range driving lamps, the fog lamps and my high beams all at

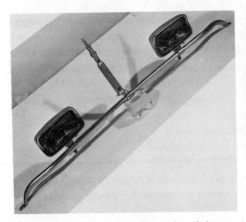

This light bar is great for mounting lights on the roof. The optional CB antenna mounting bracket puts your antenna in the center of the roof without a hole (Courtesy, Superior/Ideal, Incorporated)

Accessory lights are: two Marchal 950 long range driving lights on the roof, two H-4 replacement headlamps, and two Marchal 950 fog lights on the bumper

once. That's six powerful lights using about 330 watts and 25 amps. Since my alternator is over 50 amps this is no problem. Other lights are so ridiculously powerful that they use 100 or 150 watts each. There is no way you can light up more than a pair this way.

Relays are also important. Marchal has a 514 relay that is made for auxiliary lighting systems. It also has a built-in 25 amp fuse. With one of these relays on every pair of lights, you can switch on all your lights and not worry about burning anything out or overloading your electrical system. If the load is too great the relay will shut the power off. You don't have to buy Marchal lights to get this relay. You can buy the 514 relay separately and wire it to your KC Hilites, Perlux or other lights.

Mounting the lights is also important. Spot and long-range driving lights should always be mounted high, preferably on the roof or roll bar. Fog lights should be mounted low, on the brush guard bumper. They can even be mounted upside down under the bumper if that is the only place you can put them. My fog lights are mounted on my Hickey winch mounting platform.

A good balanced lighting setup should include fog lights, spot or long-range driving lights, replacement headlamps, and some sort of rear illumination.

ENGINE ACCESSORIES AND MODIFICATIONS

The engines found in the new four wheelers are the same engines that can be bought with other models made by the same manufacturer. Chevy uses Chevy engines in their four wheelers, Ford uses Ford engines, etc. The accessories available in the showroom are limited to an enlarged heater, larger capacity alternator, more effective air cleaner, larger capacity cooling system, and perhaps a transmission cooler. These items are tacked on to the otherwise typical automobile engine.

Off roading puts greater demands on the vehicle, and the engine is no exception. Along with the transmission and differentials, it makes the biggest difference to overall off-road performance. Because the engines are made by the same factory that makes the car engines, the stock four wheeler performs essentially like a car, running most efficiently at 55mph. At this speed it gets the highest fuel efficiency and highest horsepower as well as torque. Off-road running requires that you reverse the engine's performance curve. Instead of running most efficiently at high rpm, it should run most efficiently at low rpm (1,500–2,500rpm range).

More torque is needed at lower rpm, the engine must cool itself properly at low vehicle speed, and gas is wasted by gunning the engine to get the power you need to push through thick mud and up steep hills. You can correct this situation by choosing the best engine option for your off-road needs.

Once you have selected a good engine, you can modify it to suit your special off-roading requirements.

Your other alternative is to swap engines, and modify it if necessary. The third and least desirable alternative is to live with a sluggish, gas-gulping, poor-performing engine.

A popular accessory for boosting horsepower and performance: dual exhausts. Shown here is a system for 1975 Ford 4WD pickups (Courtesy, Hooker Headers)

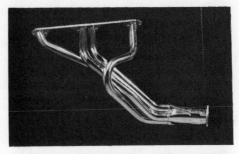

This chrome-plated Advance Adapters header is half the pair for the Jeep 304 V8 (Courtesy, Advance Adapters, Inc.)

Modifying Stock Engines

HEADERS

Most guys opt for the improving-their-present-engine alternative. This is much easier and less expensive than swapping, and involves less fabricating and custom-fitting of linkages, etc. To start with, most modifiers install headers. These are fairly easy to install; they simply bolt on to replace the old exhaust manifold and head pipe. Install them when the engine is cool and make sure the gasket is fitted properly. Torque down all the bolts from the center out to the edges, alternating from left to right as you move away from the center. That's all there is to it. The benefits are increased acceleration and slightly better gas mileage (although your tendency to take advantage of the better acceleration will offset this a little). Headers remedy the exhaust constipation characteristic of stock exhaust setups.

I use an Advance Adapters header on my Scout four-cylinder engine. Some people say that I am wasting my time putting a header on a four-cylinder engine, but I reply that it needs all the help it can get. The headers give improved acceleration and gas mileage, and has helped keep the engine from stalling out in low rpm situations. The engine has good torque, but the header makes the most of it. My four cylinder never conks out on steep hills, as I've seen some sixes do.

CARBURETORS

The second item usually replaced is the carburetor. The most popular brands are Holley, Rochester and Carter. You'll find enthusiasts who swear that one or the other is the best, but it depends on the application.

An off-road carburetor requires a low cfm (cubic feet per minute) output. The lower cfm improves engine efficiency at low rpm by delivering less combustible air-fuel mixture. The mixture will burn more cleanly and thoroughly. Popular Holleys with this capability are the 600cfm Model 4160, available for Chevy, Ford, and Chrysler. It comes in emission or non-emission versions. They feature an electric choke, vacuum operated secondaries, emission provisions, side pivot floats, and a single inlet fuel bowl. For Chevys they fit the 350–402 engines from 1970–72, the 350–454 engines of 1973–74, and the 350–400 engines of 1975–76. Models for the Ford 1970–72 302, 360, and 390 engines, the 1973–74 302, and the 1975–76 351 engines are available. Chrysler engines can use models designed for the 1970–72

318, 360, 383, 400, and 413 cubic-inch engines. The 1973–74 engines in the 318, 360, 383, 400, and 413 displacements fit this model, as well as the 1975–76 318, 360, and 440 cubic inch sizes. The spread-bore 450cfm is also a good choice for a low cfm and good street performance.

INTAKE MANIFOLDS

A good carburetor can only do its best when coupled with a good intake manifold. Edelbrock manifolds are very good, while the Offenhauser Dual-Port 360 is popular because it provides for off-road and street performance with a two-stage air-fuel mixture design. This can be coupled to a Carter 625cfm, Holley Model 4160 four barrel or Rochester Quadrajet. A good carburetor/intake manifold combination should be fed well and smoothly. An electric fuel pump is a good choice for providing a constant even flow of fuel over the entire rpm range.

CAMSHAFTS

For some, a new camshaft is the start of engine modifications. For others it's the last thing they want to get involved in. While headers and a new carburetor and intake manifold will improve any engine's performance, real power comes when these changes accompany a new camshaft. Fitting these components together is very difficult, and to some extent is a trial and error process, with too many turning it into a big mistake. Since so many combinations of these components are possible, and only a few possible combinations will really work well, you have to be very careful about the combination you use. Crower camshafts are very good for improving off-road performance, particularly the specially designed Baja Torque-Master®. It gives good low-end and mid-range power and has a silent hydraulic grind. The issue with cams is to get the right lift, duration, and timing. An off-road camshaft should provide a quick lift so the air-fuel mixture will reach the combustion chambers rapidly. The Crower Baja Torque-Master accomplishes this. Other Crower camshafts feature varying lifts and durations for better mid-range performance and street performance. You have to really know what you're doing to pick the combination that's right for your engine and your driving habits. The valve train components, including the springs, lifters, and shims, also must be replaced. You cannot replace a camshaft and think that you're finished. The whole package either works perfectly and efficiently or you've wasted your time and money and could have gotten comparable results with just headers and a new carburetor and manifold.

IGNITION SYSTEMS

For perfect timing and a good spark you must get a good distributor. Some aftermarket distributors are considered very good, although everybody now goes with an electronic system. Accel makes a good magnetic electronic ignition system, although some people prefer a light-actuated system, such as the Mallory Unilite® ignition system, which uses a small beam of infrared light as a trigger instead of a magnet. It is simpler and easier to install, and you keep your old distributor. But it doesn't have the complete reliability and high performance ruggedness and accuracy of the systems that replace the entire distributor with a high performance unit. There are also magnetic add-on kits.

Electronic ignitions do produce a hotter, more accurately timed spark for today's lean-burning emission control engines. You can adapt your old distributor to a new breakerless system, and complete the job with a set of Accel "yellow jacket" plug wires and super coil. The plug wires deliver full voltage, unlike conventional wires, for full power and clean emissions. They're not affected by extremes of temperature or grime, but may play havoc with radio or CB reception. The yellow jacket plug wire set even includes a crimping tool for clean, solid connections.

Engine Maintenance and Cooling Systems

A more efficient engine needs to be maintained well and kept clean. This means clean oil, clean air flowing into the carburetor, and a good engine temperature. The oil should be changed about every 2,000 miles, or less if you run into very dusty roads or run the engine at high rpm for many hours off the road. The stock paper air cleaner element is little better than nothing at all, and should be replaced with an oil-soaked foam filter such as that made by Filtron. The alternative is to get the oil-bath air filter option, but this is only available on some Dodge and Ford models.

Clean the foam cover after each off-road outing, and check it periodically if the day is particularly dusty. It can be cleaned by soaking in solvent, and squeezing it gently like a sponge until the solvent flowing from it is clean. It will take several soakings if it's really dusty. Wring it out as much as you can and replace it on the filter element.

There are two ways to keep the engine running at a good temperature; by keeping the coolant at the proper temperature, and by cooling the oil. Check out the coolant and change it at least twice a year. A 50 percent water/antifreeze mixture is good. In the summer, the temperature of the air near the ground where the engine is located is hotter. The fan isn't given much of a chance to cool off the engine since much less air is being forced into the radiator at low speed off road. The increased engine speed only makes it worse. Having the air conditioning on on hot days also makes the engine run hot, but hot days are when you need it the most. What can you do to cool the engine? Keeping the cooling system filled and in good shape helps, as does an increased capacity radiator—a must with air conditioning.

For cooling the engine oil several factors are important. Keep enough oil in the engine. If it gets to the ADD mark, add a quart. Don't let it get so low that the engine parts are grinding and slapping into one another. Keep the oil fresh, changing it every 2,000 miles. If you have a large engine and air conditioning, you could probably use an engine oil cooler. This looks like a miniature radiator and cools the oil by giving it some contact with the cooler outside air. These attach to the engine at the oil filter mount.

Another way to increase oil cooling is to carry a larger volume of oil in the oil pan. Accessory oil pans are available which carry up to eight quarts of oil compared to the normal four. The pans just bolt on under the engine in place of the old one, and the oil dipstick works normally. The only thing to watch for is to make sure the bottom of the pan will clear the ground and any skid plates you may intend to install. Keeping your oil running cooler is the best thing you can do to extend the life of your engine, since high temperatures break down the lubricating properties of oil.

Heavy-Duty Electrical Systems

If you plan to use your off roader as a service station vehicle, a larger capacity alternator or two alternators will give you extra generating power. Two alternators can be installed on your engine by using a larger fan belt and a mounting point on the other side from your present alternator. With this extra amp-producing capability you can give jump starts to others easily and keep your own battery up on cold days. This is also a great idea if you use an electric winch which drains the battery heavily. You can add a second battery, too. Mount the battery away from engine heat and close to the starter; next to or below the existing battery is a good idea. Connect the two batteries in parallel, that is, with negative to negative and positive to positive. This will give you extra cranking power on cold days when the battery puts out only one-third of its capacity. It will give you extrta juice for jump starting other engines and using your electric winch.

Engine Rebuilding

Finally, some of the less glamorous modifications include rebuilding your old engine to perform at like-new standards. I had the cylinder head on my Scout rebuilt at 70,000 miles. As it turned out the valves were all in excellent shape and it just needed a little grinding and new shims. Later I found that the engine ran with the same power at lower rpm. This saves on gas and engine wear in the long run. While I had the head off I replaced the lifters, push rods, and rocker arms for top efficiency, and the effort paid off. I kept it stock, since the 152 four cylinder can't be beat for toughness and durability, although it suffers in the power department. At one time, International offered this same engine with a turbocharger, so it should be plenty tough.

Few off roaders opt for the complete high-performance package on their street machines. The reason is that you don't need tremendous power in normal off roading since the terrain greatly limits the speed and kind of driving you can do. In fact, most off roading, I would say 90 percent of it, is done at about 15mph. And as you know from experience, the more highly tuned an engine is, the shorter its life span is and the more delicate it becomes. Toughness is preferrable in the long run. The only exception would be off-road racing, but that's a different matter. Here the vehicle's engine and transmission has to be built to meet high performance expectations. Even then you'll find yourself spending a lot of time under the hood before and after each race.

Beware of muscle-car mechanics telling you how to modify your off roader. For them good performance is high horsepower at screaming rpms, and this kind of setup doesn't cut it off the road. This kind of engine just slips 'n slides through the mud and digs the vehicle into the sand. There are some situations that demand high horsepower and rpm, like running up a steep dry hill. But don't expect to power up a hill in the mud. To get the best out of your engine, if you're really high performance oriented, take it to a shop specializing in high performance off-road machines.

Accessory Gauges

The best way to keep track of your engine's performance and the functioning of your electrical system is with a set of high quality, accurate gauges. The idiot lights used on newer models only light up when it's too late. By the time your oil light goes on you have already done some damage to your engine by not having adequate oil pressure. And you have no way of checking your alternator's output, particularly under the strain of an electric winch and accessory lights.

You can correct this situation by using gauges. I use five Sun gauges, and I'll describe the function of each one so you can see how you will benefit by using them.

OIL PRESSURE GAUGE

Probably the most important is the oil pressure gauge. In a 60 degree dial range it goes from 0 to 100psi. About 40–50psi is the highest my engine reaches when it's running high idle at start-up. After the oil heats up, the pressure lowers to about 35psi. By checking up on oil pressure once in a while I know if any oil is leaking or if I need to add a quart. The oil pressure gauge will show a sudden drop in oil pressure so you can correct a leak before it does any damage.

AMMETER

Another very useful gauge is the ammeter. Mine goes from -60 amps to $+60$. Since my alternator puts out a maximum of 55 amps, this gauge is just right. It is very important to have this gauge if you have an electric winch or accessory lights. You can watch the gauge and see if you're draining too many amps from your battery. The gauge should show about +5 amps while driving, so you know that the alternator is supplying amps to the ignition system. Constant discharge in the negative range indicates that something is wrong with the alternator or voltage regulator. Your gauge will indicate this before you run your battery down and get stranded somewhere.

VOLTMETER

My voltmeter has a range of 10–16 volts and shows the voltage being put out by the battery. A normal battery should show about 12.3 volts; a drop to 11.1 or lower shows trouble. The battery and charging system should then be checked.

WATER TEMPERATURE GAUGE

The water temperature gauge helps you keep track of the temperature of your engine, particularly when driving on gear-grinding trails on hot days. The normal water temperature of your engine is about 180°; deviation from this means overheating or a possible coolant leak. It can also mean an inoperative water pump.

TACHOMETER

The tachometer, probably the most popular accessory gauge, is very useful for gear shifting while off roading. When driving through a muddy trail at high rpm, you want to make sure you don't over-rev your engine. Gear shifting should be done at the proper rpm range. You may think you have the feel for shifting gears, but trying to do it smoothly off the road is another matter. Here you can't depend on the speed, sound, or feel of the gas pedal. The only way you have of knowing the engine's rpm is with a good tachometer. I use one with a range of 0–5000rpm. For my four cylinder this is the best choice, since it redlines at 4000. It is marked in tenths between the larger numbers, so it's accurate to within 100rpm. Less accurate tachs are marked in 200s, but I would recommend the 100 spacing for accuracy.

Since these are all electric gauges, they are easy to install. You will have to put in a new water temperature and oil pressure sender, but this is no problem. You can use mounting panels for the gauges for a neat appearance under your dash or on top of it. I use two mounting panels since each one will mount two gauges and I have four. Having these five gauges will give you the peace of mind of knowing that your engine and electrical system won't pull any surprises on you on the road or off.

Engine Swapping

With the medium and larger four wheelers, you can get such a good selection of engines that you don't have to worry about swapping for a more powerful V8. It's so much easier to put on headers and a new carburetor and intake manifold than to go through the headaches of complete swapping that you probably won't bother. People with smaller four wheelers, however, aren't as lucky. If you own a Scout, the older Ford Bronco, a Jeep, military Jeep, or Toyota Land Cruiser, you most likely aren't satisfied with the power you have, although in recent years the Jeeps and Scouts have been available with bigger engines. Land Cruiser owners are stuck with the six-cylinder 258. Rather than go to a larger vehicle, you can put in a larger, more powerful, engine.

Before you run to the junkyard looking for the nicest engine you can find, you should consider what swapping gets you into. In the first place, you need a good engine complete with the clutch housing, standard flywheel and clutch pressure plate, and all the accessories such as the carburetor, alternator and fuel pump. You need a radiator of sufficient capacity to cool the new engine. Intact radiators are hard to find in the junkyard, and rebuilt or new radiators are expensive. Still, your best bet is to use the radiator that comes with the engine. Usually another engine will fit right into your military or civilian Jeep, except the older military models which are small in the engine compartment and may need some modification. It can be done.

You'll also need the proper engine conversion kit, which includes all you need to make the conversion except the motor mounts and throttle linkage. These must usually be fabricated. A throttle linkage is also necessary. The conversion kits usually cost around $100, but some can run as high as $300.

Expect to spend about $1,000 on the whole operation, and about a full week, working full time every day, to do a good job. Dropping in the engine and matching up the splines is the easy part, since the conversion kit will take care of that. What's time consuming is all the small things like the fuel line, throttle linkage, exhaust, radiator hoses, wiring, etc. Add to this any time you'll want to spend cleaning up the engine compartment and frame and rebuilding the junkyard engine. Aside from mechanical skills you'll need a welding torch and some fabricating ingenuity. To make it really easy on yourself, consult someone who's done an engine swap. If you're really lucky, you might be able to find somebody who's done the same swap you intend to do.

A wide variety of kits from several manufacturers are available for swapping engines into Jeeps, Scouts, and Toyota Land Cruisers. I'll list the engines and models for which kits are available, starting with the Jeeps.

SWAPPING JEEP ENGINES

Here is a list of the early and recent Jeeps that can be converted:

MB military Jeep with T-84 transmission

All four-cylinder 4WD Jeeps, S/W, P/U & FC150 with T-90 transmission and $^{15}/_{16}$ in. main drive gear

All early 2WD Jeepster, S/W & P/U with four and six-cylinder engines

All four-cylinder 4WD Jeeps, S/W & P/U with T-90 tramsmission using long (1⅛ in.) main drive gear

All 6-226 and 6-230 OHC S/W & P/U with 2WD

All 6-226 4WD S/W, P/U, and FC170

6-230 OHC Gladiator and Wagoneer with T-90 three-speed or T-98 four-speed transmission

6-230 OHC Gladiator and Wagoneer with three-speed H.D. T-89 transmission

Note: All of these must have standard shift bell housing. Here is a list of engines that may be swapped into the above models with adapter kits available from companies such as Hoosier Machine Products Co. or Advance Adaptors.

YEAR	ENGINE
49–64	Ford or Mercury V8
64 and later	Ford or Mercury V8
49 and later	Ford six cylinder (223 and larger)
62–64	Ford, Fairlane, Comet, V8 (221, 260, 289)
64 and later	Ford, Fairlane, Comet, etc. V8 (221, 260, 289)
60 and later	Falcon, Comet six cylinder (144, 170, 200)
55 and later	Chevy six cylinder
55 and later	Chevy V8 (265, 283, 327, 396, 409, car or truck bell housing)
62 and later	Chevy II four cylinder (153)
	six cylinder (194)
Pre-1959	Buick, Olds, Pontiac large V8
59 and later	Buick, Olds, Pontiac large V8
1961–63	Pontiac Tempest four cylinder
1961–1964	Buick, Olds, V6 (198, 225)
	Buick, Olds, Pontiac V8 (215)
64 and later	Buick-Olds V6 (198 and 225 CID)
1940 and later	G.M.C. six-cylinder truck (inline and V6)
55 and later	G.M.C. V8 truck (all)
1940 and later	Studebaker six-cylinder Champion (car only)
51–58	Studebaker V8 and six cylinder Commander
1959 and later	Studebaker V8
1950 and later	Rambler six cylinder (196 and 199)
63 and later	Rambler six cylinder (232)
40 and later	Dodge, Plymouth six cylinder
60 and later	Plymouth, Valiant, Dodge Dart, Lancer slant six
53 and later	Dodge, Plymouth, Chrysler, DeSoto V8 (bell housings vary, so send template with bolt holes and diameters)

Chart courtesy Hoosier Machine Products Co.

As you can see, you'll have no trouble fitting most any kind of engine into your old Jeep. For complete information on what kits fit what models, write to a company that specializes in conversion kits.

Of course recent Jeeps can accept the larger AMC Jeep engines since these are available as options. The transmission fit should be checked with the parts man at your local AMC Jeep dealer, to make sure you don't run into any problems. Motor mounts are available for the most popular engines to help the swapping, so you don't have to fabricate your own. For example, Desert Dynamics makes a Jeep motor mount kit for mounting any Chevy V8 or 221 through 351 Ford engine in a Jeep, including models MB, CJ2, CJ3A, CJ3B, CJ5, CJ6 and C101. Chevy and Ford V8s are relatively easy to come by in good shape at junkyards and are some of the easiest conversions. Hoosier Machine Products also makes a universal mount for Chevy small block V8 engines to be installed in Jeeps only.

SWAPPING SCOUT ENGINES

Conversion kits are also available for swapping engines into Scouts. This is particularly desirable for owners of early Scouts who were stuck with the 152 four cylinder as the only available engine. Although this is an excellent hard-working engine and will stand up in the toughest conditions, it doesn't have the highway power a lot of people like.

The firewall on Scouts is a bit more forward than it is on other vehicles, so you have to be careful about the engine you choose. Hoosier Machine Products says that any inline six-cylinder engine will fit if the radiator is moved to the forward side of the crossmember. Of the V8 engines, the Ford 221, 260, 289, and 302 fit very well, as do the Chevy small block V8s. Hoosier makes three kits for Scout conversions, just write to them to find which one you need. On the Scout II, several six-cylinder and V8 engines were available. The best bet with a Scout II would be to put the 345 V8 in in place of the standard 196 four cylinder if you want more power. The International 345 has the best low-end torque of any stock engine, as I mentioned before. It delivers 292 ft. lb. at 2,000rpm, as compared to the best competitor, the Chevy 400, which delivers 290 ft. lb. at 2,800rpm. With a little modification you can imagine what you can do with that engine in the Scout II.

SWAPPING LAND CRUISER ENGINES

Many owners of Toyota Land Cruisers become dissatisfied with the Land Cruiser's six-cylinder 258 standard engine not only because it doesn't have the power to pull big tires through the deep stuff, but the replacement and tune-up parts for it are sometimes hard to get and expensive. The answer for a lot of them has been to install a Chevy or Ford V8 via the conversion kits available from Advance Adapters, a specialist in Land Cruiser conversions. There are adapters available for using the standard three-speed or four-speed with Chevy or Ford engines, as well as a great variety of motor mounts. Just about any Chevy or Ford V8 can be used, but the Chevy 327, the classic V8 swapping engine, is one of the best. Bellhousing adapters as well as transmission adapters are available to make the swapping as easy and accurate as possible. Get their catalog for an education in the possibilities of Land Cruiser conversions.

DIESELS

The newest thing in engine swapping is installing diesels into vehicles with gasoline engines. This gives an advantage in mileage, as well as plenty of low-end and mid-range torque. The disadvantages of diesels are formidable. Diesels last much longer but cost two and one-half times more than a gas engine. Since you can't get many junkyard diesels you'll have to pay the parts man his high price for a brand new engine. This runs over $3,000. Diesel fuel isn't available on every street corner, but an enlarged fuel tank and a little research into the closest diesel dealer will help you out.

The first diesel to appear on the American market was the Nissan inline six optional with the 1977 Scout II. This little item cost $2,300 more than the standard 196 four cylinder. With this kind of initial cost, I doubt very much if you would realize any fuel savings over four or five years. This is one of those items that will have a small following until gas prices jump completely out of sight.

You may have gathered from this list of engine conversions that although there are many options available, you'd better pick an engine that can be fitted with presently available adapters. You can, of course, fit any engine you want into any vehicle you want, but be prepared to pay heavy bucks for a custom conversion. For most of us the exorbitant expense isn't worth it. The best bet is to do your homework from the beginning and pick a sensible conversion project for which the adapters and motor mounts are already available.

TRANSMISSION AND TRANSFER CASE ACCESSORIES AND MODIFICATIONS

Automatic Transmissions

There are several reasons why you might want to modify your automatic transmission. It might be that you want an automatic instead of your manual transmission in your four wheeler. Maybe you put a V8 in your vehicle and want a good automatic to go with it. Or it could just be that you want a more heavy-duty automtic to go with the rough use you put your rig to. There are a few things you can do to your automatic to improve its performance and extend its life.

TRANSMISSION COOLER

The most common modification is the transmission cooler. The greatest enemy to long automatic transmission life is excessive heat. Running your Blazer or pickup at high rpm on a hot or even a warm day really keeps the automatic spinning at high rpm, causing excessive heat buildup. On the bigger rigs, you probably have huge tires and lots of weight which combine to increase the strain on that transmission. This tough use is murder on the seals, gaskets, and clutch discs inside the transmission. You have two alternatives. Early transmission breakdown and a costly transmission overhaul, or a transmission cooler to extend the life of the transmission to what it would be under normal driving conditions.

A transmission cooler is a small radiator, about the size of a big heater core, that has two hose connections to the transmission. Transmission fluid is pumped to the cooler, which is mounted in front of the coolant radiator but behind the grille. The unit isn't difficult to install, although on some applications you might have trouble finding enough room inside the grille. A little wiggling around will fit it into place. This unit costs about $65. While it is a necessity on the bigger rigs like a Blazer, Bronco, and pickups, it is a matter of choice with the medium and small rigs. Another preventive item in the heat department is a larger transmission pan. This will hold a larger amount of fluid, keeping it running cooler, and has ridges and fins built into it to distribute heat more quickly.

REPROGRAMMING KITS

Another worthy modification is the installation of an automatic transmission reprogramming kit. This kit "reprograms" the transmission to stay in first or second gear at any speed, if desired, and also enables you to shift back into first or second at any speed. This is a very useful function as anybody who's driven up hills or towed a camper up a hill knows. When you get about two-thirds of the way up you start to lose momentum, and the engine doesn't have the rpm to give enough torque to keep you moving. The reprogramming kit allows you to shift back into second, stay at high rpm, and have the power to pull yourself up that hill.

This reprogramming kit can be installed without dropping the transmission, and according to the maker can be done by any competent mechanic. It's available for GM Turbo Hydra-Matic 350 and 400 transmissions, as well as Ford C4 and C6, Torqueflite®, AMC and International automatics. This covers just about everybody. The kit has heavy–duty gaskets, seals, and other frictional components and is a real bargain at $40. This and the transmission cooler are all you need to insure good off-road or towing performance and a long transmission life.

SWAPPING AUTOMATICS

When should you consider transmission swapping? If the trans you have feels too small for your truck or if you have a large V8, chances are that you want a heavier-duty transmission. You might also want to put an automatic in your Jeep or Scout.

With the help of hardware from companies such as Advance Adapters, you can install the GM Turbo Hydra-Matic 350 3-speed in your Jeep, Scout, or Toyota Land Cruiser. Other popular automatics for conversions are the GM 400, the Ford C4 and C6, and the Chrysler Torqueflite. Advance Adapters has 38 adapters available for transfer cases alone, they can help you with any conversion you have in mind. Another supplier of transmission adapters is B&M Automotive, who have their own heavy-duty transmission as well as adapters, and even a heavy duty torque converter. Remember to research the possibility of adapters, and to see if your conversion project is feasible before you start taking out your engine and transmission.

Finally, your automatic conversion will not be complete without a transfer case adapter. These can be purchased from the sources already mentioned. For example, an adapter is available for the transfer case of the early Bronco (the Dana 20) so that the GM Turbo Hydra-Matic 400, the Ford C4, or the Ford C6 can be used. This will enable you to install a larger V8 and a tough automatic in your Bronco. Here again, do your homework ahead of time.

Once you have your new automatic installed you might want to add the accessories I've already mentioned and even improve its performance with a new torque converter. Accessory torque converters such as the Holeshot from B&M improve off-road performance by allowing a higher stall speed, giving you a chance to attain higher engine rpm and better low-end torque in tough off-road situations. In crude technical terms, stall speed is the engine speed at which the torque converter stops multiplying engine power and starts delivering power at about a 1:1 ratio. This is

This adapter kit allows you to install a GM Turbo Hydra-Matic 350 three-speed automatic transmission to Jeep and Scout transfer cases (Courtesy, Advance Adapters, Inc.)

The Rough Country Part-Time Conversion unit enables you to convert your full-time New Process Model 203 transfer case to part time operation. It is said to offer a 5 to 10 percent saving on gas (Courtesy, Rough Country, Inc.)

sometimes called the lockup speed. It has nothing to do with stalling the engine. Installation of a new torque converter is a little more involved than the other modifications I've mentioned and most people don't bother to do it unless they're really high performance oriented and know what they're doing.

Transmission mounting brackets, shifting linkage kits, and the like—necessary to complete the job—are available with the adapters and can be ordered from the same distributors. They are the crucial final touch and require more time and effort than installation of the transmission itself.

There's one more accessory you can add to the transfer case that goes with the automatic transmission: the Rough Country Part-Time Conversion unit for the New Process Model 203 full-time 4WD transfer case. If you have a full-time system and don't own a Jeep Qudra-Trac, then you have a New Process Model 203 transfer case. Before this conversion unit came around, those who wanted an automatic transmission in a Chevy or GMC had to go with the full-time system. You just couldn't get an automatic with a part-time system. Since most of us like automatics, we were stuck with the full-time system. GM said that you shouldn't get poorer mileage with the full-time system, but my experience shows you'll suffer about 5–10 percent worse mileage with any full-time system. And there was nothing you could do about it. I say *was* because now there is a conversion unit that bolts onto the NP 203 transfer case and through a cable connection enables you to switch from part to full-time 4WD. If you're familiar with your transfer case, or want to attempt the bolt-on conversion, all you need do is take apart the front and back plates and fit the new unit onto the chain. It's not a cinch, so be sure to read the instructions carefully. If you're not too confident of your mechanical ability, you can have it done by a competent mechanic or at an off-road shop. The unit itself costs about $400. Add to that any labor charges that might be necessary, as well as a couple of quarts of oil. The full-time capability is disengaged by pulling on a handle connected by cable to the transfer case conversion unit. Push the handle back in and you're back in full-time again. Locking hubs can be used as with conventional part-time 4WD.

Is the conversion worth it? If you like driving on the road with the full-time system, and many do, then it's not worth the money. Is it worth it in gas savings? Figure out for yourself if you'll break even in four years. For example, if you spend $1,000 a year on gas, a 10 percent savings would amount to $400 in four years. At that time you'll break even with the cost of the conversion. By then, though, you might want to sell your rig or trade it in on a new one. You can take the conversion unit out and install it on your new NP 203 unit if you get one. It's really up to you, and the highway handling factor may be more important than gas savings in the long run.

Manual Transmissions

Manuals are preferred by some off roaders because they're tougher than automatics and more can be done with them. They are used almost exclusively in off-road competition where they are favorites because of their toughness and flexibility. You can use optimum engine rpm at almost any speed with the proper gear setup on a manual.

An automatic, on the other hand, delivers a constant flow of power for gentle acceleration up hills, through mud, etc. This makes the issue of automatic swapping pretty irrelevant, unless you want to go with one of the heavy duty units I've mentioned. They're all three speeds and the gear setups are nearly identical. There is no reason to change an automatic just because you don't like the gear ratios.

Manuals are a different story. Here the gear ratios are very important. You don't have a constant flow of power and constant engine rpm pulling you through. When you make shifts and disengage the clutch, there is temporarily no engine torque going to the wheels. You then shift up to a higher gear ratio, let the clutch in, and hope the engine rpm at that new ratio is enough to get you up that hill. A close ratio gearbox is the answer for most off-roading needs.

If you don't like the gear ratios you have, you can do one of several things. You can do nothing at all, you can install an overdrive to stretch out the third gear for good highway mileage and reduced engine wear, or you can swap your transmission for one with more deisrable gear ratios.

OVERDRIVE UNITS

Since the top gear of any transmission is suually a 1:1 ratio, the engine must run at 2,800rpm for the transmission output shaft to spin at 2,800rpm. It is very desirable to reduce that last transmission gear still further to .70:1 or so. This will result in a reduction in engine rpm at the same speed.

Right now three overdrive units are available, two from Advance Adapters and one from Warn Industries, the makers of the Warn winch. The Warn overdrive unit, the Warn All-Range Overdrive is available for installation on Jeeps through 1971 and the 1961–1965 Scout 80. It will fit no other applications (at the time of this writing). You should keep an eye on these, though, since new applications are constantly being developed. Your vehicle may have a Warn overdrive made to fit it in the near future. Since these vehicles are characterized by low gear ratios and low differential ratios (like 4.27:1) they really drag on the highway, over-revving the engine and consuming a lot of gas. The Warn overdrive has a gear reduction of .75:1, which will cut down the engine rpm at any speed by 25 percent.

The unit is actuated by a shifter. The gear ratios on your transmission are "split" giving you double the number of forward and reverse gears. Since the overdrive unit replaces the main drive gear of the transfer case and fits into the transfer case just behind the transmission, you don't have to worry about shortening or lengthening the driveshafts to accommodate it. It's a bolt-on job all the way. Specifically, a Warn overdrive will fit all of these Jeep models:

Warn Overdrive Model 33-26	Warn Overdrive Model 33-29
M-38	4-75 4x4
M-38A1	CJ-3B after serial no. 54-12506
CJ-2A	CJ-5
CJ-3A	CJ-5A four cyl.
CJ-3B to serial no. 54-12506	CJ-6
4-63 4x4	CJ-6A four cyl.
4-73 4x4	6-226
4-75 4x4	6-230

Warn Overdrive Model 33-V6	Warn Overdrive Model 33-14
These Jeeps with V6 engine:	These Jeeps with V6 engine and
CJ-5	Warner T-14 three-speed
CJ-5A	synchromesh transmission:
CJ-6	CJ-5
CJ-6A	CJ-5A
	CJ-6
	CJ-6A

Model 33-26 replaces the 26-tooth transfer case main drive gear. The other three models replace the 29-tooth transfer case main drive gear. The Scout model 80 uses the Warn Overdrive unit Model 33-29, replacing the 29-tooth transfer case main drive gear. If you own a Jeep, the Warn overdrive unit is for you. For other transmissions the Ranger Overdrive Series 10 (for manual transmissions) might fit. Here are the specific transmission model and year applications for the Ranger Overdrive, sold by Advance Adapters, Inc.:

CHEVROLET

Chevy-Muncie Series 420, 1962–67 four speed
Chevy-Muncie Series 465, 1968–76 four speed
Chevy-New Process 435, 1964–67 four speed
Chevy-New Process, 1968 and up four speed

FORD

Ford-T18, 1965–75 four speed
Ford-New Process 435, 1964–75 four speed
Ford-T&C three & four speed, late bolt pattern 1965–77, all Bronco-Jeep
    three speed 1976–77
Ford-T98, 1953–66 four speed, diesels 1965–66
Ford-New Process 435, 1967–75, four speed

INTERNATIONAL

T18, 1965–75 four speed

DODGE

New Process 435, 1966–75 four speed

TOYOTA LAND CRUISER

Six cyl., 1965–73 three speed
With Chevy V8 engine, 1963–73 three speed
With 6 cyl., 1974 & up four speed
With Chevy V8 engine, 1974 & up four speed

SAGINAW & MUNCIE

Three and four speed, 1963–1975

If you own one of these transmissions you can use the Ranger Overdrive. Please note that there are different models of the Ranger Overdrive, and many different parts in addition to the overdrive unit itself must be ordered. Consequently you must consult the Advance Adapters catalog for all specific information. Special units can be ordered and custom-made by Advance Adapters. These will naturally be more expensive than the stock unit, which costs about $800, not including installation and any special parts you may need. These units can also be adapted if you swap engines.

Unlike the Warn Overdrive, the Ranger Overdrive fits between the bellhousing and the transmission. This is somewhat more difficult to install, since it may require shortening the rear driveshaft and lengthening the front, as well as relocating the shifting mechanism. An oil hookup, which is supplied when needed, must be installed to the existing transmission. You have to be particularly careful about lining up the overdrive between the bellhousing and the transmission. A dial indicator must be used. The advantage is that you can adapt the unit to various conversions, such as the popular Ford-Chevy match, by mixing the front and rear input and bolt patterns and drive splines. The unit is a full synchromesh .73:1 overdrive, and has a direct (non-overdrive) and neutral position. When the overdrive is engaged, it provides a direct 27 percent reduction in rpm, usable with both the low and high transfer case ranges, in two or four-wheel drive. You can shift into overdrive at any speed. This unit is an excellent choice for the man who wants top off-road performance but likes to run often at highway speeds.

For automatics, the Ranger Overdrive Series 100 is the only overdrive unit I know of that can be used. Unlike the Series 10 for manuals, the Series 100 tags onto the end of the transmission with a special adapter plate. The output shaft of the automatic must be changed, and a seal keeps the gear oil of the overdrive separate from the transmission. Whereas the Series 10 has a shifting lever, the Series 100 is activated with a push-pull button installed on the dashboard and connected to the overdrive by an 8-foot cable. The output is a 32-spline shaft, which is compatible with the late style General Motors Turbo 400 yokes. If your transmission is different, a yoke will be required. Drive shaft shortening is required for every installation.

The Ranger Overdrive Series 100 fits the Ford C4 three speed, the Ford C6 three speed, the GM Turbo Hydra-Matic 350 three speed, the GM Turbo Hydra-Matic 400 three speed, the Torqueflite 727 three speed, and the Torqueflite three speed 1976 and later. Other applications will be available in the future. These are the best choices for putting an overdrive on your automatic, resulting in reduced engine rpm, better gas mileage, and reduced drivetrain wear.

Don't despair if the overdrives available don't fit your vehicle. You can still go to taller tires or a lower number on your differential gear ratios to get better mileage and reduced engine wear at highway speeds. This will affect your off-road performance, particularly in the area of low and mid-range torque and acceleration. The advantage of the overdrives is that they can be used for the highway and not cause a loss of off-road performance. You have to balance the advantages and disadvantages. Should you want to go with different differential gear ratios, you can check out the next section on differentials and axles and see what can be done.

SWAPPING MANUAL TRANSMISSIONS

Your third alternative is to swap your manual transmission for a different one. This requires two adapters, one from the engine to the transmission and one from

TOYOTA, JEEP, AND SCOUT ENGINE ADAPTERS

	GENERAL MOTORS ENGINES					FORD ENGINES	
TRANSMISSION	ALL V8 1955 AND UP	CHEVY II FOUR CYL	BUICK V6	JEEP & BUICK V6 1964 & UP	VEGA FOUR CYL	1949–64	1965 TO DATE
T84 three speed 1941–1945	X			X			X
T90 three speed 1946–1965	X	X	X	X	X	X	X
T86 three speed 1966–68 V6	X			X			X
T89 three speed 1965–1966	X			X			
T14 three speed 1969–71 V6	X			X			X
T15 three speed 1967–75 St6	X			X			X
T18&T98 four speed	X			X			X
Jeep three speed 1976–1977	X						stock
Toyota 4WD three speed	X			X			X
Toyota 4WD four speed	X						X

Information courtesy of Advance Adapters, Inc.

the transmission to the transfer case. Setting up the engine-transmission-transfer case combination you want can be pretty hairy. I suggest that since most transfer cases have about the same high and low range gear ratios, you pick from the other two the one you want to change the most. If you're really dissatisfied with your engine's power, then change only the engine, if you can. If you're dissatisfied with your transmission, then try to keep your stock engine and see if the manufacturer has another transmission available that will suit your needs. If there isn't a suitable transmission available, and you have a Toyota Land Cruiser, Jeep, or Scout, then you can check out the following engine adapters from Advance Adapters and see if they can help you out.

If an "X" appears under the engine of your choice, then an adapter is available for fitting the transmission listed on the left to the engine. For extremely rough off-roading conditions, such as those encountered in racing, Hoosier Machine Products Co. recommends that only the Ford all synchromesh three or four speed be used. They have found that this transmission is the toughest and the strongest available for installation in a Scout or Jeep, two of the most popular off-road racing machines. The transmission may be bolted onto any 1949 or newer Ford V8 engine "as-is," or with minor modification to any 1959 or newer GM (Chevy, Buick, Olds or Pontiac) engine. The holes for installation of a Hurst Shifter are already drilled. If you prefer to use a Chrysler Corporation engine, then the four-speed Chrysler transmission is a good choice. Transfer case adapters are available and you must say what year and kind you have for a proper fit.

The next step, of course, is to match the transmission to the transfer case. Here are some transfer case adapters that will allow you to use different transmissions from the stock models with your present transfer case:

TRANSFER CASES

TRANSMISSION	DANA 18 JEEP/ SCOUT	BORG/ WARNER QUADRA- TRAC	DANA 20 BRONCO	NP205 BLAZER	LAND ROVER	DATSUN	TOYOTA L/C THREE SPEED
Muncie four speed	X			X	X		X
Borg Warner four speed 110	X	X	X				
Saginaw 3 or four speed	X			stock			
Ford T & C three speed	X		stock				X
Ford T & C four speed	X		X			X	
Chrysler A833 four speed	X						X

Information courtesy of Advance Adapters, Inc.

Four-Wheel Drive Conversions

So far in this section on transmission and transfer case accessories and modifications I've been talking about additions you can make to your present 4WD system. In other words, you already have a front driving axle, transfer case, and transmission suited to off-roading and want to improve upon it. On some vehicles, such as the Datsun and Toyota mini-pickups and the Postal Service surplus Jeeps, four-wheel capability does not exist; there is no transfer case, no front driveshaft, and no front driving axle.

Is it possible to convert these to four wheel drive? The prospect looks good; these vehicles are lighter, less expensive, have cheaper insurance, and are known for toughness and good gas mileage. As far as I know, no bolt-on 4WD conversion exists for the Toyota mini-pickups. One is available for the Datsun, though. It's called, appropriately enough, the "Four-Wheel Drive Kit for Datsun Pick-Ups" and is sold by Low Manufacturing and Distributing Co. It costs about $2,000 and is a complete bolt-on unit. No welding or cutting is required, nor are any frame modifications necessary. The kit can be installed in about a weekend by a good mechanic and includes a Dana/Spicer model 30 front axle and a Dana 20 transfer case with gear ratios of 1.0:1 high range and 2.4:1 low range, giving excellent gearing for off-road use. The rear end used should be 4.37:1 and the front has a ratio of 4.27:1, allowing for good-sized tires. Included are Warn front hubs; the suspension is the leaf-spring type using four KYB gas adjustable shocks for excellent handling and long off-road life. You can add the high riser kit for an excellent off-road runner. The real advantage to this Datsun 4WD pickup is that even though you retain the stock engine and transmission, you can be sure of good off-road performance because of the exceptional light weight of the vehicle. With the 4WD apparatus tacked on, the pickup will weigh only 2,600 lb., giving you a better engine power to weight ratio than any pickup. It would just about equal the power and weight of any army jeep, and handle very well off the road. You can complete the job with a roll bar, lights, and other accessories for a relatively inexpensive and good performing off roader. Up to now a 4WD conversion was a custom job, costing twice as much as the kit and only possible in a complete automotive workshop with welding equipment. Professionally converted new mini-trucks are available from some dealers. These might be a better deal if you're not up to doing such a big project on your own.

Those who want to convert their Postal Service Jeep to 4WD are in for a much more difficult time. The main problem is the small size of the vehicle. It's so narrow that stock axles, even some Jeep axles, won't fit. Your best bet would be to pick up an army surplus jeep and cannibalize the front axle and transfer case. Fitting the transfer case to the transmission might be a problem. I suggest you contact the adapter manufacturers I've listed here for advice and possible suggestions. They might be able to do up a special adapter job given enough information. If you picked up a Postal Service jeep in good condition and want to make a four wheeler out of it, this is the only way to do it.

How about regular market vehicles? If you bought a 2WD Blazer, for example, and wanted to convert it to a four wheeler, could you do it? Yes, maybe you can. The main difference between a 2WD and 4WD Blazer is the transfer case, the front driveshaft, front suspension, and Dana 44 front driving axle. The frames are different enough to present problems. You would need some sort of adapter for the transfer case and you would have to install a different steering linkage. The cost would be great; the front axle alone would cost about $900, and the front driveshaft another $125. The transfer case would be another $800 or $900, and the shifting linkage and lever another $100 or so. You would have to connect the front brakes, of course, and check to see if you use the old brakes on the new axle. You would also have to convert to leaf springs in the front.

The price would be in the $2500–3000 range, more than the price of the 4WD option. You'd probably save money by trading in your vehicle for a used or new four wheeler and have less bother in the long run. I've seen 4WD conversions on Datsuns and Chevy LUVs and several companies will convert 2WD vans to 4WD. Aside from all the trouble, it's a great expense. Anyway a 2WD pickup, Blazer, or Jeep can make a good off roader just as it is if the driver knows how to use it.

DIFFERENTIALS AND AXLES

In the first chapter you read about how differentials affect off-road performance. Since each wheel of an axle turns corners at a different speed, the gears in the axle have to differentiate between them. This differentiation is handled by the differential, naturally. There are several types, the open type, the limited slip which incorporates frictional discs to control wheelspin, and the locking differential, which uses gears to achieve positive locking.

Because of lubrication problems, the limited slips may not be a great idea, as I explained earlier. The best are the locking types, available on new GM four wheelers. If you have a limited slip and it gives you problems, or you don't like your open differential and want to get a locking type, you can replace your differential with a locker but, right off the top I'll tell you that a new differential costs $300–500, which may dampen your enthusiasm somewhat.

The most obvious reason for buying a new differential is to improve off-road performance. You may also need a new differential because your old one is worn out. With a gear oil change once a year, the differential will usually last as long as any other part of the vehicle and probably longer. Sand, mud, water, and dirt particles can ruin a differential if the axle is submerged for long enough for water or sand to seep through leaking axle and differential case seals. This is rare, and usually you can count on the differential to function perfectly for the life of your vehicle.

Locking Differentials

Off-road performance can be improved with a locking differential by eliminating the spinning wheel problem characteristic of open differentials. The regular open differential is designed to give the spinning wheel the most engine torque, while the slower wheel gets almost none. When you get off the road and into a slippery situation, the wheel that slips will get virtually all the engine torque, while the wheel with more traction gets almost no torque at all. If it seems like a pretty backward approach to the slipping problem, it is. But this is what happens when you apply street technology to an off-road problem.

Installing a locking differential can correct this slipping problem. When one wheel begins to slip with a locking differential, the differential locks in both wheels, so torque is distributed evenly. The Eaton locking differential will do this only at lower speeds, making it ideal for highway use. Unfortunately, the Eaton locking differential is only available as a GM option at this time, not as an aftermarket accessory, so you probably can't put this excellent differential on your present vehicle.

One locking differential that is available as an aftermarket accessory is the Triple-D Dual Drive. This is a gear type, not a limited slip, so it has no friction clutches that will wear out. It can be used with full or part-time 4WD systems, and works on the front or rear axle. Best of all, it will fit almost any recent model four wheeler, since it fits the Dana 44 or 60 housing, Ford, 12 bolt GM, Toyota Land Cruiser, and racing quick-change axles. If you have a Toyota Land Cruiser and which to install the Dual Drive on the rear axle, then you'll have to buy an extra installation kit. The same goes for the 12 bolt GM with C-locks. This covers just about all the models there are. Since it is a gear type it requires no special lubrication. Just add regular gear oil, as you would to your transfer case or regular differential.

Installation can be a problem and there is no substitute for experience when setting up rear axles. Unless you consider yourself an experienced mechanic, you'll be better off having the job done professionally.

The Triple D Dual Drive kits can be purchased from almost any well equipped four-wheeler shop.

Limited Slip Differentials

Another differential is available for Toyota Land Cruiser, a Gov-lok® positive traction (limited slip) unit from Hickey Enterprises. Although it is not a locking differential, it will still provide vastly improved traction over the regular open type. It fits all 30 spline axles in 1969 and later Toyota FJ-40s and FJ-55s. Some 1968 and earlier axles with 10 splines won't fit the differential, so for $80–110 you can get a new axle and put in the limited slip. The differential itself costs around $300, but is a good improvement to the off-road performance of the Land Cruiser.

Another limited slip differential is the Tru-Trac® made by Detroit Automotive. It is a gear type like the Dual Drive and is similarly designed to fit the Dana 44 axle. You can determine, incidentally, if you have a Dana 44 by looking at the bottom right-hand side of the axle housing web. If it has a "44" stamped on, it's a Dana 44. This unit replaces the standard Dana/Spicer Powr-Lok or Trac-Lok differential supplied as an option with the Dana 44 axle. Although these original equipment differentials are very good, they have the lubrication problem I spoke of before and don't function as positively or last as long as the gear unit. Installation is similar to the Dual Drive; you must take out the old differential and bolt the new one to the ring gear. They recommend replacing the carrier bearing since it may have lose its press fit when it is removed from the old case. Shims must be packed properly and the backlash checked to specifications as with the other differential units available.

One thing you should note carefully about the Tru-Trac—it can't be used on a tire with more than a 32-inch diameter, which rules out the super huge Gumbo Monster Mudders and some of the other giant tires on the market.

You probably noticed that I said the Tru-Trac is a limited slip differential, not a locking differential. There is a difference. A limited-slip like the Tru-Trac doesn't lock in both wheels when one begins to slip. Instead, when one wheel slips the differential quickly develops a controlled spin resistance and most of the torque is then transferred to the wheel that isn't spinning. Still, the Tru-Trac is superior to the conventional limited slips that use friction plates and clutches that eventually wear out and make noise.

As a guide to differential applications, you can check out this list and see if your vehicle has a Dana 44 front or rear axle:

FRONT AXLES

MODEL		YEAR
Chevrolet	Blazer, Chassis Cab, Suburban, Pickup, K-10, K-15, K-20, K-2500	1965–79
Dodge	Ramcharger, Pickup, Power Wagon, Chassis Cab, Club Cab, Crew Cab, Conventional Cab, AW-100, W-100, W-200, W-300 series.	1959–79
Ford	Bronco	1971–79
	Pickup: F-100, F-150, F-250	1959–79
GMC	Jimmy, Pickup, Suburban, Chassis Cab, K-10, K-1500, K-20, K-2500	1964–79
IHC	Scout II, Traveler, Terra	1973–79
	Pickup: Travelall, 900, 1000, 1200	1961–75
Jeep	Wagoneer, Cherokee, Chief, Light truck, medium truck, heavy truck, FC-150, FC-170, J-10, J-20	1966–79
Plymouth	Trail Duster	1974–79

REAR AXLES

MODEL		YEAR
Chevrolet	Chassis Cab, Suburban, Pickup: C-10, C-15, K-15	1968
Ford	F-100 pickup	1967–68
GMC	Pickup: C1-1000, K-1000	1967–68
IHC	Scout, Scout II, Traveler, Terra, Metro, Travelall 900, 1000, 1100	1960–76
Jeep	Jeepster, Commando: C-101, HD	1969–72
	CJ-5, CJ-6, CH-7	1966–75
	Post Office: DJ5, DJ6, DJ7	1969–74
	Wagoneer, Cherokee Chief	1966–76
	J-10	1975–76

The Detroit Tru-Trac fits all Dana 44 axles with 30 and 19 splines. It will not fit Jeeps that use the 10-spline Dana 44 axle.

Detroit Automotive also makes the famous Detroit Locker differential. This is a locking differential that works by locking in both wheels on the axle all of the time and disengaging one when the vehicle turns. This allows one wheel to move faster than the other. As you turn, the ratcheting mechanism makes a clicking sound that you can hear. For some people this is a nuisance; others aren't bothered by it. It is an option on some Chrysler four wheelers but can also be bought from Detroit Automotive for installation with virtually any Dana 60 axle. I would recommend installing the Tru-Trac if your vehicle can fit either. It works more quietly and smoothly.

Differential Accessories and Modifications

When shopping around for differentials, there are several specifications you must know. You must know the number of splines, the Model number (such as Dana 44 or Dana 60), the gear ratio, and the ring gear diameter. Only on borderline applications will you need to know more than the model number of the axle and the number of splines. Can you get a custom-made differential from a manufacturer? You might be able to. The addresses needed are:

Triple-D Inc.   Detroit Automotive
P.O. Box 5166   P.O. Box 882
Cleveland, OH   44101   11445 Stephens Drive
(216) 281-2786   Warren, MI   48090
                                 (313) 759-3850

Call or write to these folks for information on their products and applications as well as any custom needs you might have. I would suggest that you first try to obtain a differential from your local off-road shop, since these brands are both distributed throughout the U.S.

One popular differential accessory is the differential cover. This is available from many speed and off-road shops and is easily installed. The purpose of an accessory differential cover is to provide a greater volume of gear oil for cooling and lubricating the differential gears and to give added protection to the differential. They are available in painted steel, chrome, or aluminum, and will fit the popular 4WD models. A cover should not be considered a replacement for a front differential skid plate. The skid plate gives much better protection than a cover alone, although the cover will help extend the life of the differential, particularly on larger vehicles, due to its larger gear oil volume.

There are several accessories made for the axle itself. The most popular one is the axle truss, a sturdy steel rod bolted to the bottom of the U-bolts under each end of

The front differential can be protected by a solid, steel skid plate (Courtesy, Hickey Enterprises)

Freewheeling hubs for the highway can be added to your vehicle. The most popular makes are Selectro, shown here, and Warn (Courtesy, Husky Products Co.)

the axle. This serves to reinforce the axle against bending and flexing, which occurs in situations of great strain like jumping or hitting a steep embankment or rock. You can put one on the front or the rear. Most off roaders get one for the front only since it is needed more than one in the back. The front axle hits an obstacle first and takes a greater pounding than the rear.

One other modification you might want to make on the front axle is the installation of freewheeling front hubs. With the Rough Country conversion kit you can convert your full-time NP 203 system into part time, and to make the best use of this you will need front locking hubs. The hubs made by Warn and Selectro are the most popular, and installation is not difficult. Converting to a part-time system will give you slightly better gas mileage.

PULLING, LIFTING AND WINCHING

By far, the most important accessories you have are the ones that get you out when you get stuck. Unfortunately, most off roaders don't think about getting stuck when they're in the showroom picking out the options they want on their big, beautiful four wheeler. At the time, they're concerned with the looks of the machine and the size of the engine. Getting stuck is the furthest thing from their minds. They figure that 4WD is enough, that they won't get stuck and if they do, they can rock back and forth or gun the gas pedal and slip out of the bad situation. Nothing could be farther from the truth.

Everybody gets stuck. You'd better learn that now because it's a lot easier than learning it later the hard way. Getting stuck with a four wheeler is not like getting stuck with a car. If a car gets stuck in the snow, you rock back and forth and eventually ease it out. A four wheeler drives through the same depth of snow, and much more, like it wasn't even there. This makes getting stuck with a four wheeler that much worse, because with a four wheeler you either move or you don't. You get such good traction that you can fly through all the situations that would cripple a car, so you attempt situations that you would never try with a car in a million years, like deep snow, thick mud that you would sink up to your knees in, deep water, soft sand, and everything else you can think of. This is the challenge, this is the fun, of four wheeling. But the fun loses its appeal when you're up to your door handles in mud and have no way of getting out. Suddenly it occurs to you, like slamming into a brick wall, that you just might never get out, and you'd have to leave your expensive machine, which isn't even paid for yet, out in the boonies to rot. I know, this happened to me.

How much pull does it take to get you out? What kind of equipment will give you the necessary pull? There are different kinds of accessories designed to get you out when you get stuck—accessories designed for pulling, lifting, and winching.

Winches

Do you need a winch? Actually, there isn't much of an argument about the usefulness of a winch; most people would want to have one. The only thing that keeps them from buying one is the expense. An electric winch costs $600–700, and you can spend more or less if you like. The PTO winches cost about $350 plus accessories and have some advantages as well as disadvantages. I'll compare the two shortly.

To give you an idea of the odds you're up against when pulling to get yourself out,

I've compiled the following list of situations and the amount of pull I estimated was necessary to free the stuck vehicle. Although these are estimates, I'm sure that they are fairly accurate, accurate enough to serve as a guide to the kind of winching equipment you should buy for the kind of off roading you intend to do. After reading this over, I'm sure you'll think more seriously about buying a winch.

SITUATION	PULL NEED TO GET VEHICLE FREE
Mini-pickup stuck in mud up to hubs.	2,000 lb., another vehicle with a chain or a come-along.
Scout or Jeep stuck in mud up to hubs and high-centered.	4,000 lb., a pickup with a nylon strap or tow chain.
Ramcharger stuck up to rocker panels in mud.	7,000 lb., a big pickup with Mudders and a nylon strap, or an 8,000 lb. winch.
Pickup high-centered.	8,000 lb. winch.
Pickup stuck in muddy water up to grille.	8,000 lb. winch with snatch block, total pull 16,000 lb., did the trick.
Pickup under water up to windows.	15,000 lb. tow truck winch.
Pickup sunk in bog up to door handles.	Caterpillar bulldozer with monstrous chain did the job.

These are all situations that actually happened, and the type of pull that did the trick was what was necessary after trying to use less powerful methods. In other words, using a pickup with a nylon strap didn't help to get out the guy stuck in muddy water up to his grille. And using the winch at 8,000 lb. didn't help either. What finally worked was using a snatch block with the winch, which made the winch pull half as fast but at almost twice the power. If you were stuck in clay, which has a suction effect that holds the tires down, it would take probably even more pull to get you out. The great thing about a winch is that it has a constant pull, which is much more effective in getting a vehicle out than the temporary jerk of a pickup yanking on a chain or nylon strap. The constant steady pull puts great tension on the vehicle and helps it overcome the suction of mud and the resistance of mud piled up around the tires. The pickup gets squeezed out slowly rather than jerked out suddenly.

If your off-roading ventures bring you into this kind of stuff then a winch is not just a good idea, but a necessity. The standard pulling capacity is 8,000 lb., while some smaller units pull 2,000 lb. or less.

————————————————CAUTION————————————————

A word about using winches. The winch exerts tremendous pulling power through the cable. Be sure you stand well clear of the cable. If a cable breaks—it happens—it can whip around with sufficient force to cut through small trees, a fender or your body. See the "Safety Tips" at the end of chapter 5.

As with all parts, obtain a complete specifications sheet or write to the manufacture for specifications and applications. These are the most popular winches.

Electric Winches
HICKEY SIDEWINDER III

The outstanding characteristic of this winch is that it has a vertically rather than horizontally mounted drum. This gives it a narrow shape that can fit under and

This is all the winch you'll need for your mini-pickup, the Warn Model 3000 with a 3,000-lb. pull. With a snatch block, it can handle up to 6,000 lb. (Courtesy, Warn Industries, Inc.)

The Sidewinder II winch from Hickey mounted on a Toyota Land Cruiser (Courtesy, Hickey Enterprises)

behind the front bumper rather than on top of it and in front of the grille, in full view. It has a spring-loaded cable packing mechanism that keeps the cable tightly and evenly wound around the drum. You control it with a hand-held switch. It lets out the cable under tension and pulls it back under tension, locking when the power is turned off. It works from the vehicle's battery, like the other electric winches in this section, so the engine should always be kept running when using the winch. However, using the battery's power is to your winch's advantage. When you are under water and the engine conks out, you can still run your electric winch while the PTO winch would be incapacitated. This is more easily done, of course, if you have an auxiliary battery.

The Hickey Sidewinder III pulls 9,000 lb. at 17 feet per minute (fpm) without a load, and slows down to 4fpm when under the full load of 9,000 lb. It comes with 120 feet of 5/16-inch cable and a 90-day warranty. It lists at about $550 and is available for around $470 at off-road shops throughout the country.

Mounting kits for the Sidewinder III are available for every popular four wheeler from about 1969 on, and kits go back to 1955 for Jeeps, 1961 for Land Rovers, and 1966 for Broncos and Land Cruisers. Kits vary in price, the price being lowest for the recessed mounts at about $70, going up to twice that for the large platform mounts for Scouts and some Dodge, Ford, and GM pickups. If you have an older vehicle you can readily adapt the kit to fit. Most vehicles would take the cheaper recessed mount.

Test Report: The Hickey Sidewinder III

While I was writing this book, many four-wheeling friends told me that they would like to see the major brands of winches tested to see if they actually performed up to the claims made in their advertisements. They had noted a curious lack of test results on electric winches in the 4WD magazines, and wondered how good the winches actually were. They had seen some winches at work and were disappointed in them. I can say the same for myself.

Vic Hickey of Hickey Enterprises agreed to provide a Hickey Sidewinder III winch for evaluation purposes, which I tested along with a Superwinch SH8000SR and ATV1500, appearing later in this chapter. Other winch manufuctures were invited to participate with the evaluation, but for various reasons declined. While I had seen other winches at work I had not seen the Sidewinder III perform and this gave me a chance to both test the winch and compare it to others I had seen before in similar winching circumstances.

Installation

Mounting the Sidewinder III is a bolt-on operation. It has been designed to mount securely on your frame using the frame's existing bolt holes, so all you need are a few wrenches. All the necessary hardware is included. This is important because you can save $50 or more by installing it yourself, making the winch cheaper than winches that have an initially lower price tag.

The electrical connections are very easy. A $9/16$-inch wrench is all you need. There are three 4-gauge wires going from the heavy-duty control box to the winch. These are color coded so you won't mix them up. One 2-gauge wire goes to the positive terminal of the battery. For maximum performance they suggest that you wire the engine to the frame, since the frame provides the ground. You should also shorten the wires going to the winch motor, if you can, for maximum performance. The winch performs full power without this, but for those who are perfectionists this is one thing that can be done. I was planning on making these changes but once I saw the winch work I knew it wasn't necessary.

Operation

The winch is very easy to use and sets up rapidly. A remote switch operates the winch via a 12′ cable. One end of the switch is a four-way connector that plugs into the control box under the hood. A small latch fits into the spring-loaded cover of the control box connection so the cord won't be pulled out of the control box accidentally. At the other end, a three-position toggle switch controls the winch. It says simply "IN" and "OUT." You must keep finger pressure on the switch for the winch to run; it will not run by itself. This is a good safety feature. If you were to slip and fall in front of the truck it will shut off so you won't be run over by your own truck.

A spring-loaded cable packing mechanism ensures that the cable is wound on the drum smoothly and evenly. I was told by some people that this didn't work very well. However, when I played out about 90 feet of the cable and wound it back by pulling a truck out, it wound up perfectly even, like a good fishing reel. The cable packing mechanism also makes it very convenient to free-spool cable out. When you disengage the clutch to free spool the cable, the cable packing mechanism keeps the cable from suddenly uncoiling since it is no longer under tension. Consequently, you are more apt to free-spool the cable out because it won't birdnest on the drum. This is good for two reasons: 1) You can play out the cable very fast by grabbing it and running to the truck that's stuck. This came in handy once when a truck I was trail riding with got stuck in the sand on the shore of Lake Michigan. He drove near the water to be on the firmest sand, got stuck, and the waves began washing the sand out from under his rear wheels. Each wave would wash out a great deal of sand, and every second his truck sunk deeper into the lake. I drove up to the beach and free-spooled the cable out very quickly before his truck started floating out toward the lake. If I had to unwind it under power, it would have taken five minutes more, and every second counted. 2) You can conserve valuable battery power. You need the most power when you start pulling the other truck out. If you drain your battery unwinding the cable under power, you won't have much battery power when you need it the most.

Performance

The power of the winch is awesome. Without a snatch block, I pulled a pickup that weighed twice as much as my Scout out of a bog. Propped up against a tree, I pulled out a pickup that was stuck up to his rocker panels in a bog. He had dug himself in so that his axles had sunk 6 inches into thick bog mud and clay. When I pulled him out, his axles plowed up the clay and mud while I winched him in, leaving a clean scrape as if a bulldozer had pushed through a foot of the mud and clay. I had seen other 8,000 lb. winches barely pull out a pickup in this situation with a snatch block. It seems as though the winch develops its full power more rapidly and uses more of its power. The electric motor has a great deal of torque, and this is not wasted on a high fpm rating. Other winches have more of a whining sound, and their motors seem to have less torque. I would rate this winch as the best I have seen. It is easy to install, made of the highest quality materials including strong and lightweight aluminum for the winch and drum, is easy to set up and use, and has tremendous power. Every person who saw it pull out that pickup without a snatch block said it was the best performing winch they had seen.

Accessories

Extras you can buy to get the most out of your Sidewinder III are a Hickey snatch block for doubling the winch's pull to 18,000 lb., an Ever-Wear Paul Bunyan Tree Trunk Protector® for protecting the bark of trees, and an Ever-Wear Snatch'Um Strap® rated at 20,000 lb. This can be used to act as a buffer between the winch and the vehicle being pulled out, and will also extend the reach of the cable by 30 feet. Of course an extra 100 feet of cable is a good idea. I have an extra 150 feet. If you have the bumper platform mount like I do, a mount cover is a good idea to keep the winch clean and protected from the weather.

WARN WINCH

The Warn winch is a popular winch and is available on several new models of 4WD vehicles. It has a fast no-load speed of 65fpm and slows down to 17fpm when pulling 2,000 lb. It can be installed on virtually any four wheeler and has the control box on top of the winch. The list price is $472 (1978) with hawse-type fairlead and $496 with the roller-type fairlead. The fairlead is the guide that keeps the cable from scraping the front of the winch where it exits the winch. The roller type is the best since it avoids having the cable scrape against the sides, as is the problem with the hawse type. This scraping can wear and break the cable if it happens excessively. Avoid winching to extreme side angles and you will prolong the life of your cable with a hawse-type fairlead.

Several accessories are available, such as the Winch Lock. Since the winch is mounted with a few bolts that can be easily taken off, theft may be a problem for city dwellers who park their vehicles on the street at night. The Winch Lock is a good investment. Another good accessory is the reversing kit, which enables you to use the cable under the vehicle so you can pull backward as well as forward. This is more functional than it sounds when you are driving into a swamp, get stuck, and the only suitable tree is behind you. Other extras include a choker chain and Warn snatch block, which has a unique swivel feature. This has the advantage of making cable hook-ups to the snatch block easier than taking out a pin or loosening a wing nut, but has the disadvantage of allowing you to use only cable or snatch straps with a hook, since the closed ends will not allow you to hook onto a looped nylon strap.

The Warn winches come in two models, the 8274, which has a capacity of 8,000 lb. and the 3000, which has a capacity of 3,000 lb. The winch is guaranteed for a year by the manufacturer, Warn Industries. The winch will also lock when the power is off, preventing slippage and accidents. I'll cover the 3000 more thoroughly with the smaller winches. With the low price and wide variety of mounts and accessories available, it's no wonder that the Warn Winch is the most popular winch in use.

DESERT DYNAMICS

This is another winch in the top class. It has a strong 9,000 lb. pull, a self-locking worm gear drive, powers in and out so you can lower yourself down a hill as well as pull yourself up, and fits 150 feet of ⅜-inch cable, which is stronger than the common ⁵/₁₆-inch. It comes with a choice of drum widths 8 or 11 inches, depending upon the application. Its mounting kits fit a great variety of applications, but the cable, hooks, and fairlead must be ordered separately, adding significantly to the prices of $460 for the 8-inch drum and $480 for the 11-inch drum model. The standard fairlead is the roller type, and the remote control assembly must be ordered separately. It's built to very sturdy specifications and will give a lot of service under years of tough use. One thing that is noteworthy of the Desert Dynamics winch is that it has a low profile on the vehicle, while still allowing you to see how the cable is wrapping on the drum. In other words, it's not hidden under the front end like the Hickey Sidewinder, and it doesn't jut out over the bumper and in front of the grille like the Warn Winch. It's set in the middle, not too obvious but still there.

Here's the most widely used winch, the Warn Model 8274. It pulls with a reliable 8,000 lb., and can be doubled to 16,000 lb. using their snatch block. You can also pull your vehicle backward with an accessory that runs the cable under the vehicle (Courtesy, Warn Industries, Inc.)

Another good winch in the 9,000 lb. class is the Desert Dynamics winch. It has some unusual applications if your vehicle is hard to fit (Courtesy, Desert Dynamics)

RAMSEY ELECTRIC WINCH

The Ramsey electric comes in two models; the 2000 which features a hawse-type fairlead and the 2001 which has a roller-type fairlead. The prices are $572 for the 2000 and $599 for the 2001, but this includes 150 feet of galvanized wire rope with hook, fairlead, and remote control switch, things that are extras on other models. The no-load line speed is 20fpm, which drops significantly under load, of course. The winch features power-in, power-out, free spooling, and is self-locking when the power is off. The mounting kits are extra as they are with all winch models. The stall point is a hefty 10,500 lb. and the complete shipping weight, including cable, is 112 lb. for the 2000 and 114 lb. for the 2001, making it one of the lighter heavy-duty winches. It has a low profile, so it does not protrude up or out in front of the vehicle too much.

Ramsey is now developing underslung (hidden) mounting kits for those who want their winch out of sight like the Hickey Sidewinder. Mounting kits are available for most four-wheeler models.

VIKING ELECTRIC WINCH

Another 8,000 lb. winch, the Viking electric, features power-in, power-out, and is self-locking with the power off. The remote control switch is attached to a generous 15-foot cord and it comes with an available roller-type fairlead. The price of the winch is $448. Including roller-type fairlead, 140 feet of $5/16$-inch cable, and switch it comes to $550. The no-load speed of the winch is 22fpm. Similar to the Ramsey in appearance, it has an unobtrusive low-profile look that will not be too obvious in front of the vehicle. Viking makes a lot of winches for tow trucks and other commercial uses, so you can be sure that the Viking electric is a strong, well-made winch.

KOENIG ELECTRIC WINCH

Koenig Iron Works makes some tough winches for tough commercial applications. Their winches are heavier and more rugged than most others. The Koenig electric, which pulls 8,000 lb., has a free-spooling clutch and an optional worm brake for hoisting. If you're hoisting something with it, you can stop the cable and hold it under load at any point. This is a good option for those who would use their winch as part of their job as well as for getting themselves unstuck. The price you pay for this capability is a slow cable speed of 10fpm. The winch costs $552, not including cable and hook which cost an additional $60. The remote control switch on a 15-foot cable is included, but mounting kits are extra. The winch has an upright appearance like the Warn Winch, so it's not for those who want to keep it out of sight, but is a workhorse if you expect to use your winch in a variety of applications.

Smaller Electric Winches

In this section I'll cover those electrics that have a pull of under 8,000 lb. These would be the best choice for somebody with a mini-pickup or boat trailer, or somebody who doesn't expect to get himself into a bad situation. As far as I'm concerned, though, you can't have too much winch power when you get stuck. The choice is up to you. Although there are times when even the 8,000 lb. winch won't get you out, you can still get out most of the time with a 3,000 lb. pull if you snatch it to 6,000 lb. You can get a lot of use from one of these winches if you're careful about the depth of mud you get yourself into.

WARN 3000

This is the little brother to the popular Warn Winch. It can pull 3,000 lb., power-in, power-out, has a dynamic brake, but is not self-locking so it is not wise to use it as a hoist. It comes with a remote control switch on a 12-foot cord, with 40 feet of $^3/_{16}$-inch galvanized aircraft cable with a safety hook. The safety hook is a good idea and should be chosen whenever you can get it. The hook has a spring-held latch that keeps cable, chain, nylon straps, etc. from slipping out before the cable is under enough tension to hold the hook straight out. This might sound like a trivial point, but nothing is more aggravating than having the cable come unhooked and drag along the ground. The winch bolts to your frame so you needn't buy an additional mounting kit. You can, if you wish, buy a grille guard or bumper guard for $55. The whole thing costs about $265, so you get a lot of pulling power for your money, particularly when doubled with the Warn snatch block. This winch is available on some new models as an option, and is a wise choice since it's easier to include it as part of your payments than to buy it with cash.

POWERWINCH VR-192

This can be installed permanently or temporarily on your vehicle. It pulls 3,500 lb. directly, but is free-spooled out. In other words, you release a ratchet and the drum spins freely, allowing you to play out the cable. The disadvantage to this is that you can't lower anything with it. It locks automatically with the power off, a good feature for a winch of this size. You can use it temporarily with a trailer hitch ball adapter. This way you can pull from the rear or the front, if you have a trailer ball attached to the front end. Also included in the $300 price are a remote control switch with a 10-foot cord, an emergency hand crank, 50 feet of $^7/_{32}$-inch cable, and a safety hook. Since you can double the pull to a hefty 7,000 lb. with a snatch block, it is a very useful little item, particularly since it can be carried in your truck where it can't be stolen. The no-load line speed is not given by the manufacturer but I would imagine it's not too fast.

The smaller brother to the VR-192 is the VR-182 which pulls 2,000 lb. It has all the features the bigger one has, but pulls 1,500 lb. less. Since it costs only $40 less than the bigger one you get much more for your money when you get the bigger one. Brush guards and grille guard are available, but I would use it as a portable with the trailer ball adapter.

SUPERWINCH

Superwinch makes two winches useful to the off roader. The larger, more powerful, model is the SH 8000 SR. This unit pulls 3,000 lb. and can be snatched to pull 6,000 lb. It comes with a trailer hitch to fit a 2-inch trailer ball. By tightening a nut under the hitch the unit will fit a 1⅞-inch ball. Its line speed is 10fpm, and it comes with 50 feet of $^3/_{16}$-inch galvanized aircraft cable. Standard equipment includes a snatch block and 25 feet of electrical wire with a battery clamp on the end. This is for hooking up the positive connection. An 8-foot negative lead is provided in case you want to use the winch on someone else's vehicle or on a vehicle where there will be no ground connection. Circuit breakers insure that the unit will not burn out. As an option you can buy a remote control switch with a 10-foot cord. It can be mounted on the dashboard so you can operate the winch in very cold or rainy weather inside your cab.

The Superwinch is ideal for mini-pickups or light applications with any vehicle (Courtesy, Superwinch, Inc.)

Test Report: The Superwinch SH 8000 SR

I tested the Superwinch SH 8000 SR on my Scout and on a Chevy ¾-ton pickup. The winch pulled the Scout out of a boggy area when it lost traction and dug itself in. The line had to be doubled for a net pull of 6,000 lb. to do this. With the single line, the winch can pull my Scout out when stuck in sand, since sand does not have the resistance heavy mud has. The pickup was pulled out when slightly stuck. This occurred when the wheels hit a muddy area and would not grab. The vehicle did not dig in very far and was not hung up on the axles or frame. If your vehicle is hung up this way, I would say that the SH 8000 SR could not pull it out. You would have to jack it up and fill in under the wheels to raise the frame. Therefore, this winch is limited to pulling out vehicles under 4,000 lb. when moderately stuck. If your off roading is not too wild, this winch may be for you. It is very light and portable and doesn't use much battery amperage.

The cable unreels very easily when the handle is on "free" and automatically holds the line locked when you let it go. For pulling in, just pull the handle forward to the "haul" position. There is no power out, but you don't need this since freewheeling the line out is much faster.

The total cost of the winch with remote control switch is about $360. You may find a cheaper price from a discount distributor.

SUPERWINCH ATV 1500

The smaller Superwinch is the model ATV 1500 which features a 1,000 lb. pull. This winch can be permanently mounted or mounted on the swinger bar using a 2 or 1⅞-inch ball. When mounted on the vehicle permanently it can be mounted vertically or horizontally. A cable guide is available for swinger mount or permanent mount applications. You can free-spool it out or power it out, and power it in. When it stops it locks for safety. The switch can be mounted on the dashboard for convenience. It has a no-load line speed of 25fpm, which is halved when using the snatch block (standard). The ³/₁₆-inch cable is 35 feet. You should use a Snatch'Um Strap® or two for an extension, or get a 100-foot length of cable so you can reach trees. The Superguard brush guard is a good locking and useful accessory and a Superlock anti-theft lock will deter theft. The winch costs $180, but I've seen it on sale for $100 at discount stores.

ATV 1500 Test Report

When doubled with a snatch block, the power of the winch is 2,000 lb, so it has less pull than the SH 8000 SR single line, in the previous section. This limits the winch to lighter vehicles such as a mini-pickup or small Jeep when only slightly stuck. If you have an old, small Jeep or mini-pickup with small tires and lose traction, the ATV 1500 will pull you out. Any badly stuck situation or larger vehicle would not benefit from this winch. Many of these are sold; it is the most popular winch, so a lot of off roaders are finding uses for it.

Power Take-Off Winches

So far I've been talking about electric winches, those that run off your vehicle's battery. These winches have the advantage of being simple to install and can be transferred to your next truck when you trade yours in. The disadvantage is that they put a heavy strain on your battery. You must have a standby battery or keep the alternator running to recharge it during use. If your vehicle is stuck in water up to its headlights and the engine won't run, you can still run the winch for some time to get yourself out. On the other hand, the electric winches may need to be rebuilt once in a while. The Warn Winch can be rebuilt with a winch-rebuilding kit after a long period of use.

Other winches are mechanically run and are much simpler in construction, needing less maintenance. These are the power take-off winches, or PTOs. Rather than running off a geared-down electric motor, they run off the transfer case or transmission via a long skinny driveshaft. The PTO is extremely durable and reliable. Since it's just another set of gears, it will last as long as the transfer case. It is the answer for long, extended use. If you're the type of off roader who wants to go trailblazing and use a winch all day long to pull yourself up steep hills and through small rivers, then the PTO is for you. It will run for hours, whereas the electrics get hot in a little while and shouldn't be run for more than 20 minutes or a half hour at a time. The only drawbacks to PTO winches are that they won't run when the engine isn't running, such as when you ford a river and slip into a deep spot, and they can't be put on every vehicle, although they will fit on most. The driveshaft also hangs a little lower than the rest of the underside parts and is more vulnerable to damage. Also, you can't take off the PTO and fit it on your new vehicle as easily as you can an electric, although it can be done if you plan carefully and buy a new mounting kit.

Some PTOs can be operated with the vehicle in gear, so you can power your wheels as you pull, giving a little extra help. Of course, you can do the same more easily with an electric winch. With some PTOs you can also vary the speed of the winch by shifting the transmission or transfer case, an additional advantage. The basic difference is that the PTO is made for extended hard use, while the electric is good enough for occasional use.

KOENIG PTO WINCH

This winch has an 8,000 lb. pull, power-in, power-out, and hooks up to most 4WD vehicles. It has the advantage of running at all transmission speeds for increased speed on relatively flat surfaces and decreased, geared down rates for lugging your vehicle up steep hills or through deep water. You can also keep the transfer case in neutral and the transmission in gear so the wheels will stand still while the winch does the pulling. This is particularly useful at times when you don't want to dig yourself in any deeper, such as when you get stuck in sand. These winches are more expensive. While the winch itself costs only about $300, the extra hardware necessary, such as the transfer case gear unit, driveshaft, and bumper, cost an additional $300 or more, equalling the most expensive electric winch. Included with the mount is 150 feet of $5/16$-inch cable. The line speed is not available from the manufacturer, but varies greatly with the transmission speed. This winch weighs a hefty 190 lb., but is built to take the greatest punishment over a long life.

RAMSEY PTO WINCH

This is another tough, commercial-quality PTO winch. They come in 8,000 and 10,000 lb. pull capacities, depending upon the application. For example, a Scout or Jeep would take an 8,000 lb. winch, the 200 model, while the big Ford F-250 might use the 10,000 lb. winch. This is a great advantage for those large and heavy rigs, since when snatched it will pull 20,000 lb., two tons more than the regular 8,000 lb. winch. And more powerful winches are available. Since the winch is so well made, the price is higher. The winch itself costs about $300 while the mounting kit costs an additional $700–900. As a result, you don't see too many of these around. You can also get a PTO from Ramsey with a smaller capacity, down to 1,000 lb. These winches have a low-mount look, not being too conspicuous since they don't have to include a bulky electric motor.

On the accessories line for the Ramsey, you can buy cable, tow ropes, a snatch block, and hooks. Only the winch kits for Jeep vehicles include 150 feet of $5/16$-inch cable, all others do not include a cable or hook. Ramsey winches have the power-in, power-out feature for sure hoisting and pulling action. For larger vehicles, which includes anything bigger than a Scout or Jeep, I would recommend the optional ⅜-inch cable since it is stronger and can take the pull necessary to use your winch on a Blazer-size vehicle or pickup. I've seen $5/16$-inch cable break many times when used on a really large vehicle, such as a pickup. It breaks at 9,800 lb., and since the stall point of many winches is over this, it will break when you need it the most. If you belong to a club and will use your winch often to get your buddies out of the mud, get the ⅜-inch cable. The larger cable is also available on most electrics, so be sure to check that out. Since the ⅜-inch size is thicker, the winch drum will only hold 100 feet of it instead of 150 feet of $5/16$-inch cable, so an extra 50 or 75-foot length of cable might be a good idea.

VIKING PTO WINCH

This has a capacity of 8,000 lb., and comes in two mounts, a base mount and a front mount. The base mount has a lower profile than the front mount. The price of the base mount is about $325 and the front mount is about $335, with a roller-type fairlead an extra $36. Cable is also extra; 140 feet of $5/16$-inch cable costs an additional $65. The unique thing about this winch is its large cable capacity. It can hold up to 470 feet of $5/16$-inch cable, making it the largest capacity available on a winch of any kind. It has the power-in, power-out feature standard on power take-offs, but it is also heavier and larger than some of the other units. The price of the mounting kit is unknown to me; you'd have to find out from a dealer or from Viking. This is a winch for the very serious off roader, the type who constantly has to winch through swamps, up steep hills, and through streams. This winch qualifies itself for the toughest uses, particularly with the large drum capacity. As with the other PTOs, it's made to last the life of the vehicle and more.

OTHER ALTERNATIVES

If your pocketbook still says no to these winches, even the cheaper and less powerful models, don't despair. You can still get yourself out with less cash but more work. One of the most popular alternatives is the come-along, or ratchet hoist. This is a manually-muscled ratcheting winch. It has a long handle and a spool that winds up the cable with each lift of the handle. In effect it works like a socket wrench so that the dog can lock the drum with each pull. Dozens of models are available from everybody from Sears to special commercial manufacturers. I have what I consider to be the best and most durably made, a model C-400H made by Beebe Bros., Inc., of Seattle, Washington. You can buy it from a local distributor as I did. The reason I bought this one is that it has the greatest pulling strength over the longest cable distance, a big factor with come-alongs. Most models pull about 1,000 or 1,500 lb. over 15 feet and half this distance when the strength is doubled. So at 3,000 lb. it will only pull about 7½ feet. My Beebe come-along will pull 2,000 lb. single line for 20 feet and will pull 4,000 lb. for 10 feet, more than any other come-along I could find. It is made to super-durable standards, and has little extras like safety latches on the hooks so cable and chain won't slip out, a snap-on reversible lever for using it in any direction, and will lower a load notch by notch, which most come-alongs can't do. It also features a self-aligning cable guide, and parts like the dog that receive the most wear are made of bronze.

The price for this little beauty was $86, but with freight from Seattle, safety latches on all three hooks, and tax, it came to $100. I also have a snatch block, so I can double the pull to 8,000 lb.

It has enough power to get my Scout out of most situations, since it weighs only 3,400 lb. when loaded with me and my junk. Once in a while I have a Blazer or pickup pull me out when I don't think the come-along will do the trick, but this is more because it's so much easier to have somebody else pull me out than to get out the come-along and cable and anchor to a tree.

Come-alongs have great advantages and disadvantages. The greatest advantage is that it's cheap (mine is probably the most expensive one), it's lightweight (mine weighs only 17 lb. and again it's probably the heaviest one you can buy), and it doesn't need any electricity or engine power to work. You can pull yourself out if it's freezing and your engine won't start or if your pipes are stuffed to the headers with mud. I've seen electric winches crippled under these circumstances. The come-along always works. It's also extremely portable since it's so small and doesn't have to be bolted to your frame. I've used it to move a piano, pull out some bushes while doing a little landscaping, and loaned it to friends who used it to lift out an engine. It's a great tool to have around the house. Even with an electric winch, I

Here's the basic setup for getting unstuck: a towing cable, choker chain for attaching cable to a frame or leaf spring shackle, and a snatch block which doubles the pulling power of any winch, come-along, or vehicle (Courtesy, Warn Industries, Inc.)

The hand operated rachet-hoist, or come-along, is an effective and inexpensive way to get your vehicle out when it's stuck. This model can pull 4,000 lb when doubled up as shown

will always bring my come-along just in case. The come-along also works from any angle. You can tie it to a tree branch and pull out, tie it to a tree and pull forward, sideways, backward, and upside down. Nothing is more frustrating than to have an expensive winch and not be able to use it because the only tree in sight is behind you.

The come-along does have its disadvantages. You can only pull 20 feet single line, and 10 feet double line (using the pulley to snatch it). The pulley was included as part of the come-along. It's pretty bad when you're stuck in mud and can only pull 10 feet at a time. You have to bring an extra length of cable, wrap it around a tree, pull 10 feet, wrap the cable 10 feet more around the tree, pull on the come-along another 10 feet, and so on, until you're out. This can take an hour or so. With an electric winch, you hook it up and pull yourself 100 or 150 feet straight out. The blessing of convenience.

Is a come-along for you? Well if you don't get stuck too often and find yourself doing a lot of other handy work that needs some pulling power, then the come-along is your best and cheapest choice. I once heard of a fellow who hauled one on his backpack through the woods and used it to lug logs onto the walls of his log cabin. His come-along made an otherwise very difficult job very easy.

Then again, if you don't mind getting a little muddy you can still use a come-along even if you get stuck fairly often. It takes more work but it'll get you out. An off roader I know got himself out of Lake Michigan with a come-along, a shovel, some boards, and hard work. It can be done. Do I think it works? I own one. Everybody says they'd like to have a winch, including me, but I'd rather prefer a winch and own a come-along than prefer a winch and not have any means of getting out when I got stuck.

Lifting

There are times when lifting yourself out is the best way to get out. An example would be if your truck were high centered; in other words, sitting on the frame or axles, and no tree or other vehicle was in sight. You can take out your trusty HI-LIFT® jack and lift the rear of the truck up, swing the body over onto solid ground, and do the same with the front end. This would get you out of your rut. The HI-LIFT jack is probably your best investment in off-roading peace of mind, and one of the least expensive, since it costs about $40.

Unlike the jack you get with your new car which is only meant for changing tires, the HI-LIFT jack is a real workhorse. It can lift 7,000 lb. a distance of 4 feet, and you can get one that will lift 5 feet. It works under load both ways, so you can use it sideways or upside down. Using it is quick and easy—you slide the runner up until it contacts the bumper, from then on you jack it up as high as you want to go. It has two pins that climb up the steel I-beam post, so one is always in the locked position. There's no chance that the runner will accidentally not catch and lose the load. It has a detachable base plate so you can use it as a come-along. It pulls 5,000 lb. when used as a come-along, and this can be snatched to 10,000 lb. Of course the pull is only about 3½ feet, so it will take some work, but is better than nothing.

Accessories include a bumper lift for lifting bumpers without scratching, a Loc-Rac for locking your HI-LIFT to the front or inside of your vehicle, a jack protector for protecting it from the rain, and a plastic handle grip. This jack should be standard equipment for all four wheelers, and once you own one, you'll never think any other jack is worth the name. You can buy it at off-road shops or through the mail from any one of several off-road equipment distributors.

Pulling Equipment

TOW HOOKS

Tow hooks are essential on the vehicle being pulled out. You must have a strong anchor connected to the frame so the pulling vehicle can get a good grip on your vehicle. Never attach a chain or nylon strap to a bumper. The bumper is very weak, as you'll find out, and all you will get out of it is a funny looking bumper.

TRAILER BALL

The ball gives you a good place in the rear to loop on a nylon strap or chain. This is essential equipment for the person doing the pulling. Never use the bumper to pull somebody else, you'll just bend it out of shape or rip it off.

Every off-road vehicle should have two tow hooks in the front and a trailer ball in

The 10,000 lb. capacity Ever-Wear tow strap is good for pulling stuck vehicles. The hooks are handy for situations that don't require jerking the vehicle out

Front tow hooks are essential, and the chrome looks nice. Why a front tow ball? It's great for backing a boat into the water or a trailer into a parking space. You can see where it's going as you move the steering wheel. The cable and grab hook are from a Hickey Sidewinder winch

the rear. Hickey has a trailer ball bracket for the front brush guard that works nicely. It is particularly good for backing your boat trailer into the water, since you can see where you're steering much more easily than you can when you're backing up. This also allows you to use your winch to pull the boat onto the trailer. These pulling aids should be considered essential equipment on every off roader, not an option.

You need a flexible connection between you and the pulling or pulled vehicle. Three alternatives are chain, cable, and a nylon strap.

CHAIN

The traditional pulling equipment has always included a tow chain. Chain works great for its intended purpose, towing another vehicle, when the load doesn't exceed a few hundred pounds. If you recall, the pull needed to get a badly stuck four wheeler out is measured in tons, not pounds, so chain doesn't hold up to the job. Look at the load rating of regular ⅜-inch chain, it's 2,800 lb. While this might be enough for some situations, it certainly won't cut it when the going gets rough.

Chain is okay for chokers, when you need something strong to wrap around the frame or leaf spring shackle. Cable can be used but it may get cut scraping against sharp edges. The same goes for a nylon strap. Chain is flexible and abrasion resistant.

The disadvantages of chain are that it's heavy, expensive, not very strong, and will break if a sudden jerk is applied to it. Chain also makes a lot of noise when you're bouncing around off the road and is very annoying.

CABLE

Cable is much stronger than chain. Cable ⅜-inch thick can safely handle a load of 12,000 lb. at a cheaper price per foot than chain. It's also much lighter, easier to handle, and doesn't make a lot of noise in the back of your truck. Like chain, though, it can break under a sudden load; the steel will stretch a little but not enough. It is a good idea to carry an extra length of cable. I carry a 100-foot length and a 50-foot length, each with a thimble eye on one end and a safety hook on the other. This way I can use them to supplement the short length of my come-along, and also to hook up my HI-LIFT jack as a come-along. The great advantage of cable is that it can be used with a snatch block since it's round and thin. Chain won't work in a snatch block and neither will nylon. Don't buy cable just for pulling, but it's a great idea to have extra pieces for snatching and winching.

See the WARNING under "Winches" in chapter three and the "Safety Tips" at the end of chapter five.

NYLON STRAP

This is the best thing to use for pulling. Nylon has all the advantages where chain and cable have disadvantages. It's incredibly strong; you can buy straps that will take 18 tons without breaking. It's lighter than cable or chain and won't rattle around in the back of your truck. It doesn't stiffen, doesn't have wires sticking out of it, and won't lash back at you when it breaks like cable. It costs more and is only available in short lengths, but it's well worth it.

It's best advantage is that it doesn't break when jerked suddenly, like steel chain

Even with a winch that has 150 or so feet of cable, extra lengths of cable come in handy. They can be used with the HI-LIFT jack to make a come-along

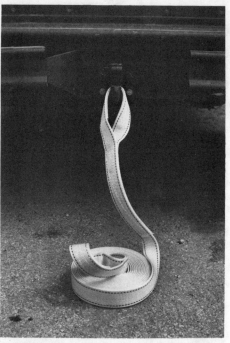

This Ever-Wear Snatch 'Um Strap® is rated at 20,000 lb. and will stretch as it is jerked, giving a slingshot effect that makes pulling out stuck vehicles easier and safer. It should be standard equipment on all four wheelers

and cable do. It's stretch allows the pulling truck to start with some slack, pick up momentum, and jerk the stuck vehicle free. The nylon strap actually increases the pulling power of the vehicle by storing up energy. The best known nylon straps are those made by Ever-Wear Products, Inc., called the Snatch-Um Strap®. These come in a 20,000 lb. and 48,000 lb. capacities. They're the original stretching straps and the best made, because they have a half-twist at the loop and a piece of reinforcing nylon sewn in. This prevents the loop from getting cut and frazzled. It also makes attachment to tow hooks and trailer balls easier. I have used the 20,000 lb. strap and can say from experience that it works very well. The 48,000 lb. size, the Big Daddy Improved Snatch-Um Strap® is really huge. It is 4 inches wide, and like the 10 ton Improved Snatch-Um Strap,® is a convenient 30 feet long. With a capacity of 24 tons it doesn't stretch too easily, but is just the thing for 4WD clubs. There's no way you'd break this one. Even stretching it is virtually impossible, but the stretch factor makes it safer to use. One other strap without the stretching feature made by Ever-Wear is the Saf-T-Tow® strap. This is primarily intended for towing a vehicle, not jerking it out when it's stuck. It has a capacity of 10,000 lb. so it's safe for all towing needs. Instead of having loops at the ends it has grab hooks, making attachment a little easier. I would recommend this strap for light pulling applications such as for mini-pickups or Scouts. Don't buy it and expect it to jerk free a 7,000 lb. pickup. Get the 10-ton strap for that job.

SNOWPLOWING EQUIPMENT

Should you get into plowing? This depends on several things: how much work you like to do, how much snow you get in your area, and how well you can manage your own plowing business.

If you don't like to get up at two in the morning and work until seven or eight when you start your regular job, then don't get into plowing. The merchants who hire you to plow their parking lots want them cleared by the time their doors are open for business. They don't want their customers to stay away because the parking lot is under 8 inches of snow. The number one priority is to make sure you're willing to get yourself up to do the work.

You must also have enough snow to make the venture worthwhile. You can't really predict how much snow you'll have. The East has been having a lot of snow in recent winters; the Midwest has been drier and colder. Usually any state north of Kentucky has enough snow to support some kind of plowing business. Try to remember if past winters have been snowy. You may even try the local office of the U.S. Weather Service for exact statistics on the inches of snowfall in each month of the winter. In most northern states the snow starts in November and lasts until the end of March. This gives you five months of plowing work.

During these five months you have to manage your snowplowing business and get the work done properly. This is the most difficult part of the plowing game. People who are successful at plowing set up plowing contracts in the fall or late summer. The terms of these contracts may vary. For example, you might have everybody pay you $50 a month to be responsible to keep their lot clear during that time. Or you may have them pay you only when it snows. This is the more personal method and is used by people in small towns or areas where they know the neighborhood merchants well enough to get by on a verbal agreement.

However you do it, you must first do some footwork and make the rounds of the

Having a plow on your four wheeler can make you some extra money. Here a Blazer plows through heavy snow, clearing a small parking lot

neighborhood merchants. Get a few hundred business cards made up so you can leave them with the store managers or owners. Most prospects will probably fall through. Don't get so many plowing agreements that you can't get the work done. You can only get so much plowing done in the hours you have to do it. If it snows heavily you'll have to start the night before, clear some of the lots, and come back to them in the morning for the finishing touch. Most plowers go with the fixed payment per month setup. This way they get paid even if it doesn't snow and earn their money when it snows heavily.

Remember also that aside from your investment in your plow you have to account for your gas, extra wear on your four wheeler, your time, and an occasional clutch replacement. Be sure to get the most heavy-duty suspension package for your front axle and springs. They will bear most of the load and punishment. An assistant is a great help. He can carry a snow shovel and clean up sidewalks, doorways, etc., but he'll have to be paid too. If plowing sounds like a lot of hard work and planning, it is. Some plowers in Chicago made only about $300 all winter. At that rate it would take them over four years just to pay for the plow, and another year to pay for the gas and other expenses. Others have made a handsome profit on their equipment investment in just one or two winters.

These are the popular plows and accessories.

WESTERN SNOWPLOW

Western makes manual and hydraulically controlled plows. With a manual plow you have to get out of your truck to angle the blade the way you want it, and hold it in place with a pin or a chain. This is a time-consuming process and takes valuable time away from your plowing operations. The more useful and popular models feature hydraulic tilting and lifting. This makes it very easy. Western accomplishes this with a single lever "T-Stick" control. It's simple to operate. You pull the t-handle to raise, push to lower, and twist to angle right or left. It mounts next to the transmission shifter for quick and easy response.

The hydraulic pump is operated by a 12 volt electric motor connected to the vehicle's battery. You have a choice of blades ranging from 6 feet to 8 feet wide. These are the popular widths from the smallest Jeep to the biggest four wheel drive pickup, covering every vehicle in between.

I think the Western plow is one of the best you can buy. The reason is that, although the blade and mounting are similar to the other plows and the price is about the same ($1,100) the single lever "T-Stick" control is the best and most dependable you can buy. It is extremely important to control the lifting, lowering, and angling of the blade easily. When you're plowing a parking lot, you must push straight ahead with the blade down, raise the blade as you back up, and angle it to push the snow to the side. Each time you back up, you must raise the blade, and each time you push snow you must lower it. Frequent angle changes are needed when plowing any kind of a confined area, like a parking lot.

You want to do the raising, lowering, and angling as quickly as possible to save time and get the job done quickly. Plowing is a race against time, especially if you have a large number of accounts and you want to gain a reputation for doing an efficient job.

The "T-Stick" single lever hydraulic control is the best because it actuates the raising and angling pistons with cables. The cables are very sure in their action and very dependable. Other brands with space age electronic controls may not be as dependable. The reason is that the electric control actuates a solenoid which in turn activates the valve on the hydraulic lowering and angling pistons. These solenoids break down after some use and do not last as long as the cable controlled units. I know of plow dealers who discontinued selling electrically controlled plows because of the money they lost repairing solenoids under warranty.

If you intend to plow with your four wheeler, the easiest thing to do is to get the right engine, clutch, transmission, and suspension right from the start. To help you choose the right options, following are the specifications listed by Western Products for use with their snowplows.

INTERNATIONAL

Specification for Scout II, Terra, and Traveler

Front suspension	Heavy-duty springs and shocks
Transmission	Three-speed automatic or four-speed manual
Clutch	Heavy-duty, 11 inch
Transfer case	Dana 20 two-speed
Steering	Power or standard
Electrical	
Battery	72 amp. hr.
Alternator	61 amp.
Tires	All-weather tread H78X15 minimum

The seven-foot blade is a good size for the Scout II.

PLYMOUTH Trail Duster or DODGE Ramcharger

Specification for Trail Duster or Ramcharger 4x4

Front suspension	Heavy-duty shocks and springs
Clutch	Standard
Transmission	Automatic or four-speed manual
Steering	Power
Electrical	
Battery	70 amp. hr.
Alternator	63 amp.
Tires	Mud and snow H78X15B or larger

The seven-foot blade is recommended for the Trail Duster.

GMC

Specifications for	Jimmy 4x4	½ ton pickup 4x4	¾ ton pickup 4x4
Front suspension			
Shocks	Heavy duty	Heavy duty	Heavy duty
Springs	Heavy duty	Heavy duty	Heavy duty

Clutch	11-inch	11-inch, six cyl. 12-inch, V8	11-inch, six cyl. 12-inch, V8
Transmission	Auto or four spd.	Auto or four spd.	Auto or four spd.
Electrical			
battery	80 amp. hr.	80 amp. hr.	80 amp. hr.
Alternator	42 amp.	61 amp.	61 amp. or larger
Tires	G78x15 or larger	H78x15 or larger	8.75x16.5 or larger

A 7-foot blade is recommended for the Jimmy and the 7½-foot for the pickups.

CHEVROLET

Specifications for	Blazer	K10 & K20	K30 1 ton
Front suspension			
Shocks	Heavy duty	Heavy duty	Heavy duty
Springs	Heavy duty	Heavy duty	Heavy duty
Stabilizer	Heavy duty	Heavy duty	Heavy duty
Clutch	11-inch for six cyl. or V8	11-inch, six cyl. 12-inch, V8	11-inch, six cyl. 12-inch, V8
Transmission	Automatic or four speed	automatic or four speed	automatic or four speed
Steering	Power	Power	Power
Electrical			
Battery	4000 watt	4000 watt	4000 watt
Alternator	61 amp.	61 amp.	61 amp.
Tires	H78x15 or larger	8.75x16.5 or larger	9.50x16.5 or larger

The 7½-foot blade is recommended for all except the 1 ton pickup, which takes the 8-foot blade.

With any snowplow on a four wheeler, always pick the larger clutch option, larger tires, the most powerful battery and alternator, the heaviest front suspension, an automatic or four-speed manual transmission, and power steering. Mud tires work well in the snow, so check the tire section at the beginning of this chapter to see if your tires do the job.

MEYER SNOWPLOW

This is another good plow. The main difference between this and the Western plow is that the Meyer is controlled by its electronic power pack, actuated by levers on the dash. The advantages are that this sytem is easier to install, since it's electrical and only requires running wires through the dash. It's very quick and easy to use since you only have to flick a switch, and the switches can be located anywhere you like. The cables used by Western have to be located where they can be run to the hydraulic unit. The center of the floor, where the stick shift for the transmission is located, is usually the best spot. The drawback, as I have indicated, is that the solenoid-activated valves have caused problems.

Other accessories by Meyer include a miniature salt spreader which attaches to the back of your pickup and can spread 600 lb. of salt from 3 to 30 feet. A snow deflector deflects the snow from the top of the blade so it doesn't go into your windshield. The plow marker kit from Meyer enables you to see where the edges of the plow are so you can judge the correct angle you need. Meyer plows are available on Jeep vehicles as an option. They set you up with the correct clutches, suspension, etc. for reliable and durable plowing operations.

As you can see, the snowplow mount hangs too low for summer off-road use. Remove it in April when the snow stops

TOWING EQUIPMENT

Pintle Hook

Four wheelers can be used for a wide variety of towing applications. I have a pintle hook on my Scout. The pintle hook towing connection is popular with people using farm and construction equipment. Another very popular type of towing connection is the equalizing hitch. This hitch extends toward the center of the vehicle and has the advantage of distributing heavy towing loads to all four wheels rather than just the two rear wheels. Overloading the rear end is a problem when towing heavy trailers with the conventional trailer hitch. The equalizing hitch can be purchased with many new four wheelers as an option, or added later as an aftermarket accessory.

TOWBAR

Some people like to keep their four wheelers for off-road use only. This requires towing it to the trail to avoid licensing fees and other legal requirements such as turn signals. The best way to tow it is with a towbar; one brand is the Kum-Along Towbar from Superior/Ideal. This is a very sturdy tow bar and can be used on most four wheelers. It is very simple to use. Just bolt two brackets under the frame of the vehicle to be towed and the towbar can be connected with two bolts. Each one connects securely with a pin. This way the towbar can be taken off when not in use.

It can also be used as an emergency towing device. For example, if several off roaders own Scouts, Jeeps, Blazers, etc., they can all buy a pair of brackets and bolt them to their frames. Then if any one of them breaks down while off-roading, they can take out the towbar, slip it on, and tow the truck home. You can do away with large bills for a tow truck.

Turn-Signal Connector

For those who want to tow four wheelers home from the army surplus or Postal Service Jeep sale, Superior/Ideal among others, has the answer to your turn-signal connection headache. They sell a light set, complete with mounting brackets and wiring, that attaches to the roof of the vehicle being towed. You can connect your turn signals with a quick connector and not have to fool around with wiring.

Trailer Ball

The most commonly used towing connection is the trailer ball. These come in various sizes, but the 1⅞-inch size is the most useful. It is also a good idea to carry the 2-inch size in case you need it.

Trailer

Another very useful item is the utility trailer. There have been many cheap models around for years, but now there is one to fit the most rugged needs of the off-roader. It is called "The Helder Off-Road" and is made by Helder Mfg., Inc. Its compact size is ideal for off-road use. Its rugged frame is made from 3-inch channel iron, and the tongue is fabricated from ¼-inch wall box steel. The 2000 lb. axle sits under special coil springs and allows up to 15½ inches of ground clearance when used with 11 x 15 tires. The body is made from 14 gauge steel as are the fenders. The tailgate is made from the same 14 gauge steel and there is a 3-inch flange around the top of the body for fitting a wide variety of covers, from a metal lockable top to a tonneau cover, all available as options. Helder also offers chrome folding tie-downs. The inside dimensions of the cargo box are 20 inches deep by 39¼ inches wide by 59½ inches long. The hubs are made of heavy steel instead of the more brittle cast iron, and a wide variety of hub options allow you to fit

The Helder Off-Road utility trailer is a most rugged and useful trailer. It's the perfect companion to your four wheeler when your activities require hauling (Courtesy, Helder Mfg. Inc.)

The tow bar can be used to tow disabled vehicles or bring your Jeep to the trails

your truck's tires on the trailer. This may come in handy if you get two flats and have to take one off the trailer.

Standard features include two 4-inch stainless steel tail lights, a tight-turning 2-inch Cartwright hitch, and heavy duty ⅝-inch steel hubs with ½-inch studs. Options include factory-installed gas can holders (you can fit two gas cans on the side steps), safety chains, hub pattern alterations, locking hinged metal top, various tire packages, and a customized paint job over filled-in seams for a smooth look. The trailer comes with a choice of primer and without tires and rims to allow the owner to choose the tires he wants.

CB RADIOS

After the initial CB fad petered out, a large number of people kept their CBs or purchased better units. These are the people who really need a CB and are grateful to the fad for having introduced them to the CB radio. Foremost among them are the owners of off-road vehicles. Because off roaders often travel great distances to their trails and need assistance in getting unstuck, the CB is a great tool. In this section, I'll discuss the basic kinds of CB radios and features. For a full treatment of how to buy, install, and use a CB, I would suggest that you get Chilton's book on the subject, *Chilton's CB Handbook.* It goes into much greater detail than I can here in a page, giving you the complete rundown on how to choose, install, and operate a CB radio.

You can spend a great deal of money on a CB, or as little as $30–40, depending on how much transmitting power you want. Most CBs are good at receiving; it's the transmitting power that separates the good sets from the poorer ones.

A less expensive and more flexible alternative is to go with a hand-held or walkie talkie CB radio. These hand held models have a three-channel capability, and come with one pair of crystals for channel 14. Other crystals, from 1 to 40, can be purchased separately at about $5 a pair. They usually have a minimum of two watts of input power, and can transmit for several miles, varying greatly with terrain and weather conditions, of course.

These hand held CBs are useful for all kinds of outdoor activities as well as off-roading. For example, if other members of your club have mobile CB units in their trucks, you only have to buy one hand-held CB to keep in touch with them on the trail. You can go off on your own and feel assured that if you get stuck or lost you will be able to contact them. The hand-held CBs run on eight AA batteries, so the converter for your truck's 12 volt system is a good idea. You can use your alternator's power while off-roading and save the batteries for when you go hiking or fishing. These are probably the most versatile CBs you can buy.

The other CB accessory you will need is an antenna. You will need an antenna with any mobile unit. Most hand-held CBs have a built-in telescopic antenna, but its effectiveness can be increased by using a roof-mounted antenna. Most of the best antennas are standard 50–52 ohm antennas, and come in a variety of mounts; magnetic, bolt, no-bolt trunk lid mount, chrome plated gutter clip mount, and bumper type mount. You can also get camper mounts and suction cup tie-down mounts. Most antennas have a stainless steel spring so it can bend horizontally and not

(Left) Here's a CB radio with excellent transmitting and receiving capabilities, as well as side-band versatility, the President Grant AM-SSB (Center) The Avanti Racer 27 antenna is a good one for off-road use. Mount it in the center of the metal roof for best results (Courtesy, Avanti Research & Development) (Right) Hand-held CB radios are great for trail use

break off. This is more critical than you think when you imagine it being bent in every direction by tree branches.

A CB radio can be your best investment in off-roading fun and safety when used to its capability. If you get stuck somewhere out in the boonies your radio will put you in communication with someone with a winch. They can come to your rescue and pull you out. If you own a winch you can use your radio to come in contact with people who need help, whether they be off-roaders or someone who slid into a ditch.

Four-wheel drive clubs use them all the time to keep their truck caravans together on outings. The first and last trucks in the line have CB radios and keep in contact with one another. If one member gets lost or held up at a stoplight while passing through town, the last member can tell the leader to stop the caravan until they catch up. A CB is also a good way to pass the day while you are making miles on a long trip.

4

Off-Roading Preparations

You've bought your nice, shiny, new four wheeler and brought it home. You've mounted your winch, auxiliary lights, roll bar, big tires on wide wheels, and you're all set. You feel a little anxious and a little worried about going four wheeling. Even though you have the vehicle and accessories you think you'll need, there still are some things you don't quite feel you've got down. Things like how to maintain your truck in top shape, how to be prepared for cold and ice, what spare parts and tools you should carry for repairs you might need to make, how to handle an emergency that might take place far from help, and how to keep your home on wheels clean and comfortable.

Your four wheeler can take you deep into the boonies

This chapter will cover all these critical areas, the ones that make the difference between having a good adventure and lots of fun or having headaches and regretting that you ever left the garage. In any sport, and four wheeling is a sport, the ones who have the most experience tend to bring along the little things that make the difference. They want to feel cozy in their truck yet be prepared for the worst emergency. This holds true if your truck is new or an old military vehicle, like mine. The best way to insure a safe and trouble-free outing is to take care of your vehicle for as long as you own it—through a good maintenance program.

PRE-TRIP MAINTENANCE

Just about all of the four wheelers I know are very serious about maintaining their vehicles. Four wheeling requires too much attention to accessories and driving techniques for you to ignore the performance of your vehicle. The vehicle forces you to pay attention to it. Driving off the road is an intense experience, particularly on a rough trail. The last thing you want is for it to break down in the middle of nowhere.

We all want to take good care of our vehicles. It becomes difficult, though, because of the lack of a good checklist of things to look over before a trip. The vehicle maintenance schedule (VMS) you get with your truck is a great list of basic things to check out, based on mileage or a yearly schedule, but it doesn't really point out the specific things that undergo great stress while off roading. If you send away for the big, thick shop manual from the manufacturer you get so many pages of little things to check that you get lost and don't really know where to start. It would take you a week to check out everything on these lists. They're totally comprehensive, but impractical.

To help you out, I've compiled a checklist. This list isn't meant to take the place of your regular VMS, the one buried under the cassettes and junk in your glove compartment. It is meant to supplement it and to help you zero in on the specific things that can go wrong while off-roading. Another good idea is to pick up one of Chilton's Repair & Tune-Up Guides for your specific vehicle. Each one gives you all the specifications and information you'll need, in language you can understand.

I would suggest that you check the things on this list about every four months; twice a year at least. This way you'll be in close contact with the condition of your truck. If you go on longer trips, several days during a long weekend, or a week or two for a vacation, then start going over your rig carefully a month or so before the trip. This will give you enough time to correct all the things you should correct and order any additional parts of accessories you may need.

Keep a notebook page as a record of all the things you do, including the date and mileage. I do. This is one of those things you always read about in books but never do. This time do it. You'll be surprised how easy it is to forget if you put in a new oil filter last time you changed the oil. You can't trust your memory. After a few years you won't remember what you did.

My checklist is based on actual cases of things that can and do go wrong off roading. Read it all the way through, and check off right now the things you want to look at on your truck. You'll forget them later if you don't. Even if you already know everything on this list, it will be a good reminder. You can be sure that the one thing you overlook will be what breaks down.

I've listed the maintenance items under parts of the vehicle. This will make it easy for you to check out one part of your truck at a time.

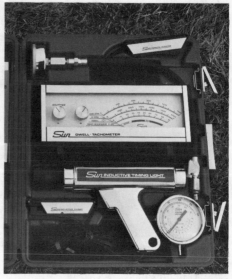

mileage	oil	plugs	points	oil filter	gas f
56,100	✓ 10w		✓	✓ 10	✓
57,500	✓ 30w				
~~58,300~~	r 30			✓	
59,875	✓ 30w July 9			✓	✓
60,400				Canada Trip (Buy oil)	
63,800	√25w Sept 10				
66,100			✓		
66,440	40 10w 10w40			✓	
67,450		✓			
69,000	10w 40				
70,200	✓ CANADA TRIP			✓	
73,500		OK			
77,250	10w 40 Valvoline				

Keep a maintenance schedule sheet like this one for tune-ups and oil changes. Otherwise, you'll forget when it's time for an oil change or tune-up

This complete tune-up kit by Sun has everything you need to keep your truck in top condition and to detect mechanical malfunctions

Engine

Tune your engine and check its performance about every 8,000 miles. Of course, you need some equipment to do this. Sun Consumer Products makes an excellent, high quality tune-up testing equipment kit. This includes an inductive timing light, dwell/tachometer, compression tester, vacuum gauge, and remote starter switch —all packed into a molded suitcase-style case. You can perform tests on the starting system, mechanical systems such as vacuum and compression, ignition system, fuel system, emission control system, and charging system. The kit does have limitations and it may not be able to diagnose all problems but it can, however, give you an excellent idea of where the problem might be and what might have to be done to correct it. For example, I had an ignition problem with my Scout. It would run rough when it reached 2,000rpm or more. I first checked out the tune-up specifications. They were perfect. The next possibility was that it could have been a mechanical problem, such as a sticking or cracked valve, or a compression leak. The vacuum gauge was easy to hook-up and I found that the engine was running perfectly at 20 inches of vacuum. The next possibility was the timing advance in the distributor. Following the instructions, I tested both the centrifugal advance and vacuum advance, and found that both worked fine. The only possibilities left were a defective distributor or coil. I had the engine analyzed and it turned out to be a defective distributor. Since the engine was 12 years old I just bought a new unit instead of rebuilding the defective one. When analyzing a problem the most difficult thing is to pin down exactly what it is. The Sun tune-up equipment gives you a good start on pinning down problems and will enable you to solve most of them yourself. There is even a wall chart included for reference. You can use this chart to go through a complete checkup of your engine at tune-up time and the Chilton books will tell you how to go about performing all these maintenance chores.

Check radiator for leaks. Also check heater core for leaks. Drain radiator and replace coolant with 50 percent antifreeze mixture if it's a year old or in questionable condition. Look over radiator hoses. If there are any cracks or checking, replace them.

Change oil if it hasn't been changed in 2,000 miles. Replace the oil filter at least every second oil change. You could use a longer mileage interval for the oil change but this is what I recommend for long engine life under off-road conditions.

Check air filter. If you can't see the sun through your paper element, replace it. Flush out foam air cleaners with cleaning solvent or kerosene. Clean out your oil bath filter, if you have one, and fill with fresh oil.

Check gas filter, replace along with tune-up parts. Also replace the PCV valve at tune-up time.

Check fan belts and accessory belts for wear. If they've frayed or cracked, replace them. Remember to take along spares.

Check the water level of the battery, fill with distilled water if necessary.

Check the idle speed and air-fuel mixture of the carburetor. Clean the carburetor linkages and choke linkage with a good solvent.

Take a good look at the engine. Check for antifreeze or engine oil leaks. Wet spots on the engine or oil on the garage floor will give these conditions away.

Make sure all electrical connections, particularly those on the battery, are clean, dry and tight. Check for loose wires on the engine or unusual noises.

Make any other necessary adjustments and repairs. In other words, *fix* all those things you've been putting off.

Transmission

If you have a manual transmission, change the gear oil once a year. Check the garage floor or the street under your truck for gear oil that may be coming from leaking seals or gaskets.

If you have an automatic transmission, check the fluid level before and after every off-road trip. Drain and refill transmission fluid every 10,000 miles under rough off-road use, particularly if you have a pickup or Blazer-size truck. Off roading is very hard on automatics and you should keep your fluid at its proper level and in excellent condition to avoid any trouble.

Dana 20 Two-Speed Transfer Case

The Dana 20 two-speed transfer case is usually lubricated by your transmission's gear oil. Filling the transmission up to the height of the fill plug will maintain the correct fluid level in the transfer case as well. It is best to check the level in both gearboxes though, since some transmissions don't share the oil supply with the transfer case. Watch for leaks. The same maintenance procedures apply to all other part-time transfer cases. Use 80W90 gear oil.

Quadra-Trac Transfer Case

Check fluid level every 5,000 miles. Level should be up to the fill hole plug. Use Jeep Quadra-Trac lubricant. Every 30,000 miles drain the lubricant through the bottom drain hole, tighten the drain plug and refill with Quadra-Trac lubricant. Drive the vehicle in circles, both clockwise and counterclockwise for a few minutes to make sure that the lubricant circulates throughout the inter-axle differential.

Quadra-Trac with Low Range Reduction Unit

To service this you must first drain the Quadra-Trac main unit, replace the plug and tighten to 20 ft. lbs. Next, loosen the reduction unit housing attaching bolts and pull the housing back far enough to drain all lubricant. There is no drain plug on the reduction unit. After the lubricant is drained completely, tighten ⅜-inch bolts to 20 ft. lb. and 5/16-inch bolts to 9 ft. lb. torque. Fill the main transfer case unit with two quarts of Jeep Quadra-Trac lubricant and install the fill plug. Then add one pint of Quadra-Trac lubricant to the reduction unit through its fill hole. I would only use the special Quadra-Trac lubricant that Jeep makes for their transfer case. You'd also be interested to know that stick-slip or chattering condition can be cured on the Quadra-Trac by replacing the lubricant. Drive around for a while to make sure the lubricant is warmed up and circulating before you drain it.

New Process Model 203-Full-time Transfer Case

Recommended oil changes are every 32,000 miles. I would change it every year. As with the Quadra-Trac, draining is a little tricky. Loosen the bottom left bolt from the front output bearing cover if there isn't a drain plug. This bolt is covered with a sealant that may wear off after it's loosened a few times. If it leaks, some Loctite 242 will work. General Motors recommends that you remove the power take-off cover from the side of the case and use a suction gun to make sure most of the oil is out. Refill with 9 pints of SAE 10W30 or 10W40 engine oil. Yes, engine oil, not gear oil. The filler plug is located near the front left. Check the filler plug hole occasionally to see if it's filled to the top. If not, top it off. No special additive is required.

Driveshafts

Every six months you should check the driveshaft splines and lubricate them with grease. Pump grease into the grease fitting until it comes out the loose end. Also check the U-joints; if there's any looseness at all, replace them. A U-joint is either solid or it's ruined. The double cardan (constant velocity) joint is more difficult to lubricate. It is usually used on the front driveshaft of a 4WD vehicle. First see if there are arrows on the pinion yoke and driveshaft for correct alignment. If not, mark each side with white paint or scratch a mark on each part. Disconnect it from the front axle. Move the shaft over to one side as far as you can. Rotate the shaft until the lubrication hole in the center bearing can be seen. Lubricate the grease fitting using an adapter such as Alemite Adapter No. 6783. Align the marks on the driveshaft an the pinion yoke, slide them together, and connect the front U-joint again. GM recommends that you don't detach the driveshaft, but turn the grease fitting up and use a flex hose and needle nose adapter. Check the surface of the shafts. If there is any tar or heavy undercoating on them, clean it off with paint thinner. The extra weight of the undercoating, even an extra ounce, will throw the driveshaft out of balance at high speed and prematurely wear out the U-joints.

Axles and Differentials.

Check the level of the gear oil in the differentials every six months. It should be up to the filler hole. Only check the differential level when you haven't driven the vehicle for a while since it will expand under the heat build-up of use and look filled when it isn't. Refill using 80W90 gear oil once a year. If the axles are submerged in sandy or muddy water, drain the gear oil and refill.

Check pinion shaft seals at differentials for leaks. If it is new and leaking, give the seal a month or so to break in. If it leaks after that, replace it.

Take off the rear brake drums and see if there is any bearing or axle grease around the seal. If the seal is leaking, replace it. Check the seal after submersion.

Check the spindle nuts on the rear axle and see that they're torqued properly. Hard off-road use loosens them. Also check the bolts on the axle housing flange. They also work loose after a few years.

Check the wheel studs. If they're worn to an oval or the threads are wearing off, replace them.

Check the axle U-bolts for tightness.

If you have free-running front hubs, twist them and see if they engage properly. If they bind excessively take them apart and check for proper lubrication. Check the wheel bearings to see if they're properly lubricated.

Suspension

Check the leaf springs for alignment. If the leaves are shifting or crooked tighten the U-bolts and check for a broken center bolt.

Grease the leaf spring eyes twice a year if they have grease fittings.

Check the mounting studs of the shock absorbers. Replace them if they're bent or excessively worn.

Take off the shocks and compress them in your hands. They should compress smoothly and firmly, but be more difficult to extend. If they bind, get stuck or move very easily, replace them, preferably with gas-filled shocks.

Check the mounting bolts on the leaf spring shackles. If they're worn, replace them. Also replace bushings at this time if necessary.

Tires and Wheels

Rotate your tires every 5,000 miles, every 2,500 miles if you have a limited slip or locking differential. For bias and belted bias tires move the rear tires up to the front on the same side and put the front tires on the rear of the opposite side. For radial tires, just switch the front and rear tires on the same side. For example, put the left front on the left rear and the left rear on the left front. If you wish to rotate all 5 tires, put the spare on the right rear and take the right front tire and use it as your new spare. Rotate all the other tires normally.

Get a good dial or pencil type air pressure gauge and check the pressure of your tires about once a week. Don't trust the gas station gauge to be accurate.

Check the wheels for dents and cracks. Replace a wheel if it is developing a crack. Check the stud holes. If they're worn into an oval replace the wheel and in the future keep the nuts tight. Replace any nuts that are worn into ovals.

Steering

Check the manual steering gear box to make sure the gear oil is up to the proper level. Use 80W90 gear oil. Check the power steering fluid reservoir and be sure it's filled to the proper level. Check the tie rods to see if they're bent. Grease tie rod ends with lithium grease three or four times a year.

Electric Winches

Keep the winch worm gear housing filled with 140W gear oil. Grease fittings and add a few drops of SAE 20 oil to the oil cups of the motor bearings. Follow any other lubrication instructions your winch manual may have.

Check battery cable connections and other wiring for clean, tight contacts. Unreel the cable carefully under tension, and run a lightly oiled rag over the length of it as you wind it up tightly and evenly around the drum. Trim any wires sticking out from the cable with wire cutters.

Rebuild your winch with the winch rebuilding kit if necessary. The main thing to watch for on any electric winch is to keep the bearings clean and well lubricated. This means flushing them out and refilling with clean gear oil if it has been submerged in water, or filled with dust.

Power Take-Off Winches

Keep the worm gear housing of the winch filled with SAE 140W gear oil. Once a year drain the gear housing, flush with good, clean kerosene, and refill with fresh oil. Drain and refill if the winch has been under water.

Power take-offs also have a chain drive case. Keep this filled with SAW 30W non-detergent oil. Drain and refill once a year, or after submersion.

Lubricate parts like the driveshaft that have grease fittings with lithium base grease. Lubricate the rollers of the roller-type fairlead, if you have one, by oiling the ends. The power take-off unit at the transfer case should be lubricated at the same intervals as the transfer case. Keep all mounting bolts tightened.

Electrical

Check the electrolyte in the battery to make sure it can hold a charge.

Check your off-road lights, fog lights, and other electrical accessories. Be sure they're mounted firmly and are located in a place where they won't be ripped off by tree branches.

Fix any instrument panel lights or accessory lights that don't work.

Brakes

Check the level of the brake fluid and refill it to its proper level. Check brake hoses to see if they are cracking. Replace them all if there are any signs of cracking. Examine hoses and brake lines for leaks if the brakes don't seem to grab as hard as they should. If the brakes lock, look for leaking seals or overly worn brake shoes or disc brake pads. Adjust brakes once a year if they aren't self adjusting.

Taking time to inspect and do preventive maintenance on all the things listed here will avoid about 90 percent of the breakdowns that could occur. This may seem like quite a long checklist for pre-trip maintenance, but once you get the hang of it you'll be looking under the hood and under the body of your truck out of habit.

Your eye will be trained to spot loose electrical connections, leaking fluids, and loose bolts. A half hour of inspection a month is all you need to keep your truck in top shape by catching small things before they develop into big expensive problems.

WINTER OPERATIONS

Four wheeling isn't limited to the spring and summer months. You've got a heater in your truck and there's no reason why you can't go out in the snow and deep cold of old man winter. For some, including myself, this is the best time of the year. Unlike the other months, just being there is a challenge. Getting your engine started in the morning, going for hikes through the snow, and walking and driving along frozen rivers and lakes is a great joy that can be brought to you in its fullest when your four wheeler is involved. And going places that necessitate the use of a four wheeler is what four wheeling is all about.

Having an old military vehicle has taught me just what can and will go wrong with a vehicle during the winter's cold. A few sensible precautions and preparations will insure a safe and rewarding trip into the snow and cold.

Several things in particular are important to think about. These are good traction on the ice and frozen snow, making sure your engine will start in the subzero temperatures, and keeping lighter lubricants in the engine and transmission.

Traction

After studded tires became illegal just about everywhere because of the extensive damage they did to the pavement, tire makers began looking for better ways to improve tire grip in the winter. The major innovation in this field has been the introduction of softer compounds in tires.

You may have noticed that when it gets really cold, about 10° F or lower, the rubber on your tires gets harder. They feel like solid rubber tires; they're so stiff that they slide right over ice instead of bending to get a grip on it. You can really tell the difference in the morning, when the part of the tire contacting the street seems to freeze in that position, leaving a flat spot on the tire until the weight of the vehicle and the rolling movement round it out.

Recent efforts to correct this have resulted in softer rubber compounds, rubber that doesn't get as hard when it gets cold. Just about every major tire manufacturer has a tire available with this softer compound. Sears calls it Tractionex and it's available in several tires, including retreads. Goodyear has a tire called the All Weather Radial that incorporates this rubber in the tire.

I haven't seen four wheelers going to these tires. They are designed mainly for cars, not vehicles with 4WD. The reason is that cars are very poorly designed for obtaining traction in difficult situations. Consequently they are off balance, and are too light in the rear where the driving wheels are. Four wheelers are balanced better and have a tighter stance on the road. They get better traction since the front axle also delivers drive. Since most of the weight is up front, this makes a big difference. Any four wheeler gets much better traction than any car with winter tires using a softer rubber compound. Since most four wheelers also have traction tires designed for off-road use, they are getting very good traction in the snow anyway.

What this all adds up to is that if you have a car, the softer compounds will give you better traction. For a four wheeler, the difference won't be worth the bother and expense. You're better off getting a good set of off-road tires and keeping them all year round. They are made of a good compound that doesn't get as hard in the cold.

Chains

There's only one way to get any kind of traction on ice—the old fashioned tire chain. There are two things to watch for when you buy tire chains. Getting the right size and getting a good quality chain. Getting the right size is important, particularly if you plan to go to a larger tire size. For example, if you now own H78 x 15 tires or L78 x 15s, and you want to go up to 10 x 15 with your next set, you'll have a hard time finding chains to fit both. The 10 x 15 size will fit up to 11 x 15 or 10 x 16, but are too wide for H78 x 15. It's easier to go to a taller tire, since you can buy extra lengths of tire chain to connect to the ones you already own. Width is the determining factor. Your chains must be wide enough to go up to a larger tire width. Be sure to check this out before you buy them.

Quality is also very important. Like most other things, chains come in cheap models. Look for high quality chains that have steel bars welded to the cross sections. These give much better traction in the snow and greater braking power on ice. The other thing to look for is the hook that fastens the chains together. If it's a little S-hook that you slip on, forget it. There are hooks that provide more positive locking action, such as the E-Z hook fastener on Campbell chains.

For most driving situations a pair up front will work well. They will help pull the vehicle up steep hills and will brake more quickly. Remember, up front is where most of the vehicle's weight is. For really rough going get chains on all four tires; nothing beats them. Don't forget you can also use them for that slick thick mud in the summer. You'll blow everybody else off the trail when you come in with chains on.

Starter

The starter has to be in top condition for winter use. In cold weather the battery is putting out less power, as you'll see shortly, and the engine oil gives the starter greater resistance. Even the lubrication inside the starter itself, around the ends of the armature, is thicker and drags down the torque of the starter motor.

Play it safe and have your starter in top condition. If it has 45,000 miles or more on it, take it apart and check out the brushes. Be sure they're making good clean contact, and are covering the starter shaft completely. If not, you can buy a pair of new ones for under a dollar. Break these in for a few months before the winter weather starts, since it will take some time for the new brushes to wear down and make good contact. If your four wheeler has 60,000 miles or more on it and the starter isn't in top shape, the wiser thing to do is take out the old starter and replace it with a rebuilt one.

Battery

It is a very good idea to get an increased capacity battery and alternator with your new four wheeler. If you have an old truck, get an increased capacity alternator on a trade-in and a better battery next time around.

Check out the battery. Most electrical problems arise from corroded battery terminals, old cables, or loose connections. There is nothing difficult about cleaning off the terminals. Just buy a good battery terminal brush and scrape off the corrosion until the terminals shine. Then clean off the cable connections as well. Finally, and this is important, disconnect the ground cable from the body and clean it off. This is often overlooked, but it is the major cause of poor battery performance.

If you have an older battery, check out the density of the electrolyte with a battery tester. If it is not up to par, I would buy a new one. If the battery is more than 2½ years old and used for frequent four-wheeling, I'd feel safer with a new battery, rather than risk failure in the boonies.

After much careful research and years of putting up with lousy batteries, I've found that one of the best for off-road use is the Prestolite model 2495X, which comes in sizes for all off-road vehicles. The main problem with batteries on off-road vehicles is that the vibrations and mechanical shocks destroy them. The Prestolite 2495X combats this in two ways: by using a black hard rubber case which is more flexible and durable than plastic, and by bonding the internal elements to the battery container with a special epoxy compound. Thus the cells are permanently bonded in place and protected from vibration, which can shake the active material from the plates and short the cell. These batteries also have the traditional fill from the top design, instead of being maintenance-free. I would not recommend a maintenance-free battery for off-roading. They are subjected to very harsh use and you cannot keep track of the water they are losing—they do lose a little water. The Prestolite must be filled up about three times a year, making it a low-maintenance battery, a good compromise between the old fill-it-every-month type and the new maintenance-free variety.

The main reason the starter turns slower and slower as the temperature drops is that the battery's output is a function of the temperature of the electrolyte. Just like you, it works better in warm weather. The table below shows how the output of your battery drops as the temperature goes down:

Electrolyte temp. (°F)	Output (percent)
+80	100
+60	88
+40	75
+20	62
0	45
−20	20

All figures are for a new, fully charged battery.

There is something you can do to correct this decreased battery output. Up in Minnesota, they do connect two batteries to the starter. These are connected in parallel to double the amperage. The problem with these wiring setups is that while they do work, they put an excessive load on the alternator. While both batteries discharge to give twice the cranking power, both batteries must also be recharged simultaneously. This can damage your electrical system if the batteries were drained and need a lot of recharging.

There is a better and more reliable way. You can install an automatic dual battery isolator. I have been using one made by Blackstone Manufacturing Company. This will isolate one battery from the other. If one battery drains down, it will switch to tap the second battery. When the engine is running it will control the recharging of the batteries, one at a time. Your electrical system will not be damaged, but you will still have two batteries on hand. Blackstone has several models of the battery isolator available for various needs. They also have wiring kits, battery trays, and a battery box. The most difficult part of mounting a second battery is finding a place to put it. The Protector 100 wiring kit is also great for installing the second battery. Some makers of battery isolators forget that you have to put the battery someplace and wire it in.

The advantage of the isolator is that you have two batteries to give you more starting power. Although the battery isolator will give you two batteries, it does not double the amps available for starting, it only allows you twice the cranking time. The parallel connecting method allows you to draw on both batteries at the same time, doubling the starting amps. Each system has its advantages and disadvantages. Actually you can use jumper cables to connect one battery to the other with the battery isolator. The auxiliary battery is jumped to the main battery, giving you twice the power if you need it. The battery isolator is also useful for lights, a winch, and other electrical power drainers. It's a good thing to have no matter what your uses are.

You can also install a second alternator on your engine if you do a lot of jump starting. Some people make extra money in the winter doing this. All you have to do is buy another alternator mounting bracket and find a bolt hole in the right spot. You can tap your own if you know how to do it. Another alternative is to install a larger capacity alternator. A friend of mine has two short lengths of copper pipe connected to his battery. When he gives jump starts he doesn't even have to open his hood. He just connects his jumper cables to the two copper pieces and he's all set.

Engine and Transmission Lubricants

When the temperature drops, the oils in your engine and transmission get gooier and thicker. This not only makes it harder for the starter to turn the engine, but the thicker oil is harder for the oil pump to circulate. The engine doesn't get lubricated as well as it should. What starts out as 20W20 oil becomes 80W when the temperature drops to zero. You can't get rid of this problem completely, but you can alleviate it by using a lighter viscosity oil. The following table shows you how to adjust your engine oil to the temperature:

LOWEST ANTICIPATED TEMPERATURE	RECOMMENDED SINGLE VISCOSITY	RECOMMENDED MULTI-VISCOSITY
Above 40°F	SAE 30, 40 or 50	SAE 10W30, 10W40, or 20W40
Above 0°F	SAE 20W20	SAE 10W30 or 10W40
Below 0°F	SAE 10W	SAE 5W20 or 5W30

If you change your oil every three or four months you can adjust the engine oil viscosity to the seasonal temperature very easily.

I have heard that you can get a 40W gear oil, but I haven't seen any in stores yet. Disengage the clutch when you start your engine and you will relieve the drag of the gear oil on the gears and shafts. Automatic transmission fluid does not need to be changed for winter use.

The gear oil in the differentials and the bearing grease also have a significant effect in winter weather. They slow down the vehicle. This doesn't affect starting, though, only the vehicle when it's in motion. I once ran my Scout at −20° F and the drag on the axles was so great I had to start it in low range. After a while the gear oil warmed up and got thin enough to run in high range. Twenty or thirty degrees below zero is about the limit for starting a normal well-prepared vehicle. Anybody driving in weather colder than this should be examined for masochistic tendencies. In really cold weather in Alaska, they leave their vehicles running all day and night, knowing that they could never get them started again. There are a number of electrical heating devices available to keep the coolant or engine oil warm, but these won't help much if you don't have a place to plug in.

SPARE PARTS

If you perform all the pre-trip maintenance checks I've listed here, then you shouldn't have much trouble with breakdowns off the road. Occasionally, something does go wrong, and you never can predict in advance what it will be. You can bring along a good stock of spare parts that will help you correct what went wrong or get around it. Ideally, you should be able to keep your vehicle running to get to a garage or parts store for permanent repairs.

What parts you bring along depends on several factors. The first is how capable you are as a mechanic. If you don't know how to change oil, you'd best not venture too far from help. Bring a CB along and keep within range. Even if you can't repair your vehicle, most likely the next guy will know how. For the most part, most off-road problems occur with the battery and ignition system, the carburetor, and the suspension. If you have a good idea of how these systems operate, then you've got a pretty fair chance of correcting anything that can go wrong. Bring along enough parts to take care of anything that can happen with these things and you'll be all right.

The second factor is how far from civilization you expect to go. Don't worry about breaking down if you won't get farther than a few miles from a gas station. You can always walk for help. On these short trips, following the pre-trip maintenance schedule will head off any problem you might have.

On the other hand, a venture for 100 miles into the mountains or the wilds of Canada will necessitate a complete set of spare parts. Not only are the chances of finding help slim, but you have a much better chance of something going wrong. I've stuck my neck out several times with my army Scout, and nothing worse than a flat tire has happened. On the other hand, I've had the pleasure of going into the garage in the morning to drive to work and finding the antifreeze all over the floor from a burst water pump seal. If something is going to go wrong, I'd rather have it happen in front of my house.

The third, and probably the most important factor, is how worried you are about your vehicle breaking down. You don't want to venture into the boondocks and worry all weekend about something happening that you can't fix. Like bringing along a winch, spare parts give you peace of mind. I call this the "breakdown anxiety" factor. Breakdown anxiety varies with the condition of your vehicle and particularly with your mechanical experience. Someone with a brand new Blazer feels that nothing can go wrong; he's a little over-confident. Actually I don't trust any new vehicle until it's been broken in for at least 5,000 miles. It has to be put to the tough off-road test before something breaks. As far as the warranty goes, you're better off pushing it and running it hard the first month you have it. If there are any defective parts, they'll go while it's still under warranty.

Breakdown anxiety increases as your vehicle gets older. When it gets around 70–80,000 miles, you begin to expect things to go wrong. The remedy here is to keep a watchful eye on all the pre-trip maintenance items I've listed, and replace any worn parts before they break. It might seem expensive to buy new parts just to keep something from going wrong, but it's a lot cheaper than getting towed to a garage later.

The remedy for breakdown anxiety is to keep a good maintenance schedule, check out the pre-trip points I've listed here, and bring all the parts necessary for peace of mind. You want to have fun and adventure while off roading, while meeting new traction challenges and putting your vehicle to the test. You don't want to ruin your fun by worrying about breaking down all the time.

Giving all these factors due consideration, I've compiled the following list of spare parts necessary to both peace of mind and the repair of most of the things that can go wrong while four wheeling. The list includes not only recommendations from manuals, but those things that actually have gone wrong with my vehicle and the vehicles of many other people. The list is categorized by vehicle components. You'll also find the parts listed under two sections: a short trip section and a long trip section.

Engine Parts

Here's a list of the things that can break and bring your engine to a dead stop. Major engine wear and breakdowns usually take a long time to develop into a problem and you should be able to detect these through engine noises and poor engine performance. You can always make it home on a burnt valve, but if a small thing like a fan belt breaks you're in real trouble. Don't worry about major repairs, it's the small things that cause most engine breakdowns.

SHORT TRIP

Fan belt—Bring along spares for all vital belts. About the only non-vital ones would be for the air conditioner or air pump, if it is driven separately.

Radiator hoses—The molded ones from the dealer's parts counter are the best and the easiest to install. You can bring one of the universal kind if you have to.

Thermostat and gasket—The thermostat may stick and cause the engine to overheat. It's easy to install but be sure you bring along a gasket.

LONG TRIP ITEMS

In addition to the short trip items, these items will be necessary on extensive off-road trips:

Radiator sealant—This isn't good to use in your radiator, but far better than nothing in an emergency.

Spare parts shown here are spark plugs, U-joint, gas filter, fan belt, radiator hose, thermostat, gear oil, brake fluid, and weatherstrip adhesive. These are a good investment; you will use them for regular maintenance anyway

Extra antifreeze and an oil filter are necessities for longer vacation-length outings

Fuel pump—This isn't too expensive and it's good to have around.

Master carburetor rebuilding kit—It's cheaper than a spare carburetor and will correct any carburetor problems you may have.

Two gallons of antifreeze mix—In case the radiator leaks.

Permatex No. 2—Necessary for use with any gasket.

Three feet of gasket material for making your own gaskets—This is sold by the yard at good auto parts stores, like fabric. It's great if you need a gasket and don't have one; you can cut out your own.

⅛-inch rubber sheeting for gasket making—I used this to insulate one of the battery cables where it was contacting the body. I found it at a hardware store.

Oil filter, enough oil for an oil change and 2 quarts more—Any trip lasting a week or two will mean at least one oil change.

Air filter—You'll need at least one for dusty roads. If you have a foam type or oil bath you'll find yourself cleaning these out at least once if the conditions are dusty.

Transmission and Transfer Case

Gear oil—You won't need to drain the oil unless your truck gets stuck underwater for a few days. Otherwise, bring a couple of quarts along in case one of the seals begins to leak, just to be on the safe side.

Suspension and Drivetrain

Center bolts for leaf springs and nuts, four of each—Breaking the center bolt isn't uncommon, it's the best way to break a leaf spring.

U-bolts for leaf springs and nuts, four of each—These can be broken as well. It's best to have a pair on hand for each axle since it's hard to find a substitute.

LONG TRIP ITEMS

U-joints, one for each driveshaft—Don't buy two of the same size; the front are usually smaller than the rear U-joints.

Grease gun—A hand grease gun applied to U-joints and leaf springs at the right time will save extra wear and tear.

Mounting studs for shocks—Usually the front studs are replaceable; they aren't necessities but will make the ride home a little easier.

Axles

Wheel bearing—Carry an extra one for the front axle. It's easy to install and you might need it.

Gear oil—You might spring a leak at the pinion seal of the differential.

Axle seals—Carry a pair for the bearing seal. They're easy to install and might need replacement if your truck is under water often.

Tires and Wheels

Spare tire—Carry one for short trips, two for very long trips to the wilderness.

Pressure gauge—Useful for letting the right amount of air out of your tires for soft surfaces.

LONG TRIP ITEMS

Tire valve cores and an installation tool—This might be necessary on older tires if you hit heavy gravel or rocks.

Wheel studs—You may shear off a few. Carry 10 or 12, enough for two complete wheels. They're inexpensive necessities.

Brake fluid—In case you spring a leak at a wheel cylinder.

Brake tubing—Carry an extra piece in case you break the line at one of the front wheels. A 6-inch stock length will work.

Tire repair kit—If you have tube tires you can bring one along, but I can't see how you'd get the tire off the rim to use it. A plug kit for tubeless tires can help, though.

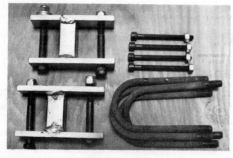

These spare suspension parts can be carried on the really rough trails. Shown are Advance Adapters shackles, center bolts, and U-bolts. Off-road stresses can break these components, particularly if your vehicle is old or has a suspension kit

If you find yourself in deep mud and water a lot, a hub rebuilding kit is a necessity (Courtesy, Husky Products Co.)

Electrical Parts

Tune-up kit—Points, rotor, condenser, distributor cap. Even if you just tuned your ignition, you never know if the parts are defective. You can bring along the old parts just in case.

Electrical connectors—Solderless type, for fixing little breaks in the wiring without solder, as well as installing your accessory lights, CB radio, speakers, gauges, etc. The best way to make sure you have all the terminals you need is to get a complete kit. I've found that a good one is the K-180 by Waldom Electronics, Inc. Chicago, IL 60632. With this kit you get 120 insulated solderless terminals and a high quality universal crimping tool with built-in wire stripper, cutter, and bolt cutter. It comes with a nice plastic case so you can throw it in your toolbox and have it when you need it.

Shrinkable tubing—This is great stuff for repairing broken wires, making stronger connections, etc. The kind I have is made by Russell Industries, Inc. and can be bought at electronics stores. After you solder two wires together, slip a piece of shrinkable tubing over the exposed connection. Light a match and hold it under the tubing. It will shrink and form a tight insulated cover over the wires. They also have shrinkable tape that can be used for all sorts of electrical connections. The tubing comes in various sizes. I use the ⅛-inch and ¼-inch sizes, along with a 10-foot roll of shrinkable tape.

LONG TRIP ITEMS

Coil—This might go at once and there's no way to fix the old one. They aren't expensive.

Bulbs—Various sizes to fit your turn signals. Bring along an extra headlight. They get broken easily on gravel roads when other cars kick up the gravel. These parts aren't necessary for mechanical reasons but will keep you from getting annoying traffic tickets in other states.

Electrical wire—18 gauge, insulated, about 25 feet. For small electrical repairs, use with the solderless connectors.

Spark plug wires—Bring along spare spark plug wires. You can buy them singly or in complete sets.

Odds 'n Ends

These are useful for getting rid of annoying rattles, rain leaks, doing minor body repairs, and patching up anything else that might go wrong.

First aid kit

Assorted nuts and bolts—Bring along sizes that fit your vehicle's engine.

Sheet metal screws—You might want to make minor modifications while on your trip.

Epoxy—Good for filling holes and gluing metal, Loctite® ribbon epoxy works great and is very easy to use with no mess.

Duct tape—Great for repairing drafty holes and a million other uses.

Weatherstrip adhesive—Great for fixing loose bolts as well as repairing tent rips and loose weatherstripping. Get the Permatex® part no. 80S.

Spare parts and tools can be stored in a handy tool box like this Sears Craftsman No. 6512

The Chilton line of Repair & Tune-Up Guides is essential for long vehicle life. Get one for your vehicle and keep it with your tools or in the glove compartment

Silicone sealant—I've found General Electric silicone products to be the best. The black Auto Seal is great for rain leaks and wiring, and the clear glue and seal for general repairs.

Rubber hose, ⅛-inch inside diameter, and clamps—Good for repairing a leaking gas line or vacuum hose.

Baling wire—For holding anything together that's coming apart, such as a loose muffler or exhaust pipe.

Cable clamps—Essential for repairing steel cable when it breaks.

The most important spare part is a repair manual for your make and model year. Chilton has a complete line of Repair & Tune-Up Guides for all four wheelers, as well as for pickups and vans. These can be found in auto parts stores and book stores, as well as many discount stores. They are inexpensive and worth a hundred times their weight in repair bills and aggravation.

BUYING SPARE PARTS

It might seem to you that this list of spare parts is too long. Well, it isn't as bad as it seems. In the first place, for a short trip you have to carry only a few things; it's on the longer trips that I recommend you bring all the spares.

Space doesn't need to be a problem, either. You can fit almost all of these parts in a large-sized tool box. I carry spare parts in one tool box and my tools in another. (Of course larger items such as your spare tire, anti-freeze and gear oil, have to be kept separately. For these I use a wooden box mounted in my Scout. If you're a pickup owner, a bed mounted tool box will hold everything.

Most people are simply too lazy to take a few minutes to plan things out. They need to have something simple break down and not have the spare part to learn to bring spare parts. Not having something when you really need it will increase your break-down anxiety. You'll be motivated enough to bring along the parts you need the next time.

As far as the expense goes, these parts are really not that expensive. They probably don't amount to more than two hundred dollars. The important thing is to spread out your payments, like you do with other things you buy. For example, next time you buy tune-up parts, buy spare points and a condenser. Keep the old rotor and distributor cap as emergency spares. If one headlight burns out, buy two. The same goes for turn signal bulbs and fuses. Decide that one month you're going to go to the dealer and buy the suspension spares you need. Next month get a fuel pump. Go to a parts store and pick up a coil and the fan and accessory belts you need. Spend ten or twenty bucks each time and in half a year you'll have all you need. Gradually building up a spare parts supply through a program like this is much better than rushing out before your vacation when you've got a thousand things to do and trying to remember them all. You'll end up forgetting the one thing you really need.

As far as quality of parts goes, four wheeling puts a tremendous strain on a vehicle. Cheap parts can wear out quickly or break when the going gets tough. If you're in a discount store and want to save a few cents on a cheaper part, stop and think if you'd want that el cheapo substitute to ruin your weekend outing. I don't think you would. Substitute parts can be just as good as dealer brand name parts, and cheaper, but buy them only if you know from your own or somebody else's experience that they will hold up. You don't want to find out in three feet of mud on a dark cold night.

Spare Parts Philosophy

Always buy parts that are a little better rather than a little more cheaply constructed. They will cost a little more, but on the whole you get what you pay for. Always include that little extra part you think you might need, rather than forget it because you might not need it. It's obvious that you might not need *any* spare part you bring. But you bring spares because if you do need them you'll need them badly. And remember that most, if not all, of the spare parts you buy will be used up in the course of normal maintenance and repairs anyway. So you're preparing for the future.

TOOLS

No matter how many or how few of the spare parts listed here you bring, they're absolutely worthless unless you bring along the right tools to install them. Nothing is more frustrating than to break a fan belt, have a spare on hand, and not have the wrench you need to loosen the tension bolt on the alternator mount. Remember it's not the big things that cause trouble on the road but the little ones. A mistake like this could cost you hours and a lot of money having a tow truck come out to get you. If this happened on a lonesome trail you could lose a day or more.

As with the spare parts list, you can bring more or less than is listed here depending on your needs. If your truck is new, you can get by with the short list of tools in a small tool box or tool roll. This can be made from a piece of heavy cloth folded over one-third and sewn up the folded side to make pockets. Then it can be rolled up and tied together with a shoelace. Some hardware stores sell these complete with tools. If you don't own any tools, a complete tool roll will suit most of your automotive needs.

Here is the short list of tools that will suit most of your one-day outing needs. You can add or take away from this list, of course, as your personal needs and judgment dictate.

Short Trip Items

Vise-Grips® jaw type—Get the original Vise-Grips® brand name or a comparable high quality item.

Lug wrench—Don't overlook this basic tire-changing tool. Some people get a simple flat and find they left their lug wrench in the garage the last time they changed their tires. I use a ½-inch drive extension handle, a 6-inch extension, and a socket. The socket fits the lug nuts better than the poorly made lug wrench.

Open-end wrenches, ⅜ to ⁹/₁₆—Don't bring bigger sizes, they'll add a great deal of bulk and weight and you won't need them.

Dial-type air pressure gauge—Get the kind that has a hose for bleeding the air. You can control the amount of air you let out so you can go down to 20psi or less for running through soft mud and sand. The pencil-shaped one is cheaper, but not as accurate. Try using it when it gets clogged with mud and sand.

⅜-inch drive socket set—It's small and stores neatly in its own case.

Box-end wrench set—You need these to go with the open end set. The same sizes, ⅜ to ⁹/₁₆, should be included.

Six-inch adjustable wrench—This is the handiest size. You can bring it instead of the open end and box end wrenches if you like, but often you need a wrench at both ends of a bolt to loosen and tighten it.

Screwdrivers—Small and medium slots, and no. 2 Phillips.

Pliers—Six-inch size is handy.

Long-nosed pliers—For any electrical work you may have to do.

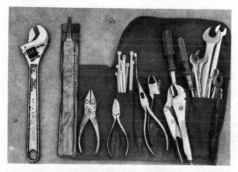

For everyday use, a small tool roll like this is all you need. All the tools in this set were carefully selected from years of experience to include enough for most problems without excess bulk

The front wheel bearing nut (spindle nut) sockets are a must for all four wheelers. They enable you to loosen the nut so you can replace or adjust wheel bearings and replace axle seals (Courtesy, Husky Products Co.)

If you've done your pre-trip maintenance, this is all you will need. Some off roaders get by with even less, bringing along just a couple of screwdrivers, an adjustable wrench, and a pair of pliers. The point is to bring as many tools as you'll think you'll need, without carrying a portable garage. If your vehicle needs that many repairs you should rebuild it before venturing out. Bring a small tool box and stash it behind the seat. Be sure it's in a secure place, and snugly tied down so it doesn't fly around on rough trails and create a safety hazard.

Long Trip Items

Aside from the short trip tools, I looked in my bigger tool box and found the following extra tools very handy on longer excursions. These are used for trips over a day, so I'm sure to have what I need to take care of any possible situation.

Vise-Grip®, chain type—This is great for grabbing anything, from two pieces you have to hold together tightly for welding to loosening super-tight oil filters. It's expensive, but nothing beats it when you need it.

Open end wrenches—Sizes 9/16 to ¾, the ones you didn't include in your short trip tool box. Again, you don't need the big ones such as 1 inch, so don't bring them. They weigh several pounds each and take up a lot of space in your toolbox.

Box end wrenches—Bring the sizes you didn't have in your short trip tool box, 9/16 to ¾.

Oil pan drain socket—If your trip will be over 2,000 miles you'll need this to change the oil.

Mechanic's hammer—When nothing else works you can always throw it at a tree or bang something to bits with it in frustration.

Liquid Wrench® no. 2—For loosening bolts, nuts, and anything else that freezes with rust. Also great for protecting metal, squeaks, and drying out wet engines. A universal tool.

Spindle (wheel bearing) nut socket—This is a very large socket for removing the nut from the front axle. It attaches to an ordinary ½-inch drive wrench. The nut must be removed whenever you replace the front axle seals or service the wheel bearings. Husky Products makes the one I use.

Hacksaw—On one trip to Canada I left mine home by accident and had to use a file to cut the lock from my spare tire. The lock froze and wouldn't open. At the time I wished I had some dynamite.

¼-inch drive socket set—For ignition, fuel line, and other little uses. These little sockets are also essential for taking the cover off your CB or stereo.

½-inch drive socket set—For heavier duty work, such as fixing wheel bearings or tightening a spindle nut. You may only need a few choice sockets as well as a long handle for leverage.

File—Can be used to sharpen a screwdriver used as a chisel, or for taking off a frozen lock when you leave your hacksaw at home. You can sharpen your ax with it, etc.

Allen wrenches—A little set of these comes in very handy when you need one.

The five-ton Walker® jack stands shown here will support most any truck. The scissors jack is small enough and has enough capacity (1½ tons) to be used as an emergency jack; it also has a wide and safe lifting platform

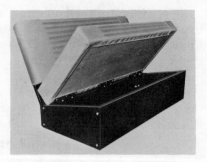

Tools, apart parts, and emergency equipment can be carried in a rear seat with a lockable compartment built in (Courtesy, Husky Products Co.)

Spark plug gapping tool—For tune-ups. It's so small it stays in the tool box.

Utility knife—You might need one for trimming off gaskets, etc.

Deep wall sockets—I carry two, ½ inch and $^9/_{16}$ inch. It seems that almost every bolt head on my Scout is one of these two sizes. They can reach into spots that you can't get to with a regular socket.

Flexible grabber—For retrieving nuts you drop into the carburetor, etc. It has a plunger at one end and a wire claw at the other. Great for retrieving things you drop into inaccessible places.

WD40®—For getting rid of squeaks, loosening binding door locks, etc. Another indispensable universal tool.

Hand impact tool—Great for loosening stubborn nuts, screws, etc. Has an attachment for ½-inch sockets. Another indispensable universal tool.

Spark plug socket—For removing spark plugs.

Small block of wood—About 5 inches long by 1-inch wide and ½-inch thick. I use it between a hammer and whatever needs pounding when the steel hammer would dent it in or can't reach far enough.

Chisels—Two; one short one ¼-inch wide, and one longer one ½-inch wide.

Putty knife—For scraping off grease, applying grease, etc. Very handy.

Torque wrench—Small beam-type or whatever you have. Useful when you have to tighten a bolt to a critical torque.

Permatex® High-Tack Spray-a-Gasket—Great stuff for sticking gaskets to the part being assembled. I often use it to hold a nut or bolt together until I can tighten it. Once you have it you find a million uses for it.

If this seems like a lot of junk to carry, it isn't. It will fit into a tool box, or better yet, if you have a Jeep or a Scout you can get a rear storage seat to hold all of your tools and spare parts. Your passengers will appreciate it too. If you are not sure that you will need all of this stuff, do what I did. Each time you do some repair work on your truck, toss the tool into your tool box or storage seat. Don't go out and buy a giant 1,000-piece tool set and throw it in the back of your truck. This way you will have only the tools you have used and will need again. After a while you will begin to accumulate all the tools and paraphenalia I have listed here. If you leave anything out when you go on vacation, you can be sure that the one thing you left home will be the tool you need the most.

Garage Tools

Here's a short list of tools that will make maintenance, engine swapping, and repair easier and safer. These are larger tools and are usually kept in the garage. It is not necessary to bring these along on off-road trips.

Jack stands—A necessity for supporting your vehicle off its wheels. Don't buy those cheap discount kind that cost $10 a pair. They don't look like they can support themselves, let alone your truck. People have been killed when these cheap jack stands collapsed. I have been using Walker professional jack stands. The two ton pair is good for smaller vehicles, but I would recommend the five ton pair for big pickups. If you have a large pickup with huge tires and a suspension kit, your axle will be too high off the ground for you to use normal jack stands. The Walker® five ton jack stands have a height of 24⅞ inches to give the biggest pickup enough reach to keep the wheels off the ground.

Tilt-a-Bar—This is a tool you can use if you plan to rebuild your engine or swap it for a different one. The tool helps you control the angle of the engine while you are taking it out and fitting it back in. It is inexpensive and extremely handy. As everyone who has put in an engine knows, aligning the splines is the most aggravating part of engine installation. This handy tool gets rid of that problem. It

The handiest garage tool for any home mechanic is a one ton floor jack. This one, made by Walker, is lightweight with a long handle for reaching under the truck

The saw and hatchet are helpful for cutting firewood or small branches to build a platform when you're stuck in mud. The shovel is a necessity for off-road outings of any length

works with an ordinary ½-inch drive wrench. As you turn a fitting at the end, a threaded shaft turns and adjusts the angle of the engine. It is available from Superior/Ideal.

Trans-jack—This is a necessity when removing a transmission or differential from a truck for either rebuilding or swapping. I recommend the Superior/Ideal trans-jack because it has a reasonable price, is well made, and has an adapter available for 4WD transfer cases. If you're going to do any of the transmission or differential swapping described in the accessories chapter this jack is for you.

Floor jack—Walker also makes a lightweight floor jack for general garage use. This is the number 93636 one ton jack. It is a hydraulic type jack, and will lift one ton up to 16¼ inches off the ground. It is very light at 34 lb. An automatic valve prevents overloading and the extra long handle (34 inches) is very convenient when reaching under pickups.

EMERGENCY EQUIPMENT

It seems that the last thing people are willing to spend money on is an emergency. Only after something happens that results in a disaster will they prepare for it. And then it's too late. This is true of off roaders as well. Most don't even carry equipment to get themselves out when they get stuck. Only after they get stuck and get slapped with a $100 tow truck bill will they put out some money for a winch or a HI-LIFT jack. As I mentioned before, the farther into the boonies you go, the more prepared you'd better be to get yourself out of any situation you get into.

Here's a list of the equipment I bring along for handling emergencies. Some things might be repeats from other sections because they serve more than one function.

Tire pump—You can use either a manual pump or a 12 volt electric that works off your car battery. Either way, a source of air for your deflated tires (when running on soft sand or mud) is an excellent idea. Most people don't bother to install an electric air pump since they don't hit trails that are too far from a gas station. But for convenience, an air pump is a great idea. I use the Miller air pump, model 3100 mini air compressor. It is made by the K. J. Miller Co., of Broadview. IL and is easily obtained through large retail stores such as Sears. You can permanently mount it inside your hood, and it has two alligator clips for connection to the battery terminals rather than the less convenient cigarette lighter connection. It comes with a 12-foot hose so you can reach all four tires easily. You might need an extension hose for the bigger trucks. It sells for about $50 and is a good investment since you can put it into your next truck. This pump inflates tires faster than any other you can buy, a great help in the cold or the rain.

Jacks—I recommend bringing along two. One should definitely be the HI-LIFT jack, and the second jack should be a scissors-type. I prefer it mainly because the lifting platform is wider and safer than the small round head on hydraulic jacks. It can be made very useful by mounting a piece of ¾-inch plywood on it. Then

When you let your tire pressure down for soft terrain, this Miller inflator pump can air them back up. It operates from the vehicle's battery. It is compact, fitting readily under the hood of the author's Scout

You can carry all your unsticking equipment on the front. Here is a Jeep with a Warn winch and a HI-LIFT jack in a handy place. HI-LIFT brackets were used along with an extra bracket

when you use it in sand or soft dirt it will have enough support to lift the vehicle. A square detachable platform for the HI/LIFT jack is also a great idea, and it's easy to install since the jack platform has holes in it.

Jumper cables—You'll use these all year. Occasionally someone may kill his battery using a winch without the engine running, or clog up his exhaust and drain the battery trying to restart. Get a good set of jumpers. Don't buy the cheap models, they have thin gauge copper wire and cheap clamps that break in cold weather, when you need them the most. Better sets cost from $15–20, but won't break, have thicker copper cables, and the cables are insulated with plastic that remains pliable in really cold weather. They last years longer.

Emergency road reflectors—This is required in most states as a standard piece of emergency equipment. They are used to alert other drivers of your breakdown so they don't run into you. The widely available red reflectorized triangle type with a heavy steel base is very good. You can also use them to mark trails when the

You can carry your spare parts, tools, emergency equipment, and 50 gallons of gas in this tool box (Courtesy, Hickey Enterprises)

These emergency items should be carried by every vehicle. Shown here are: flashlight, first-aid kit, fire extinguisher, and emergency reflector

road takes a turn to the left and right. On your way back, the marker will tell you which way is the correct route back, keeping you from getting lost in unfamiliar territory. While towing my Scout back from the army camp, I wired one onto the hack so cars could see that they should use caution.

Fire extinguisher—A friend of mine flooded his engine and spilled the gas out the float bowl release valve. A flame shot up through the carburetor and burned his whole truck. Now he carries a fire extinguisher. I carry a 5 lb. powder type, which is good for paper as well as chemical and grease fires. If the caked-on grease and oil on your engine ever catches fire, it will be impossible to put out without a fire extinguisher. It is refillable and is a great investment. With all the money you pay for insurance, you may as well spend a little on something that will actually help you in an emergency. Your insurance policy won't help you put out a fire. A 5 lb. extinguisher costs about $23.

Gas can(s)—At least one is a good idea. But make sure you fill it when you need to. Any time you go on an outing with a club, or go on a longer trip by yourself, be sure to fill the can. That extra five gallons will get you to the next gas station, or will take you where you're going if the gas stations are closed and you need a little extra mileage. A larger gas tank on your new vehicle is always a good idea, or a new auxiliary tank on your older truck can also help. The classic GI jerry can is the best can. When you buy one make sure that it has a good rubber gasket at the top as well as a hole for the gas vapors to vent through. For a while some plastic ones were sold, but the steel cans are better. You can expect to pay about $12 for a jerry can. I've seen some for as much as $18, but this is a ripoff and there's no difference in quality. Be sure to spend an extra two bucks on a filler extension tube. This screws onto the gas can lid when the cap is taken off. This is absolutely essential since it's impossible to get the gas into your tank without a long nozzle.

Ground cloth—Bring one along for the times when you have to scoot under your truck to check the suspension, change a tire, or do any kind of work. You can buy one, but a relatively clean, old throw rug works fine. It is also useful for spreading on the dirt when you want to take a break from driving and sit out in the sun. A heavy rug is also great when you have to push somebody out. Between bumpers it will keep both from getting scratched. It's also necessary to use a throw rug or a rubber floor mat when you use the jack. This prevents the jack from scraping against the paint and chrome on the front and back ends of your vehicle.

Large plastic bucket—This can be brought on longer trips. It's not only useful for carrying camping water, but can be used to carry sand to give you traction on ice, or gravel to fill in under your wheels when you get high-centered. When it's in the truck you can store things in it, such as beer cans and ice.

Paper towels and hand cleaner—Very handy for cleaning up. These items should be carried even on short trips, since you never know when you're going to get your hands greasy.

12 volt trouble light—This is the kind you use in your garage, but it works from your battery. Attach two alligator clips to your battery terminals and you've got a full-sized light bulb in a trouble light housing. Everybody should have one, particularly when you get stuck at night and can't see what you're doing.

Cordless soldering iron—This is a great little tool to use for soldering connections when you install your lights, repair a speaker wire, etc. I have one made by Weller®. The unit is light and has fine tips for delicate work. It comes with a set of three tips, solder, recharger, sponge, soldering aid tool, and plastic case. It lasts through a Saturday afternoon of repair work, and can be recharged indefinitely with its NiCad battery. You can use it for emergencies, of course, but I find that I use it all the time, since I don't have to worry about an electrical cord. It even has a small light bulb that lights your work, great for working in the dark or under your dashboard.

In addition to all this, add the unstuck equipment I mentioned in the last chapter. As with the spare parts and tools, remember that this equipment doesn't take up much room and it can be easily stored in a large tool box or storage box, the kind they sell for pickups with a lid on each side. You could also borrow a lot of these things from other people if you'll need them for a long trip.

If you find yourself frequently going on outings with a partner, you can split the load. You'll each have to carry less and you can save some money this way. Four wheeling clubs should take some kind of inventory before each trip to be sure that this equipment is carried by somebody. All too often everybody assumes that somebody *else* brought along a certain piece of equipment.

Storage

Nobody wants to carry all this equipment around if they don't have a good spot to store it in. If you have a four wheeler like a Jeep or a Toyota Land Cruiser, you might want to use the back space for a cooler, and not have a big box in the way. What I keep my come-along, extra cable, jumper cables, ax, and the like in an old navy duffel bag. I can throw it in the back of my Scout before I leave, and take it out when I get home, without spending an hour walking back and forth from the garage to the Scout to store everything. The duffel bag also keeps everything from rolling around. I keep my HI-LIFT jack under the duffel bag for the same reason. Everything is easy to get at and stays put. This not only prevents theft but keeps that 25-pound jack from getting thrown around in the back of your truck.

The biggest storage problem is caused by the gas can. It seems that carrying a gas

A homemade tool and equipment box, like the one in the back of my Scout, will ensure a custom fit

If you like to carry an outside-mount gas can, keep it and the gas clean with a gas can cover, available to match the tire cover (Courtesy, Husky Products Co.)

can outside your truck has become a status symbol. I don't think that carrying around a full gas can in the back of your truck is a good idea for three reasons. First, the can will get full of road dirt and crud. This will find its way into the gas tank and carburetor where it will clog up jets. Second, you don't really need to carry a gas can if you live near a gas station, and most people do. The third reason you shouldn't carry a full can is the fire and explosion hazard. If you carry a full can on a swing-away tire and gas can carrier, it could explode with the force of ten sticks of dynamite if you get hit in the rear.

Since a rear gas can carrier looks bad with just a spare tire on it, carry your can but carry it empty and covered. Covers are stocked by RV stores and come in white or black heavy vinyl. You can attach the cover to your can quickly and easily since there's an elastic strap sewn into the back of the cover. The cover even comes with a choice of left or right spout applications.

I carry my gas can inside the back area of my Scout, covered with a black cover, and tied down with some rubber tie-downs. I only fill it if I plan on being away from a gas station for half a day or more.

HOUSEHOLD ITEMS

If you are going out on a three week trek into the wilderness, or you just intend to spend a few hours on the beach having a picnic, the experience is much more memorable and enjoyable when you've brought along some comforts. I call these household items. They help you to keep clean and have a good time.

Cooler—The one universally essential item for all trips, long and short. Particularly useful in the summer for keeping your beer cold. Also used for storing food and keeping your film cool when you want to take a few pictures on hot and muggy days. Coleman makes good coolers, and they last. Expect to pay about $25 for a decent one.

Small whisk broom—This is an optional item. It will help you sweep out the floor and bed on your truck on those house-cleaning days when you want everything to look neat, shiny and clean.

The cooler is always the center of activity after a day of trail riding

A few items that come in handy on longer trips are the rags, whisk broom, squeegee, and rope shown here

Flashlight—A very handy item. It will help you look around for lost keys, change at the toll booth, etc. Fill it with alkaline batteries so it works when you need it.

Drink holders—Available from off-road equipment suppliers in sizes to fit most four wheelers. Great for when you park somewhere, but don't bring an opened drink on a rough trail. You'll soon be wearing it.

Raincoat—Another optional item for those who want to keep dry. Even if I remember to bring one along, I never bother to wear it.

Insect repellent—Necessary in every state of the U.S. during the summer. If bugs like you as much as they like me, I'd carry a bottle of Deep Woods Off. This stuff works great. It's expensive but a little plastic bottle goes a long way. Another good insect repellent is the one made by Cutter laboratories. This works well on mosquitoes, as does the Deep Woods Off, but I think the Deep Woods Off works a little better and does a good job on black flies.

Calamine lotion—This is an old favorite for relieving the itch of mosquito bites. I've found that the brand by the name of Caladryl works best. One dab of this stuff on a swollen mosquito bite and it won't itch any more. An essential item. It should have a prominent place in the glove compartment with the Deep Woods Off.

No-pest strip—Great for hanging in your truck when you park near a lake and bugs swarm into your truck on a hot day. Just keep this inside and you'll get rid of all the bugs that got in. It isn't too healthy to breathe this stuff in a small enclosed space, so only hang it up when you're not inside. Otherwise, store it in an airtight ziploc plastic bag.

First-aid kit—Optional, but could come in very handy in a bad situation, like when working with a winch.

All-weather camera housing—Many four wheelers carry 35mm cameras on their trips to record sights and the situations and action they encounter while off-roading. The problem has always been, though, that 35mm cameras are very delicate and can be ruined by the flying mud, dust, and water on off-road trails. Now there is a perfect solution to this problem. It is the EWA marine, underwater, and all-weather camera housing. This is a heavy duty PCV bag for protecting your camera from the elements. It features heavy-duty construction, a large window in front to allow light into the lens and a smaller window in the rear for using the camera's viewfinder. A large built-in glove allows easy handling of film advance, focusing, and exposure controls on the camera. You can attach a motor drive or a flash with no problem. It can even be taken underwater for a depth of 10 meters. I use it now every time I go four wheeling to keep dust, water, and mud off my camera. I only have to clean the optical glass windows on the camera housing. It can be found in camera stores and is very light and much less expensive than the old heavy skin-diving housings, and comes in sizes for virtually every 35mm camera and 8mm movie camera.

Off-roading is less organized than many other sports, particularly other automotive sports. For example, you can go to campsites specially set up for camping trailers and other recreational vehicles, but you can't go to an admissions gate, pay a couple of bucks, and use an off-road trail near a big city. I think this might come about in the near future. Without organization, you're on your own. Consequently most four wheelers are good mechanics, take care of their vehicles, and are prepared to handle most emergencies. If they don't want to do these things, then they usually don't stay in four wheeling for very long. Four wheeling is for independent people who have the courage to strike out into the unknown and take care of themselves. Follow these lists of emergency items and you'll avoid an off-road tragedy.

5

On the Trail

DECIDING WHERE TO GO

If you've just bought your first four wheeler you'll encounter a problem you've never had before: finding a place to go. All the time you were driving a car you were driving on paved roads, and it never crossed your mind that you might not want to drive your four wheeler on a paved road. Sure, 4WD helps you in the snow and in tricky handling situations on wet pavement, but you really want to go where the trails are rough or where there are no trails at all.

The best place to start is to ask a fellow four wheeler where he goes. He'll be able to clue you in on the local trails. Don't be surprised if he isn't willing to tell you all he knows. Everybody has a trail or two he likes to keep secret. This isn't out of selfishness, just common sense. If everyone went to a nice, out of the way trail it would soon be ruined, local residents would complain, and the trail would be closed to everybody. Respect the right of fellow four wheelers to keep their favorite trails a secret and they'll respect yours.

To find out where to take your four wheeler, join the local 4WD club. They'll have outings every two months or so, and small groups of friends may go out once or twice a weekend. These are usually year-round activities with some members going even in the wettest, coldest, and snowiest weather. Others stay home if the weather doesn't suit their fancy. Your preferences will be similar to what they are now. If you love the snow, you'll want to go four wheeling in it.

Going out with a club will also ensure that you get back, since somebody will usually bring along a winch, nylon strap, chain, jack, shovels, etc. for getting people unstuck. The club may also make some demands on you, such as paying your dues and helping others when they need help.

Private Land

Wherever you go it seems that somebody was there before you to buy up the land. In different parts of the country, such as New England, ownership may go back as much as 300 years. Most of the Midwest was settled by homesteaders in the early and mid 1800s, and many of the original families, particularly the most successful ones, still own the original homestead.

Since they own the land, they can do what they want with it, as long as they stay legal and pay their income tax, and they also have the right to keep you off it. To announce this fact to you they have to put up a NO TRESPASSING sign and enfore it. In this technicality lies the loop hole big enough to drive through.

Before you go driving over a bunch of NO TRESPASSING signs, you should understand why the signs were put up in the first place. Most farmers, the major landowners throughout the country, want to protect their crops, keep their cows, and keep hunters off their land. The farmers may not care if you drive over the unused parts of their land, the sections along rivers, on steep hills, and in swamps where crops can't be grown. You should be courteous and ask a farmer if you can drive on his land if it looks rough and untilled. He may give you permission. Farmers are often concerned that you will hurt yourself or damage your vehicle and sue them for it. So they have a justifiable reluctance to let people drive over their land.

Other farmers don't give a hoot and never say anything. Usually the local four wheelers know who they are and drive on their land without any hassles. They have respect for the land, don't tear it up, and don't tell anybody but their friends about the trail. Several of my rural friends have taken me on these trails and they were interesting driving. If you come upon a trail leading down to a large river and there's no NO TRESPASSING sign on it, you can most likely head down the trail and won't run into any trouble. If the trail has a nasty steel gate with barbed wire and a threatening sign on it, then respect that person's right to privacy and stay off the trail. Remember, farmers like people to be courteous and honest as much as you

Trailblazing on your own can be a lot of fun. Before attacking the foliage on somebody's property, get permission.

It pays to know where you're going. This guy wisely stayed away from the water. It turned out to be about five feet deep. But when he stopped to take a look, he lost his momentum and flotation in the deep mud and got stuck. He didn't get out until after midnight

When you see a sign like this and a fence, respect it. This time there was a good reason: fire hazard

do. If you ask a farmer if you can drive on his land, he may say yes and tell you about a section of swamp, a sand hole, a steep hill, or a riverbed where you can have a lot of fun. Don't expect them to understand why you want to drive on dirt and sand; they have to drive on it with their tractor and consider it part of their everyday job.

Another way to play it safe is to ask a passing police car or four wheeler where a local trail is. The policeman or fellow four wheeler will either help you or tell you where to go. This will give you some hint as to the local attitude toward four wheelers. The officers may direct you to some state land where anybody is allowed to drive. Be prepared to follow their directions with a good local map. You can get lost easily following a confusing list of country roads.

What's around the bend? In this case, it was a river. The lure of unpaved roads is irresistible to the four wheeler. This one was on private property, but the lack of NO TRESPASSING signs showed that the owner didn't care who drove on it

Federal Lands

An astonishing amount of acreage is still owned by the Federal Government. These lands are administered by various government agencies, most of which are listed below.

Bureau of Land Management—Most of their land is in the West. For example, the state of Nevada is almost entirely public land. BLM has an open policy toward off-road use of their land, and offers a great variety of off-road terrain. The best way to find out about nearby trails is to contact the local BLM office. You'll find a list of them with addresses at the end of this section.

Bureau of Reclamation—This office administers land that has been reclaimed from the ocean, swamps and rivers. It has usually been reclaimed for a specific purpose, and is rarely open to public use. Local project managers or regional offices may be contacted for information on specific trails that are open to off-road use.

Fish and Wildlife Service—They're very strict on limiting access and activities on their land, since their sole intention is to protect the plant, fish, and wildlife of the areas under their jurisdiction. They do allow off-road vehicles on a few national wildlife reserves to enable visitors to have access to fishing and observation points. Don't plan on an off-road outing to one of these areas, though. They want to keep the areas peaceful and quiet for the wildlife. If there's one near you, check the ranger station for information on any trails that may be open.

National Park Service—This is the most famous agency that handles public lands. Areas under their jurisdiction include Yellowstone National Park, and all parks in the national park system. Since they must carefully regulate camping and vehicle movement in their parks while trying to protect the scenery and wildlife, off-road vehicle use is strictly forbidden except in those areas where the superintendent has designated trails. Even then you must stay on the trail and follow trail markings. Since national parks have been established mainly as tourist attractions, you're better off with some other public land agency.

Army Corps of Engineers—This agency controls an incredible amount of land, unknown to most people because it's not marked on maps like the wildlife refuges or national parks and forests. Their land is usually the floodplain along the rivers where they have built dams, which includes just about every river in the United States. Since the areas they administer have flooded on a regular basis, they don't worry about ecological damage or soil erosion. The only problem is finding access to the land along rivers, which is usually surrounded by private land. Look in the phone book for the nearest office to inquire about permission to use their land.

Forest Service—There's a national forest in every state. They mark off trails for off-road use, and the ranger station at the entrance is the easiest and best place to find out where the trails are. Even though most of the trails are tame by four-wheeling standards, they offer great scenery and a nice drive through beautiful forests. The trails are clearly marked with signs, and are often closed due to heavy snow, flooding, or dry brush conditions. Respect their trail closings.

More primitive trails, like this one in Wisconsin, can be found all over the U.S. open to the four wheeler

Tennessee Valley Authority—This is probably the most permissive agency, and they allow off-road use on their huge "Land Between the Lakes" region in western Tennessee and Kentucky. If you live near this area, you'll find that you can drive down just about all their paved, gravelled, and graded roads except when seasonal conditions require closings. In addition, a 2,500 acre tract called the Turkey Bay Off-Road Vehicle Area has been designated primarily for off-road vehicle use.

Regulations

In all of these areas you must conform to the regulations of the federal agency managing the areas as well as the local and immediate regulations (such as a closed trail). The best way to find out what these regulations are is to ask the official in charge. He'll be quick to tell you the limitations and areas of off-road vehicle use. Respect what the officials say and ask of you. The rules are very reasonable and are usually common sense ways of preserving the land for everybody's enjoyment. Following these rules will keep the land open for us all in the future. The vast majority of off roaders are clean, careful, and conservation-minded drivers. You always get the few who throw beer cans and ruin it for us all. It doesn't hurt to remind such idiots of their responsibility to everybody else whenever you see them violating the land.

Here are the general regulations governing the use of off-road vehicles. All federal agencies follow these rules as well as additions they may make to handle local conditions.

1. Off-road vehicles must conform to applicable State laws and vehicle registration requirements.

2. Off-road vehicles must be equipped with a proper muffler and brakes in good working condition.

3. Off-road vehicles that produce unusual or excessive noise are not permitted.

4. In most instances, off-road vehicles must be equipped with a spark arrestor.

5. No person may operate an off-road vehicle on public lands without a valid operator's license or learner's permit unless accompanied by an adult who has a valid operator's license.

6. No person may operate an off-road vehicle on public lands in a reckless, careless, or negligent manner.

7. No person may operate an off-road vehicle in excess of established speed limits.

8. No person may operate an off-road vehicle while under the influence of alcohol or drugs.

9. No person may operate an off-road vehicle in a manner likely to cause damage to or disturbance of the land, wildlife, wildlife habitat, or vegetative resources.

10. No person may operate an off-road vehicle during hours of darkness without lighted headlights and taillights. Headlights shall be powerful enough to illuminate an object at 300 feet, and taillights visible for 500 feet from the rear of the vehicle.

11. No person or association of persons may conduct any rally, meet, or other type of organized event, involving the use of 25 or more vehicles on public lands without first obtaining a permit to do so from the authorized officer.

As you can see, these rules are mainly common sense directives that anybody with a four wheeler follows. They are written to keep the junkers and noisy vehicles off public lands. They are not relevant to most off-road machines. These vehicles are most likely in perfect condition and don't have to worry about the headlight, taillight and muffler requirements. Be sure to check out the state lighting laws before you put on any auxiliary lights. The major manufacturers of auxiliary lights, such as K.C. HiLites, or Perlux are more than willing to tell you which of their lights can be used on the highway as well as off. In most states, you can disconnect or cover the illegal lights while highway driving and stay within the law.

If you belong to a 4WD club and want to find a new and interesting spot to go, you can contact the local federal land agencies and find out about nearby trails. Even the Army allows four wheelers on their training terrain, since it gets torn up with tanks, armored personnel carriers, and the like during maneuvers. You'll find the Army to be cooperative during the off-season, which is before or after the summer months.

Roads on federal lands open to off roaders often look like this, gravel roads running for miles through the woods

To help you get started, here are the states that have public lands and the number of acres under their public jurdisdiction. Some states have no public land at all, as you can see from this list:

STATE	PUBLIC LAND ACREAGE	STATE	PUBLIC LAND ACREAGE
Alabama	363	Montana	8,162,539
Alaska	277,314,772	Nebraska	7,884
Arizona	12,995,613	Nevada	48,231,204
Arkansas	1,127	New Mexico	13,185,219
California	15,592,313	North Dakota	74,835
Colorado	8,465,124	Oklahoma	7,525
Florida	367	Oregon	15,686,725
Idaho	12,113,149	South Dakota	276,571
Kansas	954	Utah	22,752,224
Louisiana	2,023	Washington	293,067
Michigan	549	Wisconsin	91
Minnesota	43,923	Wyoming	17,459,934
Mississippi	1,137		

Here's a list of the offices of the Bureau of Outdoor Recreation. They can help you locate nearby trails for your club:

NORTHWEST—Regional Director, 915 Second Avenue, Seattle, Washington, 98174. (Covering Alaska, Idaho, Oregon, and Washington).

PACIFIC SOUTHWEST—Regional Director, Box 36062, 450 Golden Gate Avenue, San Francisco, California 94102. (Covering American Samoa, Arizona, California, Guam, Hawaii, and Nevada).

MID-CONTINENT—Regional Director, P.O. Box 25387, Denver Federal Center, Denver, Colorado 80225. (Covering Colorado, Iowa, Kansas, Missouri, Montana, Nebraska, North Dakota, South Dakota, Utah, and Wyoming.)

SOUTH CENTRAL—Regional Director, 5000 Marble Avenue, N.E., Alburquerque, New Mexico 87110. (Covering Arkansas, Louisiana, New Mexico, Oklahoma, and Texas.)

LAKE CENTRAL—Regional Director, 3853 Research Park Drive, Ann Arbor, Michigan 48104. (Covering Illinois, Indiana, Michigan, Minnesota, Ohio, and Wisconsin).

SOUTHEAST—Regional Director, 148 Cain Street, Atlanta, Georgia, 30303. (Covering Alabama, Florida, Georgia, Kentucky, Mississippi, North Carolina, Puerto Rico, South Carolina, Tennessee, Virgin Islands.)

NORTHEAST—Regional Director, Federal Office Building, 600 Arch Street, Philadelphia, Pennsylvania 19106. (Covering Connecticut, Delaware, Maine, Maryland, Massachusetts, New Hampshire, New Jersey, New York, Pennsylvania, Rhode Island, Vermont, Virginia, West Virginia, and the District of Columbia).

CENTRAL OFFICE—Bureau of Outdoor Recreation, Department of the Interior, Washington, D.C. 20240

Note: All of the information in this federal land section is from the pamphlet entitled, "Off-Road Vehicle Use on Federal Lands," by the U.S. Dept. of the Interior, Bureau of Outdoor Recreation.

Here are the office addresses of the Bureau of Land Management, Department of the Interior:

COLORADO—State Director, Bureau of Land Management, 700 Colorado State Bank Building, 1600 Broadway, Denver, Colorado 80202

MONTANA, NORTH DAKOTA, SOUTH DAKOTA—State Director, Bureau of Land Management, Federal Building and U.S. Courthouse, Billings, Montana, 59101

UTAH—State Director, Bureau of Land Management, Federal Building, 125 South State Street, P.O. Box 11505, Salt Lake City, Utah 84111

WYOMING, KANSAS, NEBRASKA—State Director, Bureau of Land Management, Joseph C. O'Mahoney Federal Center, 2120 Capitol Avenue, P.O. Box 1828, Cheyenne, Wyoming 82001

Here are the addresses for the Department of the Interior, Bureau of Reclamation;

LOWER COLORADO REGION—Regional Director, Lower Colorado Region, Bureau of Reclamation, Nevada Highway and Park Service, P.O. Box 427, Boulder City, Nevada 89005

LOWER MISSOURI REGION—Regional Director, Lower Missouri Region,

Bureau of Reclamation, Building 20, Denver Federal Center, Denver, Colorado 80225

PACIFIC NORTHWEST REGION—Regional Director, Pacific Northwest Region, Bureau of Reclamation, P.O. Box 043, 550 West Forst Street, Boise, Idaho 83724

SOUTHWEST REGION—Regional Director, Southwest Region, Bureau of Reclamation, Herring Plaza Box H-4377, Amarillo, Texas 79101

UPPER COLORADO REGION—Regional Director, Upper Colorado Region, Bureau of Reclamation, 125 South State Street, P.O. Box 11568, Salt Lake City, Utah 84111

UPPER MISSOURI REGION—Regional Director, Upper Missouri Region, Bureau of Reclamation, 316 North 26th Street, Billings, Montana 59101. Mailing Address: P.O. Box 2553, Billings, Montana 59103

U.S. FISH AND WILDLIFE SERVICE, DEPARTMENT OF THE INTERIOR— Regional Director, U.S. Fish and Wildlife Service, 10597 West 6th Avenue, Lakewood, Colorado 80215, 234-2209. Mailing Address: P.O. Box 25486, Denver Federal Center, Denver, Colorado 80225

The following addresses are for the offices of the National Park Service:

NATIONAL PARK SERVICE—Room 1013, 18th and C Streets N.W., U.S. Department of the Interior, Washington, D.C. 20240

MID-ATLANTIC REGION—143 South Third Street, Philadelphia, Pennsylvania 19106 (Delaware, Maryland, Pennsylvania, Virginia, West Virginia)

SOUTHEAST REGION—Scott-Hudgens Building, 3401 Whipple Street, Atlanta, Georgia 30344, (Alabama, Florida, Georgia, Kentucky, Mississippi, North Carolina, South Carolina, Tennessee)

SOUTHWEST REGION—Old Santa Fe Trail, P.O. Box 728, Santa Fe, New Mexico 87501, (Arkansas, Louisiana, New Mexico, Oklahoma, Texas)

NORTH ATLANTIC REGION—150 Causeway Street, Boston, Massachusetts 02114, (Connecticut, Maine, Massachusetts, New Hampshire, New Jersey, New York, Rhode Island, Vermont)

WESTERN REGION—450 Golden Gate Avenue, P.O. Box 36036, San Francisco, California 94102, (Arizona, California, Hawaii, Nevada)

MIDWEST REGION—1709 Jackson Street, Omaha, Nebraska 68102, (Illinois, Indiana, Iowa, Kansas, Michigan, Minnesota, Missouri, Nebraska, Ohio, Wisconsin)

PACIFIC NORTHWEST REGION—523 Fourth and Pike Building, Seattle, Washington 98101, (Alaska, Idaho, Oregon, Washington)

ROCKY MOUNTAIN REGION—655 Parfet Street, Lakewood, Colorado 80226, (Colorado, Montana, North Dakota, South Dakota, Utah, Wyoming)

NATIONAL CAPITAL PARKS—1100 Ohio Drive, S.W., Washington, D.C. 20242

Here are the addresses and phone numbers of the offices of the U.S. Corps of Engineers:

LOWER MISSISSIPPI VALLEY DIVISION—Division Engineer, Lower Mississippi Valley Division, U.S. Corps of Engineers, P.O. Box 60, Vicksburg, Mississippi 39180

MEMPHIS DISTRICT—District Engineer, Memphis District, U.S. Corps of Engineers, 668 Clifford Davis Federal Building, Memphis, Tennessee 38103

ST. LOUIS DISTRICT—District Engineer, St. Louis District, U.S. Corps of Engineers, 210 North 12th Street, St. Louis, Missouri 63101

MISSOURI RIVER DIVISION—Division Engineer, Missouri River Division, U.S. Corps of Engineers, 7426 New Federal Building, 215 North 17th, P.O. Box 103, Downtown Station, Omaha, Nebraska 68101

KANSAS CITY DISTRICT—District Engineer, Kansas City District, U.S. Corps of Engineers, 700 Federal Building, 601 East 12th Street, Kansas City, Missouri 64106

OMAHA DISTRICT—District Engineer, Omaha District, U.S. Corps of Engineers, 6014 U.S. Post Office and Court House, Omaha, Nebraska 68102

NORTH CENTRAL DIVISION—Division Engineer, North Central District, U.S. Corps of Engineers, 536 South Clark Street, Chicago, Illinois 60605

ROCK ISLAND DISTRICT—District Engineer, Rock Island District, U.S. Corps of Engineers, Clock Tower Building, Rock Island, Illinois 61202

ST. PAUL DISTRICT—District Engineer, St. Paul District, U.S. Corps of Engineers, 1135 U.S. Post Office and Custom House, St. Paul, Minnesota 55101

NORTH PACIFIC DIVISION—Division Engineer, North Pacific Division, U.S. Corps of Engineers, 210 Custom House, Portland, Oregon 97209

SEATTLE DISTRICT—District Engineer, Seattle District, U.S. Corps of Engineers, 4735 East Marginal Way South, Seattle, Washington 98134. Mailing Address: P.O. Box C-3755, Seattle, Washington 98124

WALLA WALLA DISTRICT—District Engineer, Walla Walla District, U.S. Corps of Engineers, Building 602, City-Council Airport, Walla Walla, Washington 99362

SOUTH PACIFIC DIVISION—Division Engineer, South Pacific Division, U.S. Corps of Engineers, 630 Sansome Street, Room 1216, San Francisco, California 94111

SACRAMENTO DISTRICT—District Engineer, Sacramento District, U.S. Corps of Engineers, 650 Capitol Mall, Sacramento, California 95814

SOUTHWESTERN DIVISION—Division Engineer, Southwestern Division, U.S. Corps of Engineers, 1200 Main Street, Dallas, Texas 75202

ALBUQUERQUE DISTRICT—District Engineer, Albuquerque District, U.S. Corps of Engineers, P.O. Box 1580, Albuquerque, New Mexico 87103

LITTLE ROCK DISTRICT—District Engineer, Little Rock District, P.O. Box 867, Little Rock, Arkansas 72203

TULSA DISTRICT—District Engineer, Tulsa District, U.S. Corps of Engineers, P.O. Box 61, Tulsa, Oklahoma 74102

Here are the addresses for the U.S. Forest Service:

EASTERN REGION—Regional Forester, Region 9, Eastern, U.S. Forest Service, 633 West Wisconsin Avenue, Milwaukee, Wisconsin 53203

INTERMOUNTAIN REGION—Regional Forester, Region 4, Intermountain, U.S. Forest Service, Federal Office Building, 324 25th Street, Ogden, Utah 84401

NORTHERN REGION—Regional Forester, Region 1, Northern, U.S. Forest Service, Federal Building, Missoula, Montana 59801

ROCKY MOUNTAIN REGION—Regional Forester, Region 2, Rocky Mountain, U.S. Forest Service, 11177 West 8th Avenue, Lakewood, Colorado 80215. Mailing Address: P.O. Box 25127, Lakewood, Colorado 80225

When traveling on federal lands, always respect the trail signs. They are put up for your safety

NAVIGATION

On most of your off-road outings navigation won't be a big problem. Weekend jaunts to the local trail for a little mud running are the most common type of off-road trip. Keeping oriented is more a problem of making sure you meet your friends there and arrive at the same tavern at the end of the day.

More extensive club outings, such as weekend trips a few hundred miles away or even in another state, may pose a slight navigation problem. Make sure the caravan leader has a good state map and knows where he's going. This will save time and delays.

Once you're at the trail with your club, try to keep together. Some guys always have to go out on their own to try the muddiest spot or the steepest section of the hills. They might have a lot of fun, but the purpose of a club outing is for everyone in the club to enjoy the trail together. It's a chance to talk with the other guys and discuss the plans they have for improving their engine's power, the new tires they expect to put on, etc. When club members stick together, particularly when the trail may extend over many miles, they can help each other out and notice when anybody gets stuck. Navigation means knowing where you are and knowing how to get out if you need help.

CBs are very important in keeping the club's vehicles together on the trail as well as on the highway. Then, if trouble arises, the member with the winch can be summoned and told where the stuck vehicle is.

On longer, vacation-length trips, navigation will be a problem. If you head into the desert, mountains, or the woods, you may find yourself traveling for hours through unfamiliar territory, taking so many turns and zig-zags that you don't know what direction you've gone and where you're headed. Finding your way back isn't as easy as turning around and following your tracks. Often your tracks will be invisible, made on such hard ground that they leave no impression. On other occasions you may not even have the room to turn around. This could happen if you follow a stream bed with steep sides, or drive down a narrow canyon or along a river gorge. Before you know it, you've run into a dead end, with nowhere to turn around. On other occasions you may have to find a different route out. In any of these situations, when you're in unfamiliar territory and far from help, your only aid may be a good topographic map.

Topographic Maps

While an ordinary map shows the locations of roads, towns, rivers, and major lakes, a topographic map shows all these and more; it is a picture of the terrain. It does this through the use of symbols and map colorings and textures. This makes topographic maps the most valuable maps for off roaders and anyone else interested in exploring the land. On topographic maps, you can find the major highways, secondary roads such as county roads, improved light-duty roads such as a graded gravel road, unimproved dirt roads, which are rough car tracks, and finally trails. These last two are of special interest to the off roader. As you may have found out, it's extremely difficult to find small out-of-the-way trails on your own. You have to know someone who lives in a rural area and can lead you to one. The entrance to a little trail may be so well concealed that you have probably driven past thousands of them without even knowing it.

Here's where the topographic map helps. It will locate these trails for you, and tell you exactly where they are. Not only that, it tells the type of terrain you'll be driving in. For example, the maps show dune areas, sandy areas, mine tailings, levees, washes, gravel beaches, and stream beds. They also give you the exact location of dry lake beds, woodland, submerged marsh (swamp) orchards, mangrove swamps (in the south) wooded marsh, shore flats, rock and coral reefs, shipwrecks, railroad right-of-ways that have been abandoned, and depressions. All of these areas can be readily and easily identified on a topographic map. These are all the type of terrain that's perfect for four wheeling.

Here's how you use a topographic map. First pick out a rough area where you want to go. Say you live in Michigan and you'd like to go to some interesting places. What you first must do, after looking at a state map of the general area where you

For extensive off roading in the wilderness, the 1:250,000 scale U.S. Geological Survey topographic map and a compass will help you find old mining trails, ghost towns, waterfalls, and other attractions

For most purposes such as off-road club outings, the gas station variety of state map is good enough

want to go, is write to the U.S. Geological Survey for an index of the topographic maps of your state. The addresses differ depending upon where you live. Here are the two addresses: U.S. Geological Survey, Federal Center, Building 41, Denver, Colorado 80225 (for states west of the Mississippi river including Minnesota) or U.S. Geological Survey, Washington, D.C. 20242 (for states east of the Mississippi river).

Ask for the "Index to National Topographic Maps, 1:250,000 Scale" and the index to the topographic maps of your state. The reason you should ask for both indexes is that they deal with different scales of maps. The 1:250,000 scale is a larger scale than the 1:24,000 scale you'll find on the state index. It covers a much larger area, about 100 miles by 60 miles, so it can't show as much detail as the 1:24,000 scale map, which only covers an area of 6 miles by 8 miles. On the 1:24,000 scale you can even pick out individual cabins, power lines, water wells, and buildings. This is usually too much detail to be of good use, and I would recommend the 1:250,000 scale map for two reasons. One is that the map shows enough detail to be of good off-road use, and the second is that to cover the same area with 1:24,000 scale maps you would need ten times as many maps, and have to spend ten times the money. One or two 1:250,000 scale maps are all you need for most places you would want to go. For $1 each these maps are a great bargain.

When you get the index to the maps of your state, there will be a list of places in the state where you can buy the maps, and universities and public libraries where you can see the maps. You can save a lot of money and time by visiting a good library, going to their map room, and planning out your trip. It may turn out that you don't need to buy the maps at all. You can mark a state map with the location of the trail you want to go to and save some money. Alternatively, you can photocopy the section of the map you need, since these maps are about 2 x 3 feet and are rather large to carry around.

Once I was planning the first west to east crossing of the state of Alaska. I went to a university library that had every topographic map published by the U.S. Geological Survey, instead of buying the maps I needed. I found out that I would have to cross several major rivers, one of which was over a mile wide, and also would have to cross miles of swampland at a time. Of course I gave up the trip. Now I know why it hasn't been done before.

The same kind of maps are available for Canada. Just write to the following address: Canada Map Office, Surveys and Mapping Branch, Dept. of Energy, Mines, and Resources, Ottawa, Canada, K1A 0E9.

Ask for an index of the topographic maps available for the province you're interested in, whether it be Ontario, Alberta, Manitoba, Newfoundland, or whatever. The maps on the 1:250,000 scale from Canada are $1.50. I've ordered maps from both agencies. The indices are free, and are very good maps themselves. The service is fair, it takes about six to eight weeks to receive maps due to the slow mailing of the large cardboard tubes. The people at both agencies are courteous and helpful, and always willing to answer any questions you may have. If you're planning to take a long trip and expect to use topographic maps, then plan at least two months ahead and send for your maps so they'll get to you by the time you leave.

One final word on using a compass. The topographic maps you use will have a small diagram showing magnetic declination, or the deviation of magnetic north from true north. Most people don't know it, but the northern magnetic field is constantly shifting. It usually moves west at about 1½ degrees a year as seen from the U.S. This means that the declination correction on the older maps will be wrong. The easiest and most accurate way to find your directions is to find some landmark, such as the tallest hill, a river, or a lake and remember where it is located. Set your compass to show roughly true north and do your figuring in relation to the landmark you've pointed out. By driving toward or away from a definite point you can keep from getting lost.

OFF-ROAD DRIVING TECHNIQUES

Driving off the road is very different from driving on paved roads where the path is laid out for you. You have to create your own path, or follow the trail passed over by many others. You don't have to contend with traffic lights, stop signs, parking meters, and other traffic. In fact, the main reason most people go off roading is to get away from all this urban congestion and regulation and strike out on their own to tackle the naked terrain on its own terms.

This may mean simply following the four wheeler ahead of you on the well-worn trail, or it could mean striking out over 100 miles of untouched terrain armed with nothing but a topographic map.

Whatever your style of off roading, and whatever condition the trail or terrain may be in, you have two main goals in off-road driving: 1) to get where you're going, and 2) to avoid getting stuck. Don't get me wrong. Getting where you're going also means having a lot of fun and tackling new traction challenges to see how much better those new tires will do in the deep mud compared to the old ones.

Here are the general techniques you should use in all off-roading situations. If you're a beginner, read these over and bring this book in your glove compartment when you first start to go off roading. It will help you when you come up to an ob-

The most common obstacle on a well-used trail is a pair of deep tire ruts. If you drive in them, your axles would become hung up. The easiest way to avoid this is to drive with one of the ruts under the center of the vehicle. Here a 1978 Scout SS-II does the trick

stacle you're not sure you can handle. After about 10–15 hours of off-road driving, you should begin to get the hang of it. Getting stuck a few times will also help you to learn the limitations of your vehicle.

General Rules

1) Sit up straight in your seat in a relaxed way, and hold onto the steering wheel loosely, with your hands at the two and ten o'clock positions. Be sure to keep your thumbs on the outside of the steering wheel so the spokes won't dislocate your thumb when you hit a rock or tree stump. When not clutching, keep your left foot on the floor. Using your seat belt or harness is a good idea. It will help you maintain control over the steering wheel, as well as keep you from conking your head on the roof.

2) Keep moving through obstacles such as mud, sand, or when going up a steep hill. Don't clutch, don't shift gears, and don't give it so much gas that your tires spin. Spinning tires might be fun on the street but when you do it in off-road conditions you'll quickly dig in.

Never stop in the middle of mud, sand, or water. As soon as you do you'll begin to sink. In soft mud vehicles can sink so fast that you can watch them drop. Don't stop on a hill, either. The brakes will lock and cause you to slide. You won't be able to steer while sliding and you'll soon be sliding down the hill sideways. Next thing you know you'll be rolling down.

3) When coming to a bad traction situation select a gear and stick to it. Try to maintain an even speed and you'll get the best control and traction. For most situations second gear is the best. You won't move fast enough to power through obstacles in first and you'll lose torque and the engine will die if you try to shift to third.

4) When descending a hill, shift to first gear at the top of the hill, before you start down, and let the engine help you ease down. Automatic hubs should be locked so the front wheels can assist in the braking and help maintain control.

Whatever you do, don't slam on the brakes. You'll lose your grip on the mud and slide down, toppling over in the process.

5) The "power approach"—Sometimes crashing through an obstacle at as high a speed as possible is the only way you can get through. This will get you through a bad stretch of deep mud, soft and deep sand, up a steep slope, or through a stream with a soft bottom. The idea here is that you gain enough momentum to get through the obstacle without any traction, you just hang on and fly through.

Powering into a situation can backfire, though. The faster you approach an obstacle and get stuck, the more pull it will take to get you out. It's like driving a stake that much deeper into the ground by hitting with a sledge hammer. Once a friend of mine with a Ford F150 powered into a bog, only to find that he dove right in like a submarine and ended up with heavy mud up to his door handles. A winch and a tow truck couldn't pull him out. Fortunately he works in construction and was able to get a bulldozer to pull him out with a monstrous chain. Even then he almost pulled the frame out from under the body of the truck.

Another fellow was driving a Toyota Land Cruiser in the winter and thought he would have some fun bursting through a snow drift and watching the snow fly. Well, the drift wasn't built like a feather pillow, as he thought it would be.

With a loud crunch he stuck the front end of his Toyota into a solid wall of snow. The snow had thawed and frozen underneath the drift. He went home sitting in a tow truck with his Toyota behind. The drift had shifted his radiator back a little toward his engine. Before you have a lot of fun like this and realize it's not so funny, you should check out any obstacle you intend to power through. This includes deep mud, water, sand and snow. Take a few minutes to get out and poke a stick into the water to see how deep it is. One innocent-looking water puddle on a trail near Chicago turns out to be 6 feet deep. It's actually a ditch that the trail passes

This guy knows how to drive through mud. He gunned it and his automatic transmission and 10x15LT tires had no trouble with the more than foot deep mud

through, so it looks like a little puddle of water on the trail. Many guys have spent their afternoon swimming in that puddle. The moral of the story is, when uncertain, look before you leap.

For obvious reasons, nobody took on this obstacle. The last guy to try it is still under water

6) Learn to think in terms of ground clearance and straddling clearance. Find the lowest point to the ground on your vehicle and measure how low it is. On my Scout it's 9½ inches, from the bottom of the differential case to the ground.

Learn to recognize how wide your vehicle's stance is; in other words, how far apart the tires are. Then you will know when you approach a deep rut if you will be able to clear it. While on a trail it will help at first to get out and see if you can clear that rock with your differential case before you ram into it. Having a partner check these things out also helps. After some practice and experience you will know exactly how high a rock or tree stump you can safely clear and when to get out and check. Don't be overconfident and show off. A new axle will set you back a lot of money.

These general rules apply to all off-roading situations. Once you learn to follow the driving techniques described, you'll have no problems, except when you get stuck because your four wheeler can't handle the terrain. And remember, every four wheeler can get stuck.

To help you out with some of the worst off-road situations, I've described them with some comments on how to handle them.

Mud

You may have some trouble with the thick black mud that lies around bogs, swamps, and lakes. This mud is soft, as dense as clay so it clogs up your tires quickly, and as slippery as butter so your tires soon lose their grip on it. If your local area has a lot of this stuff, the only way to handle it is with good semi-flotation tires and aggressive tread. The Gumbo Monster Mudder is the best tire for this

Here's a lesson on how to drive through a huge mud hole. Keep one wheel on each side on level ground if you can, gun it, and hang on. Look at the tires, they're the skinny stockers! Sure, bigger tires would make it easier, but there is no substitute for driving skill

since the treads are so deep and wide apart. Another good choice that is quieter on the road is the Armstrong Tru-Trac. Both of these tires will keep pretty clean while staying on top of the mud as long as you keep moving. The trick to driving through this stuff is to put that gas pedal to the floor and leave it there. Your tires will spin, but the motion will keep them digging and your truck moving. Approaching this

Here's how to exit the mud hole

stuff in a slow cautious manner is sure death. You'll quickly sink into it up to your bumpers.

If you hit this stuff only occasionally, then bring along your tire chains. They will help you out a great deal, providing a good biting surface that will keep relatively clean of mud.

When driving on muddy roads, you can keep out of other people's tire ruts by straddling the right tire rut. This can be done by keeping your left tires on the center of the trail and your right tires on the right shoulder of the trail. Do this only if the tire ruts are so deep that you're sure you'll get high-centered. Otherwise, you'll be spoiling all the fun by taking a muddy trail too cautiously.

Snow

Handle bad snow conditions as you would handle bad mud. Get aggressive tread tires with good flotation, such as the ones I mentioned, and if constant slipping on ice is a problem, the only real solution is a set of tire chains. Chains on all four wheels work best but if you must make a choice, put them on the front tires for steering control. Watch out for your front brake discs, though.

There are three main types of snow conditions. The first is newly fallen, soft powdery snow. Your four wheeler will have no trouble with this, and you will do very well with your regular tires, such as the Goodyear Tracker A/Ts on your new four wheeler. The reason is that the snow is so light it offers little resistance to the tires, and you will easily roll right over it.

This old Jeep CJ-3B plows through the snow with Armstrong Tru-Trac tires. Traction in snow requires an aggressive tire; treat it as if it were very slippery mud

The second kind of snow hazard is wet, heavy snow. This kind usually falls in the fall and spring, when the weather isn't so cold as to make the snow dry and powdery. The problem with this snow is that it is wet and packs very quickly, making slippery surfaces. The first time over the newly fallen snow you will get very good traction, since the snow will pack under your treads and give a good grip. The second time around, though, you'll be going over hard and slippery tracks, not much better than ice. You can gain some traction on this stuff, but not enough to go up steep hills. Another problem with this snow is that it usually melts and forms muddy, slushy patches. Since the ground beneath it is usually mud, you have a slippery mud condition. Aggressive flotation tires are the best bet.

The third kind of snow condition happens in the middle of winter. By this time the ground is frozen and icy. When it snows, the snow just sits on top of the frozen ground and ice. While hard ground with grass on it will give some traction, bare or icy ground is almost impossible to get a grip on. Here tire chains on all four wheels are a necessity unless you'll only be driving on this stuff for a short way. If you get stuck on the ice, you'll have to use sand or gravel for traction, or winch yourself out. A common way to get stuck in these conditions is to get hung up, or high-centered, because the drifting snow concealed a patch of high frozen ground.

Sand

The word for soft sand travel is flotation. Aggressive tires aren't as important as they are in mud, and even smooth tires will work well if they're on wide rims, 8 to 10 inches wide, with the tire pressure down to 20psi. The worst sand conditions in the Midwest and East are in rivers and at the edges of lakes where the sand has mixed with light organic silt to make a very soft, watery mixture. You'll quickly sink to the bumpers in this stuff. For most uses, your regular tires will get you through a patch of soft sand if you power your way through.

The ultimate test of any four wheeler's capability is a steep hill of very soft sand. Here the author's Scout easily tops a small sand hill. Goodyear Wranglers and a Burbank suspension kit made it easy for the four-cylinder engine

If you drive out onto a river bed, as I have done, try to keep a steady even movement. Second gear in low range works well. It gives you good engine torque and control. Often soft sand will alternate with a bar of hard gravel, or firm granular sand. Try to stay on this bar and keep away from the silt. If you find yourself going the last 50 feet in soft sand, don't stop. If you must turn back, turn in a gentle, wide arc to avoid digging in and slowing down. The front tires will clear a shallow V-shaped path for the rear tires, so don't turn too sharply or they'll dig in.

Never come to a dead stop in soft sand. You will instantly sink in and have a hard time trying to get moving again. Never slow down unless you have to in order to avoid some obstacle, and don't change gears. The resistance of soft sand to movement is incredible. When you take the clutch out to shift gears, even for an instant, there will be no engine torque going to the wheels, and your truck will instantly halt. Don't brake, since you're in the sand you won't have to. This is just a habit carried over from traffic. If you need to slow down, just let up on the gas a little and the sand will do the rest.

If you have superwide flotation tires and a powerful engine you don't have to worry about the sand. But most of us don't have them, and we have to be more cautious. The best way to avoid a lot of trouble is to get out and scout the area before you get yourself deeply stuck. See where the firmest sand is, and mark the spot by digging a line with your foot or placing a stick there. As you walk around the area you intend to drive on, test the firmness of the sand. Stand on your heels; if you sink, your truck will. If you don't; then most likely your truck won't either. I've done this and sunk up to my knees in silty sand. Needless to say I would have spent long hours getting out of there. I stayed away from the stuff.

Deep Water

Any vehicle can ford a depth of 1½ feet with no problem. Going through water this deep, though, is not like flying through a few inches of water and watching the spray fly over your vehicle. You have to be careful to move slow enough so the resistance of the water does not become too great, and fast enough to keep moving over a soft bottom. About 4–5mph is ideal, in first or second gear low range, depending upon your axle ratios, of course.

The Hickey Sidewinder III 9,000 lb. winch easily pulls the author's Scout out of a slimy bog

Get out and check how deep the water is, how strong the current is, and how soft the bottom is. Testing the bottom is the most important factor. You can easily drive across a hard bottom, but a soft bottom or a bottom with big rocks will get you into trouble if you're not careful. Use the same standard for the bottom as you would for sand; if your heel sinks in to the ankle while standing on it, don't enter the water, or be prepared to winch out. If you think the water will be deep enough to hit the fan blades, loosen the fan belt at the alternator slide so the fan won't churn the water and spray the distributor. Immediately tighten the belt when you leave the water to avoid overheating. If the belt is wet and slips, loosen it again and dry it with a rag.

Try to avoid knee-deep water if you can. If you have to ford such depths, be prepared by taping up the distributor with the electrician's tape you brought along. The easiest and most surefire way to cross deep water is to let the engine run at 1,000rpm and pull yourself across with a winch. You won't get stuck, and the engine rpm will keep water from entering the exhaust pipe, the only thing you really have to worry about. Another thing you can do is carry a 4-foot length of rubber hose that fits over your exhaust pipe. Use a clamp to tighten it, and tie it so it points up toward the sky. This will greatly reduce the chance of the water pressure overcoming the pressure of the exhaust and stalling the engine. If your engine does stall in deep water, pull the truck out before restarting it. Check the distributor for wetness first. The contacts inside the cap should be dry. If you have an electric winch and your engine stalls, you'll have to use the battery to pull your truck out. This will take a lot of juice, so it's a good idea to carry two batteries if you intend to hit a lot of deep water.

To keep the brakes functioning, leave your foot on the brake pedal enough to keep the shoes or disc brake pads in contact with the drum or rotor. This will keep the brakes dry enough to remain functional. Any water that does seep into the brakes can be quickly dried off by keeping the brakes down once you get out of the water. The heat generated by the friction of the brakes contacting will be more than enough to dry the brakes.

The only trouble you should ever have with water is if you dive into a puddle and find that it's 6 feet deep, or if you drive into a bog and the water is a foot deep and the mud underneath is 3 feet deep. In all such situations a sharp eye and some caution will save you a great deal of trouble.

Steep Hills

The only way to make it up a steep hill is with a powerful engine and good tires. Steep hills are probably the most difficult obstacle to tackle, especially when they're covered with soft slippery mud, soft sand, or slick snow. There's no trick to getting up a hill. You have to be careful when coming down; here the danger is sliding and rolling over. To avoid this drive up a hill in a straight line, particularly if you think you may not make it. This way if you stop on the way up, you can put it in reverse and use your engine to help slow your trip down. You won't have to try to steer your way down. The same applies when descending a hill. Keep it in first gear and use the engine to help you slow down. Don't use your brakes; they'll lock and you'll lose steering control. If you have automatic locking hubs, lock them before you start down so the engine can help the front axle brake and assist in steering control.

Pulling a Trailer

There is no special trick to towing a trailer behind your four wheeler. You should pay great attention to getting the proper size and weight of trailer for the towing capabilities of your vehicle, and make sure that the engine and transmission's cooling system can handle the extra load. Don't drive too fast on gravel roads with a camping trailer, it could slide off the edge of the road, dragging your vehicle with it. Learn to get a feel for the pulling power of your vehicle and be conservative in the choice of roads you take in bad weather. You could find yourself sliding backward halfway up a slippery hill with no room to turn around.

Here's the fun way to drive through water, splashing through at 10–15 miles per hour. This splash didn't even knock out the ignition, which wasn't waterproofed. Water about 1½ to 2 feet deep is perfect for this. Did I check out the depth of the water first? No, but I did make sure that there was a tree available for winching out

Here is the safer way to approach water, keeping an even speed of about 5–8 miles per hour. This isn't as much fun as the faster way, but it does a good job of cleaning mud from your tires and body, and there's less chance of getting stuck in deep water

Getting stuck in deep mud isn't as bad when you have two pickups with nylon straps to pull you out

GETTING STUCK: HOW TO GET OUT

Getting stuck in a four wheeler is like, as the old analogy goes, getting pregnant; you can't be a little stuck. You either are or you aren't. This is because the 4WD vehicle has such excellent traction that if it can move at all, it will. If it can't move, it's stuck. It's as simple as that.

The most difficult thing about getting stuck is learning to have the right attitude about it. The right attitude is, as in other things, to face the reality that you're stuck, accept it, and learn to deal with it. And the reality of getting stuck is this: you *can* get stuck, and you *will* get stuck.

This might sound simple but it isn't. Most guys, especially when they have a new four wheeler, really don't believe that they can get stuck. They have a lot of pride in their vehicle and its capabilities, and rightly so. But this pride makes it hard for them to realize that their vehicle has limitations, that it can get stuck in the right (or wrong) circumstances. So when they're driving through deep sand and they stop moving, they don't really believe that they're stuck. They press down on the gas pedal a few more times. The tires spin some more, throw out some more sand, and dig in deeper. This makes the situation worse. Then they get out and dig some sand out from in front of the tires, thinking that this will help. Hitting the gas again, they help the tires dig themselves in still deeper and high center the vehicle. Now the tires are spinning freely in the air, throwing a few grains of sand here and there, and the vehicle is held up completely by the two long frame members. *Now* the driver realizes that he's stuck. While before it would have taken him 10 minutes to get out, it will now take him 45 minutes, providing he's brought the right equipment. And since he doesn't believe that he can get stuck, he hasn't brought along the right equipment. He'd better have some friends nearby who can help him get out.

The front end of this Dodge Ramcharger got stuck in a thick, soft bog. The grass hides the mud and water. Next to being submerged in a lake, getting stuck in a bog is the worst off-road hazard

Even with Armstrong Tru-Tracs, the mud was too soft and the water deeper than expected

Now let's reverse the film. This time we'll see the situation over again and I'll say what he should have done. As soon as he stopped moving, he should have:

1) *not* hit the gas again

2) got out and looked at the situation, and thought about whether he could get out by putting the transfer case in low range and creeping. This would be the choice if he were moving slowly through heavy sand, and came to a halt. On the other hand, if he were moving along at 10 mph or so through thick mud and stopped, putting the transfer case into low range wouldn't help.

3) realized that he is stuck, not hit the gas any more, even in low range, and started thinking about how he's going to get himself out.

There are two main ways of getting stuck. You either sink, or you become high-centered or hung up.

If you sink, you're up to the hubs in mud, or up to the bumper in mud, and can't get out under your own power because your wheels are slipping. You will have to be pulled out, although you can lift yourself out if you want to take the time to build a platform of branches and logs to support the vehicle. Nobody wants to go through this effort, but it may be the last resort if you can't pull yourself out.

Being high-centered, or hung up, is being stuck so that the wheels are not making ground contact. The reason they are in the air is that you have either driven onto a bump or dug yourself in with all four wheels. The vehicle is not resting on the wheels but on its frame and axles. It's like a turtle being supported by a rock under its belly. It can't reach down far enough with its legs to get any traction. Your vehicle must be pulled off, or preferably lifted off and slid onto higher ground.

Equipment

You need a jack for lifting, and two kinds of pulling equipment: 1) a mechanical pulling device, such as a winch or a hand-operated come-along, and 2) a nylon strap or length of cable for being pulled out by another truck. You need both of these because you may not be able to use one or the other and must have some means of pulling when lifting won't work. You should also bring along the emergency equipment listed in chapter 4.

When using a winch and snatch block, attach the end of the winch cable to the winch mount with a choker chain. Attach the snatch block to the vehicle being pulled with another chain. This arrangement nearly doubles the pull of the winch

There are four personality types in stuck situations, each with their own approach to getting out of a stuck situation, and each with their own favorite method. These four kinds are the muscle-man, the mole, the "Leonardo da Vinci" type, and the construction worker. Watch how different people act in a stuck situation and you'll instantly see what I mean.

The first kind, the muscle-man, is characterized by an obsession with power. Whatever the stuck situation, he wants to hook up a cable or nylon strap and yank the guy out. He always drives a big powerful pickup truck. He usually doesn't care if he rips off a leaf spring shackle, bends a bumper, or breaks your cable, chain, or

Two big pickups with Gumbo Monster Mudders couldn't pull out the stuck Chevy

nylon strap by pulling too hard. He loves to hook it up, gun it, and yank 'em out. He can often be seen pulling the frame out from under the body of a Toyota mini-pickup stuck in the mud and saying, "Well, I got ya out!"

The second kind is the mole. He loves to dig in the dirt. As soon as he discovers someone who's stuck he jumps out of his truck, shovel in hand, and proceeds without saying a word, to dig around, next to, behind and in front of all four tires, usually high-centering the vehicle in the process. His favorite line is, "Maybe we need to dig a little more!" You should restrain this person whenever possible. He often does more harm than good.

The third kind is the Leonardo da Vinci type. Call him Leonardo for short. He'll come up to the situation and proceed to theorize on the angles, pulleys, and direction of pull needed to get the stuck vehicle free, using, of course, the most efficient means of force. He can be found walking around the stuck vehicle, looking at the situation from all four sides, plotting the location of trees, boulders, and possible angles of approach for the pulling vehicle, all the while making complex mental calculations on how to get you out. He's always disappointed in the equipment on hand; it isn't enough for his theory to work. After a while he realizes this and says: "If only we had some more snatch blocks and cable!"

The fourth type is the construction worker. His procedure is to whip out a couple of boards and shove them under the wheels, usually getting into an argument with the mole, who wants some room for digging. They sometimes compromise. The mole builds his trench, then the construction worker lays a few boards around the wheels. After a while the construction worker will yell out, "We need some more boards!"

What's humorous about these people and their methods is not that they're doing the wrong thing, but that they just take their method to an extreme and think that

Finally, a Warn winch with an 8,000 lb. pull snatched up to 16,000 lb. got him out of the mudhole. Note how the hood is up to protect the driver and windshield in case the cable breaks

it's the right solution all the time. Actually, the right solution will usually be a combination of all of these, adapted to the situation at hand.

Stuck in Mud

This is a very common situation in the Midwest, especially since most four wheelers don't consider a trail to be a challenge unless it's good and muddy.

When you're mostly sunk, that is, you have mud up to your rocker panels and past your hubs, the easiest way to get out is to be pulled out. If the truck pulling you out has a winch on it, make sure it is straight ahead of yours, or as nearly straight ahead as possible. A winch pulls most effectively in a straight line, and will pull you toward it no matter what the angle is. In other words, if the vehicle pulling

When set up as a come-along, as shown, the versatile HI-LIFT jack will pull 5,000 lb. dead weight about 40 inches. It's not as convenient as an electric winch, but will get the job done if nothing else is available

When using a come-along, make sure the cable pulls the truck straight out. Then crank it as shown for slow but sure progress

you out is to your right about 50 feet, it will pull your truck toward it instead of pulling it straight out. It will have much more resistance to overcome from the mud around your truck if it is not pulling the wheels straight out. If this is the only possible angle, turn your front wheels in the direction of the pull. You can use a snatch block to straighten out the line if there is a tree directly in front of you. This will make pulling easier. If the pulling truck is almost at your side, it will capsize your truck rather than pull it out.

A very quick way to get somebody out of this situation is to have a truck pull them out. The truck doing the pulling has to be on less muddy ground so it can get good enough traction. A nylon strap is the best pulling line, cable is next, and chain a poor third. As I stated before, chain breaks easiest of the three.

Never attach your strap or chain to the bumper. This one was bent out by a nylon strap. The strap is now looped around the front end guard and onto the tow hook

If you have a winch on your own truck, then you should find a tree in front of the truck and tie your winch line to it by wrapping the cable around the tree trunk a couple of times and attaching it with the hook. The easiest way to attach a winch line to a tree and protect the bark is with a Paul Bunyan Tree Trunk Protector. It works great.

If none of these possibilities exist, you can use your jack as a come-along. It will pull 5,000 lb. laterally, although it will lift 7,000 lb. straight up. There is a $5/16$-inch shear bolt that will break if the load exceeds 5,000 lb. If this breaks, you can still get some more pull by using a screwdriver in its place. Be advised though, that putting this extra strain on the jack nullifies the warranty, and may break the jack causing some whiplash with a cable. You can double the pull of the jack by using a cable and a snatch block, but you won't get more than about 1¾ feet of pull this way. It might be better than nothing in an emergency.

If you're out in the boonies and have tried all of these things and still can't get out, your last chance is to use your HI-LIFT jack and lift yourself out. To do this you must first use some tree branches to build a platform for the jack to rest on. A small wood cutting saw will be helpful. Use long branches, as thick as you can find. When you start to put some load on the jack it will push the branches into the mud. Lift the jack off the branches and pile more on, etc., until the platform holds. While you lift the end of the truck, shove some more tree branches under the wheels. Doing this on all four wheels will get you out of the stuck situation, but you still may have some more mud to go through. If you don't think you can make it through the rest of the mud without getting stuck again, then cut some more branches and lay them crosswise in front of the truck. In effect you will be building your own corduroy road.

If this sounds like hours of hard work, you're right. You must realize, though, that it will work if done correctly, and it will get you out eventually. You can always walk away from your vehicle and hitchhike to a phone, but I wouldn't leave it alone longer than overnight. I've known vehicles to be stripped of tires, engine parts, and accessories when left alone too long. If you're in a rural area and can't get any help, you can always ask a farmer to pull you out with his tractor. This is a surefire way to get out and a few bucks will persuade him to go along with you back to your truck.

High-Centered

When most guys get high-centered they just ask their buddy in the pickup truck to pull them out. But before you get yanked out, look underneath the truck and see if there are any big rocks or tree branches in the way. That big rock may be what stopped you in the first place. If you're pulled off violently with a big truck, chances are that you will damage your differential or axle housing.

The safest way to get your truck out when high-centered is to lift it off. Using your jack, you can do this in two ways. One is to lift the rear up so the wheels clear the level ground. Then with a shovel or your hands, fill in under the wheels with sand, gravel, or dry dirt. Do this on both the front and the rear wheels. When you're done, you'll be able to drive away since your wheels will now be on the ground.

The other way is to lift the end of the truck, then push it off the jack sideways so the wheels fall on higher ground. This works well if your wheels fell into somebody else's tire ruts on a trail. Do the same with the front end and you can drive away.

While approaching the top of a sand dune, this Scout dug in and became high-centered, hung up on the frame

High-centered in sand. The only way to get out of this stuff is to lift both ends with your HI-LIFT jack and fill in under the tires, so that the frame will clear the sand

Steep Ditch

Once I drove onto a rocky beach in northern Minnesota on the shore of Lake Superior. There was a sharp drop down to the beach where the waves had reached their high mark. Going down onto the beach was easy, but getting up was impossible. The wall was too steep, and while I rolled down with the help of gravity, the H78 x 15 tires I had at the time couldn't climb back up. For all practical purposes, I was trapped. I didn't check the situation before driving into it, as I should have.

To back up this steep embankment, I used two boards. Getting down was easy, getting up was impossible. The other alternative would have been to dig into the embankment a little, smooth it down, and winch up. I used the boards because they were lying on the beach

I got out by leveling the crest of the rocks as much as I could with a shovel, and using two boards I found down the beach (they were washed up on the shore) as a ramp, I was able to back up the steep incline. Now, of course, with the wisdom of hindsight, I watch out for this kind of thing.

You'll be in a similar situation if you find yourself nose down in a ditch. You can't use a winch to pull yourself out (unless you have the Warn winch with the reversing attachment). What you can do is lift up the front end with your jack and fill in under the tires. You should be able to back out. Of course it would be easy if someone could pull you out from behind, but these things have a way of happening when you don't expect them.

You could also put a couple of boards under the front tires or in front of them to help you get out and over the top. This will work providing the ditch wall isn't too high and you had the foresight to bring along two boards.

Safety Tips

The force you're dealing with when you use your jack or winch is measured in thousands of pounds. When something slips or breaks, it can create a very dangerous situation. There are a few safety precautions you can take when using this equipment that will make your four wheeling more enjoyable.

When handling cable, wear leather work gloves so the broken strands on the cable won't stab into your hands. This happens particularly with cable that's five or more years old. Stay away from the winch line once it starts to tighten. When it does tighten, make sure you're well out of the way. If it's going to slip off the vehicle you're pulling, it will do it now. You can protect yourself somewhat by draping a blanket or a piece of carpeting on the end of the cable nearest you. If the cable breaks or slips off and snaps back, the carpet will lessen the impact. You can raise your hood to protect your windshield from a flying grab hook. Cable will usually fall straight to the ground when it breaks, but it can lash back and cut your arm.

Don't ever use your winch for anything but pulling objects. If you lift a heavy weight with it, such as an engine, don't ever stand under what you're lifting. Use the proper method of attaching it to a truck, which is with a choker chain or nylon strap. You can attach the grab hook directly onto a tow hook, but don't try to fit it onto a trailer ball; it won't work. Don't attach the hook by catching it on something like the leaves of a leaf spring and pulling sideways with it. The hook is made to pull in a straight line, not at angles.

Don't try funny stuff with your winch, such as pulling your truck up a tree or scaling a vertical cliff. The winch has tremendous power and reliability, but not enough to stake your life on.

Don't snatch your winch line more than once. While a snatch block will double the winch's pulling power, two snatch blocks will not quadruple it. You begin to have strange cable stretching problems and won't benefit by trying this. Limit your snatching to one snatch block for doubling pulling power, and one for changing direction, if necessary.

Always hold the cable taut when letting it unreel. The cable on the drum is under tension and will unwind and get snarled if it loosens up

Whenever you use the winch, stop and figure out what would happen if the line broke. Would it snap back and hit you in the face? Is there someone else standing in the way? Everyone wants to watch a winch at work, but it's your responsibility as the winch owner to keep people from getting hurt.

A HI-LIFT jack can also be dangerous. The main danger is that the jack will slip

When two wheels dig in or the truck is high-centered, a HI-LIFT jack can lift you out. A piece of plywood was used to keep the jack from denting the front of the truck, but the jack pushed itself into the mud instead of lifting the truck. You need a good platform of heavy planks and sometimes a bed of tree branches to support the jack

Deflate your tires when running on soft sand and mud *before* you hit the soft stuff. Let out air until the tires bulge slightly at the bottom. An air pressure gauge will measure the pressure accurately. 20psi is good for most uses, really soft stuff may require 14–12 psi. Make sure your tires and wheels are made for this low pressure before you try it on the trail

out from under its load. Have a good piece of plywood bolted under the jack or have it on a very level surface. The slightest angle can cause it to slip. If it does, it will move sideways and knock your brains out if you're in the way. Or it could slip from the bottom and break your leg. Always keep a hand on top of the jack to steady it and keep your feet clear from the sides. Make sure bystanders are not in the way. Never use the jack on ice or slippery rocks.

Come-alongs require some safety precautions too. The difficult thing to do with a come-along is to reverse the pull, or take the tension off it. It has a release lever, but you must crank the lever halfway to free it, and your fingers could get caught under the dog (the catch that holds the drum). If you have a come-along, practice releasing it and lowering loads before you put a two ton truck on it. All the winch cable safety rules apply to the come-along cable, and the methods of attaching it to vehicles are the same.

Follow the winch manual's instruction on how much cable to leave on the winch drum for safety (usually one layer as a safety factor). You can make it easy to know when you've come to the end of the line by spray-painting the last few feet with an orange or yellow dayglo paint. Then you can tell at a glance when you shouldn't let out any more cable.

6

Army Surplus Jeeps,
Land Rovers, and
Postal Service Jeeps

I've never met a four wheeler who doesn't want to constantly improve his truck. Maybe he wants a bigger set of tires, or flashier wheels, or a more powerful CB. Most likely he wants all of these. Eventually he wants to get a new and bigger or better truck. Off roading is a series of challenges, and there's no better way to meet the challenges than to get better equipment and improve your skills in using it.

Everybody has their own idea of the ultimate four wheeler, the truck that will go anywhere and not get stuck, that would last practically forever, impervious to the demons of rust and corrosion. Two vehicles have arisen in the collective off roaders' mind as fulfilling this wish; the army surplus Jeep and the Land Rover.

Just as people like to believe in the fountain of youth or the legendary treasure of the Sierre Madre, they have wanted to believe in a perfectly durable vehicle for off roading. And just like these other myths, information about the army surplus Jeep and the Land Rover has been clouded in hearsay and superstition. The confusion about the Jeep has been about how to get one. This is centered on the myth of getting 100 buyers together to pay $52.00 each for a Jeep packed in a crate in grease. Since the Jeeps supposedly are only sold in quantity, you would have to get a large number of people together in order to buy them.

As for the Land Rover, the issue is why the Rover is no longer exported to the U.S. A few guys still own them, and keep the sturdy machines going. It's not unusual to see Rovers 25 years old rolling the streets. Now that four wheeling is so popular, it would seem that British Leyland would want to help their sales by making the Land Rovers readily available to American buyers. But they have not. In fact, British Leyland discontinued their Land Rover marketing program in North America entirely several years ago. Why?

THE MYTH OF THE $52.00 ARMY SURPLUS JEEP*

Deep in the heart of every red-blooded American boy there lies, along with the dreams of being a sports hero and taking out a nice blonde, the fantasy of owning an

---

* Material in this section used by permission of the publisher of *Pickup, Van, and 4WD*

army Jeep. Army Jeep! The very words elicit feelings of awe, wonderment, and longing. Tough as nails, agile as a mountain goat, and as dependable as the sun rising in the morning, the army Jeep has been the subject of many stories.

Stories about army Jeeps fall into two categories. One category is the first hand experience story of the ex-GI who drove one in World War II, Korea, or Nam. "Yeah, they'll go through flooded creeks like nothin'," they tell us, "climb steep hills ya can hardly walk up. We beat the hell out of 'em and they came back asking for more."

The second category of Jeep story is the kind that circulates among high school students and young people looking for a cheap 4WD vehicle. This story goes like this: "Oh sure, I know where you can buy a Jeep. There's a warehouse in Peoria, IL., that stocks army vehicles. They've got tanks, Jeeps, half-tracks, you name it. The only catch is you have to buy a hundred or so before they'll sell one to you. They're packed in creosote grease in wooden crates, and you don't get a battery or tires. Otherwise you get all the engine parts, everything."

Then they go on to tell you how a guy in Minnesota or Pennsylvania got one this way. And the cost? A terrific $52! Imagine that! You could pay $7,000 for a new AMC Jeep and the army Jeeps are built tougher! I wish I knew a hundred guys who wanted one so I could get one!

The odd thing about this $52 Jeep story, though, is that I've never met anyone who actually bought one this way. Sure there are stories floating around. But if you press these for names and addresses, they don't know. Living in the city of Chicago all my life, I've never even seen one. You'd think that with the popularity of army Jeeps and 4WD vehicles these days, *somebody* would have assembled a hundred people to buy them. Nobody has.

Like other people, I thought the army Jeep would be the perfect answer to my 4WD dreams. It would be cheap, last a long time, and go anywhere I would want to go with a four wheeler. Think of the fun I would have in the summer driving around with the top off! Somehow, I had to get one.

I started to investigate how to get one, and turned to *The (Updated) Last Whole Earth Catalog* which always seems to have an address for anything I want. I found their section on how to buy U.S. government surplus (p. 139) and followed the directions to write to the Defense Property Disposal Service. After waiting the usual three months, I received notice of a sale taking place out of Camp McCoy near Tomah, Wisconsin. Only 250 miles away, this was as close as I could hope to get to army surplus vehicles.

All kinds of junk was listed in the catalog. Everything from a tank transmission to aluminum fuel tanks for jets. Scattered among the listings were fair and good condition Power Wagons, but I didn't want to go up to a pickup size. Luckily, a few International Harvester Scouts were on sale. A few were in fair condition and one was in "good" condition. The Scout in good condition seemed a good prospect, since Sears has a Jeep and Scout catalog, and International Harvester dealers are scattered all over the country with their headquarters near my home in Chicago. Spare parts and repairs were my concern, and an old army Jeep didn't seem a good prospect for readily available parts. I set out for Tomah to visit the Scouts before the sale, while they were on inspection. This way I could determine exactly what condition the Scout was in and whether all the repairs necessary would be worth the trouble.

With the help of my uncle, Jim Mattes, I went to the inspection the day before the sale. Looking the engine and body over, I found that the body was in excellent condition except for a large dent on the right front fender. The body was remarkably free from rust for a 1966 vehicle, and the engine was incredibly clean. The oil on the dipstick was as clean as if it just came from the can. The Scout had 53,000 miles on it, much less than the nearest one with 88,000 miles, although the other Scout had a body free of dents. I learned later that the Scouts were built for the navy, and so were heavily galvanized and/or zinc plated in spots. So effective is the zinc plating on the body that no rust has formed on a spot on the rear quarter panel where bare metal is exposed. And this is after the salt of four Chicago winters. Needless to say, I never have to worry about junking the Scout because of rust problems.

The next day I went to the sale prepared to bid as high as $1,500.00 for the Scout. When it was on the block, about 10 people bid on it, and all dropped out at a bid of $850 except one. This person kept bidding me higher until I reached $1,200, when he dropped out and I bought the Scout. There was one Jeep in excellent condition, a 1954 Kaiser, complete with a perfect canvas top. It sold for $1,350, a lot more than the fabled fifty-two bucks. Everyone not familiar with the surplus market, including me, was surprised at the high price. As you'll see in the next section on how to buy surplus vehicles, this is a typical price for a Jeep in good condition.

After I towed my Scout home and gave it a tuneup, which was all it needed to run, I found that the battery was almost shot. The valve cover gasket also leaked, but that was easily and cheaply repaired.

Friends of mine and people I ran into would ask if I bought the Scout in a crate for $52, as they'd heard. This aroused my curiosity again to see if the cheap Jeep was really existent. I wrote a letter to the Defense Supply Agency, the main agency that handles the surplus program, and asked if they sold Jeeps packed in wooden crates in grease. Jacalyn Gerard of the Public Affairs Office replied that the so-called cheap Jeeps never existed, that the army does not sell Jeeps packed in grease in wooden crates, and since the inception of the surplus program in 1962 never has. All of the Jeeps made for the army are made on contract by Ford, AMC Jeep, and other auto manufacturers. They are assembled on regular automotive assembly lines. They are not assembled by the army after delivery in a wooden crate. And if you think about it the wooden crate setup doesn't make sense. Why would the Army ship wooden crates overseas to Vietnam and have them assembled there? They would need a huge automotive plant and skilled workers. No other manufacturer ships vehicles in crates, they ship the whole thing. You've seen photos of Jeeps and tanks being unloaded off cargo ships complete. Even the biggest earth moving machinery is moved completely assembled. And since the army only orders Jeeps on contract to fill expected needs, there is never any surplus of unneeded vehicles. The Arms Appropriations Committee would just love to hear that the army is ordering equipment it doesn't need and dumping it under cost to the public. Right now the army pays almost $3,000 for a Jeep. It's a bargain by consumer standards, but since they order several hundred at a time this is the price they can get.

The $52 Jeep rumor is actually a widespread fraud scheme that has plagued the legitimate sales program of the DPDS since its inception in 1962. The classic pattern of the fraud is this. Some con artists would get high school middlemen to tell their friends that they heard of someone who could get them an inexpensive army surplus Jeep, if only a hundred people could each deposit $50. The balance of another $100 would be paid later upon receipt of the Jeep. The high school kids didn't know it was a fraud, and told their friends about it so they could get one for themselves. After the full price or a down payment was collected, the money would go to the con man who would promise delivery soon from West Germany, Peoria, Illinois, Lansing, Michigan, or whatever suited the story. On the day the Jeeps were supposed to arrive nothing happened. The con men were long gone with the money, ready to try the scheme on a new group of unwitting Jeep enthusiasts.

In January, 1974 there were some convictions for fraud in the Madison-Milwaukee area of Wisconsin involving the Jeep fraud. The December 24, 1975 edition of the Atlanta Journal reported that people were told that they could get a vintage Jeep from Europe if they paid $100 in advance. When asked how the fraud occurred Dick Jones, Public Affairs Officer of the DPDS told the *Atlanta Journal* that ". . . people will send the $100, arrive at a pasture somewhere, frequently on a Saturday morning when they can't stop their checks. All they find there are the usual things you find in a pasture—like bull . . ." The Jeep scheme popped up again in the Midwest in the spring of 1977. The *Chicago Sun-Times* stated that Illinois Attorney General William J. Scott is investigating Jeep scheme rumors in the state, attempting to locate their source. In this version of the Jeep fraud potential buyers were asked their names and social security numbers, as well as $125 for a non-existent Jeep. Disclosure of a social security number could lead to theft and the release of other confidential information when used by computer fraud operators,

Army surplus Jeeps lined up for sale in the property disposal yard of an army post. The Jeeps sold by the army are the most beaten vehicles, and often aren't worth the bother to rebuild

the March 3 article warned. So it seems that the computer age has hit the cheap Jeep scheme.

The myth of buying an army surplus Jeep cheaply persists, because people want to believe that there is an alternative to the expensive consumer-oriented Detroit vehicle, just as Turner said that Americans needed the myth of the wild open West as a place where they could go and live in freedom.

MILITARY SURPLUS BUYING GUIDE

Don't hang up your dreams. You can buy a surplus Jeep, just as I bought my surplus Scout. To do so you must go through the proper procedures, of course, but with a little letter writing, waiting, and legwork it can be done. You can end up with a very nice little army Jeep, the real McCoy. For those who want to go this route I've compiled the following surplus buying guide, the most complete one of its kind. It gives the real story of how to buy a Jeep with no phony leads about how you can get one for fifty bucks. You'll find all the information and buying tips you need to buy a 4WD, be it a Scout, pickup, or Jeep, made for the military.

What Does "Surplus" Mean?

Most people think that surplus means extra in the sense that if you have too much of something, what's left over is surplus. This is actually the correct meaning of the word, and it accurately described the situation of the Defense Supply Agency at the end of World War II. The United States had gone into full war production in all its industries, uncertain of how long the war would last. As a result, surpluses of all military materiel existed at the end of the war. You could buy almost anything you wanted, from military forks and spoons to merchant marine ships. As a matter of fact, it was through purchasing ships cheaply at the end of World War II that many of the Greek ship magnates became wealthy.

The price of these items barely covered the paperwork involved in selling them, and this is where the myth of buying a Jeep packed in grease started. Since other items were being bought brand new by the ton, it was thought that new Jeeps could be purchased the same way. I have heard that this was true. However, I have no evidence from the government or anyone else that this ever took place with Jeeps and other 4WD vehicles. This is just hearsay, and that, as you know from the $52 Jeep story, is not very reliable.

The current branch of the Defense Supply Agency that handles the sale of surplus items is called the Defense Property Disposal Service. Disposal is a good word since a great deal of the stuff they sell is junk. The purpose of this agency is to redistribute materiel from one fort or region to another, thus saving on the cost of new items and cutting down on waste.

For example, if one fort had more Jeeps than it needed, it would be wasteful to keep them sitting there unused. They might be needed at another fort 800 miles away. However, the government cannot afford to have its men delivering goods from one fort to another. That is not a military function. They must pay contractors from private industry to haul goods from one area to another. This is very expensive, as you might imagine. So, using their heads, the people at the Defense Supply Agency, the huge agency responsible for providing the branches of the military with their equipment, instituted the surplus sales program to pay for the shifting around of excess military goods.

The way it works is this. The DPDS sells old military items to the public. The money it gets is all profit, since the goods were paid for years ago. This money goes for paying for the removal and delivery of other military goods from one part of the country, or the world, to another. The DPDS gets so much money from the sales of surplus goods that it not only pays for the DPDS program, but is able to have something left over for the U.S. Treasury.

The system is a very good way to save tax dollars by selling old equipment, thereby disposing of it, and paying for the delivery of good equipment to areas where it's needed. The military kills three birds with one stone: It 1) gets rid of old equipment no longer useable, 2) pays for the movement of goods from areas of excess to areas of need, and 3) makes some extra money for the treasury. The military is to be commended for this efficient and fruitful system of saving the taxpayer's money.

What kind of items are sold as surplus? Well, the military rarely sells items that are in excellent condition. If they sell something, it's because there's no possible way to use it. Here's the government's official definition of surplus as defined by the agency that runs the surplus program, the Defense Property Disposal Service. Their definition of surplus as it appears in the pamphlet entitled "How to Buy Surplus Personal Property From the Department of Defense" is this:

"Property is declared surplus when it 1) becomes excess to military requirements because of changes in defense needs or unsuitable because of wear and tear or obsolescence, and 2) cannot be used by any other Federal Government activity."

So when you buy a surplus item you're buying something that can't be used any more by the government, that it won't bother to repair, and that it can't even *give* away to another branch of the government. If it doesn't sound like the stuff you're going to get is in very good condition, then your interpretation is correct. Take a look at the Jeeps in the photos, they are in typical surplus shape. The thing to think about with surplus goods is that they're built to such rugged standards that even in sorry shape they can still be rebuilt to last for many more years.

Methods of Selling Surplus Items

The next thing you should know about surplus vehicles is how they're sold. The two main types of sales are the sealed bid and the auction. Note that the government does not put price tags on their vehicles and set them out in a used-car lot for sale. If you want to buy a surplus unit you have to bid against others. There's no other way.

The first kind, the sealed bid sale, is run like this. The prospective bidders are mailed an "Invitation for Bid," (IFB) which is a catalog describing the vehicles that are up for sale, the inspection times, sale sites, etc. The catalog usually describes sales in several dozen different locations, so you have a large area to choose from.

You must mail in a sealed bid on a specific numbered item by 8:00 AM the day of the sale. The bids are opened and the highest bidder for any given item is awarded the item. The lower bidders are out of luck. The shortcoming of this kind of sale for you is that you have no way of knowing how high everyone is going to bid, especially if you're new to the game. The price list at the end of this buying guide will help you out in this area.

The second kind of sale, the auction, gets rid of this blind buying risk. With this kind of sale you are told on the IFB where the auction is being held. You must appear in person or be present through an authorized representative to get your bid in. Then you can see what the other bidders are bidding and see how high you'll have to go to get what you want. As you might guess, vehicles usually go for higher prices at the live auctions because the bidding is more competitive. Also, the government tries to get the most for their vehicles at these sales and advertises them in local newspapers. Consequently, 10 or 20 people might want the same Jeep you want. You could get lucky and have no one else bidding on the item. In this case you'll only have to pay the token starting bid of $2.50 or so. Don't count on it, though, this rarely happens with vehicles.

Principal Conditions of Sale

The last bit of official information you need to know is how to become a bidder and receive IFBs. Please note that this information, along with the other official information in this buying guide, is based on the pamphlet "How to Buy Surplus Personal Property From the Department of Defense," compiled and published by the DPDS.

The bidder requirements are very simple. You must be over 18 years of age, and a citizen of the United States. You must NOT be a member of the armed forces or involved in the DPDS sales program; or be a member of a family with someone in these agencies.

The descriptions of the property being sold in the catalogs are guaranteed to be accurate. However, this guarantee does not apply to "the condition of the property or its fitness for any purpose," which doesn't make the guarantee worth much. In short, you're stuck with what you buy. There are no 30-day used-car warranties, return policies, or any of those other protective consumer niceties. The government has no responsibilities to you whatsoever after you buy the vehicle. When the government gets rid of something, that is the last they want to see of it.

Don't misinterpret this. The government is not a fast talking used-car salesman. They are not interested in ripping you off. They strongly suggest that you thoroughly examine the items, in this case vehicles, that you intend to buy before you bid on them. This is the purpose of the inspection time offered at every sale. Their descriptions of the vehicles and their faults including missing or damaged parts, rusted out areas, etc. are very accurate and the result of hard work. You will not be misled, tricked, or pressured into buying anything. Remember the government simply wants to get rid of something, not make a big buck on it. If they sell a pickup for $1,500 or $1.50 it doesn't matter to them as long as they get rid of it. You will see this reflected in the passivity of the people involved in the sales program. If you want to buy, fine, if not, that's okay. They could care less either way.

Included in the Invitation for Bid will be the bid deposit requirement. Almost always this is 20 percent, although occasionally no bid deposit will be required.

Then again a higher bid deposit or the full price may be demanded at the sale. The IFB will have the exact rules for the sale you're concerned with. There are no definite rules governing how the deposits are handled, and the government can do whatever they like.

The bid deposit must be in cash, money order, or a cashier's check. No personal checks are accepted for obvious reasons. You are then given 30 days to pay the remainder of the bid and remove the item at your own expense. The military people will give you some assistance in removing the vehicles, and generally try to be as helpful as they can, to break the monotony of their routine if nothing else.

You must arrange the financing on your own if you do not have the full amount in cash. The government will not bother to help with this. You can take out a loan from a bank and bring a certified check to the sales office when you pick up your purchase. If you fail to pay the government within 30 days they will not just keep your deposit and forget about it. The bid is a binding legal contract and they will hold you to it. The auctioneers at the sale I was at assured us that they have a staff of lawyers who do nothing but bring in the money owed to the government. So be wise and arrange for financing before you go to the sale and commit yourself to purchasing a vehicle.

Getting on the Bidder's List

To get the wheels rolling you must first get on the bidder's list. This will put you on the mailing list for the sale catalogs. If you meet the basic requirements I listed earlier all you have to do is write to: DoD Surplus Sales, P.O. Box 1370, Battle Creek, MI 49016, and ask for a bidder's application.

Four to six weeks later you will receive three things: 1) a pamphlet called, "How

You'd best forfeit your dreams of the cheap Jeep. The condition of this Jeep is typical, with a price tag of $400

to Buy Surplus Personal Property From the Department of Defense," 2) a form with the bidder's application printed on it, and 3) a booklet called "Classes of Surplus Personal Property," which lists all the classes of surplus property available from the government. A class is simply a type of item. For example, classes include electronics, locomotives, tugs, plumbing fixtures and accessories, etc. Everything you can imagine including kitchen grease is listed here. You can buy anything you want from the government as surplus, and it is a good resource for starting out a small business if you happen to need something they have and can't afford to buy it new. For example, I was at a sale where some gas clothes dryers were sold for 27 cents each (in working order) because only one person wanted them. This person could start a laundromat or sell the dryers to a dormitory. Another bidder bought some old aluminum fuel tanks and was going to make pontoon boats out of them. The excursion boats at the Wisconsin Dells tourist area are old landing craft, the amphibious type. Office equipment and furniture are also some of the goodies available for a song. Back to the vehicles.

Since you want a four wheeler, you would circle number 2320C on the application since this class covers "Jeeps and all 4WD vehicles of less than one ton capacity." Then you circle the state you live in and other nearby areas where you would like to visit sales. Don't circle any states that you would definitely not be able to visit on a weekday. This only increases the mailing costs of the program.

Two to four weeks after you return the form you will receive a booklet entitled "Sale by Reference." This describes the terms and conditions of the sale of surplus items. It's written in legal language and is difficult to understand. Read it, but it contains the same information I've given you here.

You should start receiving sales catalogs six to eight weeks after you send in the bidder's application, or from two to three months after you started the whole process. The major part of participating in the surplus program is waiting. If you haven't got the patience to get this far, you may as well forget the whole thing. You'll only have to wait longer to find the vehicle you want in a sale close by.

Choosing a Vehicle

You've waited five months for the Jeep or pickup you've been looking for. How can you be sure you won't get stuck with some old piece of junk, or a fairly good looking jeep for which parts are impossible to find?

The best place to start is with the information available to you in the IFB. The IFB will describe the make and year of the vehicle, the kind of engine, transmission, and other essential components. It will also have a list of the parts that are missing or damaged. You can always count on there being more things wrong with a surplus vehicle than are listed in the IFB. Still the IFB is fairly accurate and is the best place to start.

To show you what you have to work with, here is an example of an actual IFB description of a pickup truck:

PICKUP: ¼ ton, 1968 Chevrolet Model
CS10704. Serial CS148S180013, six cyl.
gasoline engine, automatic transmission, tire size 8.15X15. Parts
detached but included: Door panel,
starter, driveshaft, fuel pump and
brakelines. Parts missing include

battery, headlights, right door glass,
carburetor, coil, distributor, oil cap,
belts, and heater. Parts damaged including frame broken. Extensive collision damage.

Outside-Used-Poor Condition
Total Cost $1498 (original cost to Defense Supply
Agency)
Est. Total Wt. 3,565 lb.

                                          1 EACH

There's not much of redeemable value to this vehicle. In general, I'd stay away from this and any other surplus vehicle in poor condition. That is, if you intend to drive it. If you're in the market for an old Jeep body, and you don't care what condition the mechanical components are in, then you can find a good one to work with in the surplus yard. It could be rebuilt providing that two conditions are met: 1) parts are available for it or can be substituted, and 2) the frame is sufficiently intact so that the engine, transmission, transfer case, suspension, and steering gear can be mounted. If the frame is paper thin or rusted out at these points (unlikely) you can forget salvaging unless you're very handy with welding and steel fabricating.

There are several ways of finding out if a military vehicle is reclaimable. You can look at the spare parts section of a large mail-order auto parts store, such as J.C. Whitney of Chicago, and see if the parts you will need can be obtained. Some dealers in military spare parts advertise in the major off-roading magazines. Get a catalog of their parts and the years and models they fit while you have the IFB in hand. The other route is not to worry about replacing the original parts and put in your own engine and transmission. This is the route many people take when re-building a surplus Jeep. You can then buy the engine you want and be sure that tune-up and engine rebuilding parts can be easily obtained.

The point is to do your homework and find out if a rebuilding job is possible before you go down to the sale and buy a Jeep that you can't do anything with. You'll just be stuck with a nice-looking surplus Jeep that would cost so much to rebuild that it's not worth it. The same holds true, believe it or not, for the older models of pickup trucks. Brand name pickups such as Ford, Dodge, and Chevy are sold by the government at sales. Some of these go back to the early fifties. It may be very difficult, if not impossible, to obtain spare parts for these. So be sure to check out the spare parts availability for that old pickup you want. Alternatively, you may be able to put in a different engine.

At the other end of the scale are the vehicles listed in good condition. These range from 20-year-old vehicles in running condition but damaged by an accident. Here's an example of a listing in an IFB for a vehicle in "good condition."

PICKUP: ½ ton, 1966 Chevrolet Model
C1404, Serial C1445A173598. Six cylinder
gasoline engine, three speed manual transmission. Outside-Used-Good Condition
Repairs Required

Total Cost $2821
Est. Total Wt. 3450 lbs.

                                          1 EACH

Buying Tips

The vehicles listed in good condition are good bets for rebuilding. A little work on engine accessories, such as rebuilding an alternator or a starter, and maybe fixing the brakes will usually get these in good running order. The IFB will list exactly what's wrong, if anything. The preceding IFB description shows that although nothing specifically is damaged or missing, repairs are needed.

Fair condition vehicles are also in general good order, but they'll need more repairs and little things to tend to before you can drive them on the street. There will be a short list of parts that are missing or damaged, and you can expect to repair a lot more. Still, fair condition vehicles are a good bet and sometimes a good buy.

Sometimes a real gem finds its way into the DPDS sale. This will be a jeep or pickup that needs little or no repair and in some instances can be driven right out of the surplus yard. My Scout was one such example. There are two ways that these gems find their way into DPDS sales. One is that something might be wrong with the vehicle that the military mechanics don't know how to fix or don't want to bother with. Say the vehicle has a persistently leaking radiator. Without the proper equipment, the mechanics can't fix it. Or say a novice mechanic takes apart a transmission and can't get it back together in working order. He'll just say it can't be fixed and let it be put up for sale. That is why you'll often find "detached but included" parts. The rest of the vehicle might be in perfect condition. Keep this in mind when you look over the vehicles in a surplus lot.

Another ploy the DPDS uses is to put a perfect condition Jeep in a sale to attract a large number of bidders. Like regular retailers, they figure that the bids on all the other items will go up, too, since a lot of people won't want to go home empty-handed. This happened at one sale I was at. If you notice a gem like this, grab it. It's worth the extra price you have to pay for it.

When you first enter a military base to look at the items on sale, be sure to ask the guard at the gate where the property disposal officer's building is. This will usually be numbered along with the other military buildings for easy identification. The disposal officer will direct you to the lot where the surplus vehicles are. While you are there, strike up a conversation with the disposal officer or his assistant and ask him how the vehicles were used, or where they came from . They may have some inside information on where they were used and how. This will give you a good indication of the general condition of the vehicles. Some vehicles are used for hard off-road maneuvering. There may be some suspension damage or even a bent frame. Others are used for air-dropping. These have an eye on each hub for attachment to the parachute. Needless to say, air-dropping does wonders for a suspension. Others have the military life of Riley, and are driven by camp messengers and officers. These are maintained well, kept well tuned, and the oil is changed frequently. These are the ones to buy. You can generally tell them apart from the others because the seats and bodies will be less beat up.

Examine the vehicles you're thinking of buying on the lot. Open the hood and look at the general condition of the engine. You can take off the air filter, see how clean it is, and look into the carburetor. It shouldn't be too dirty. Open the radiator cap and check for excessive corrosion. There may not be any antifreeze in the water at all. If so, you can expect a lot of rust in the water. Check the ground for oil and see if there is oil running down the engine. Take out the dipstick and look at how clean the oil is. Clean oil is a good sign of a well cared for engine. Take a look at the suspension, frame, and drivetrain to see that there's no permanent damage. Try to think of how difficult it would be to fix certain things that may be wrong. Would it be easy to find a windshield for a 1951 Ford Jeep? These are things that may look small in the yard but will make the difference later.

A 1967 Ford-built Jeep has obviously seen better days and will be sold as scrap. Rebuilding army jeeps usually isn't worth it

Surplus Prices

Now you know that the $52 jeep is a myth. What then, you might ask, is the price of a real surplus Jeep? To help you out in this matter I've compiled the following price list based on actual sales all over the country. This will give you an exact idea of what price you will have to pay for the surplus four wheeler of your choice.

First you should know that the government puts 4WD vehicles into three classes: 1) Jeep, utility, 2) Truck, utility, and 3) Pickup trucks.

Here are descriptions of the kind of vehicles each class includes:

1) Jeep, utility: These are the classic surplus Jeeps, made by Willys Overland, Kaiser, Jeep, AMC, and Ford.

2) Truck, utility: These are the longer wheel base four wheelers, such as the Scout and Ford Bronco.

3) Pickups refers to regular pickup-sized vehicles. The ones made for the Army include those manufactured by AMC/Jeep, Dodge, Ford, Chevrolet, and International Harvester.

Here are the going prices of each class of vehicle according to the condition listed in the IFB:

Jeep, utility:	poor condition	$80–$400
	fair condition	$400–$800
	good condition	$800–$1800
Truck, utility:	poor condition	$80–$400
	fair condition	$400–$600
	good condition	$750–$1500

Pickup truck: poor condition $160–$300
                  fair condition $300–$650
                  good condition $650–$1300

How many vehicles are available in each class? By far the largest number sold are pickups, and these are often sold in good condition. The majority sold are in fair condition. So your best bet is in the pickup class.

Utility trucks are the next most numerous. Most of these are in fair condition. About equal numbers are in good and poor condition.

Finally the smallest number sold are Jeeps, and most of these are in poor condition. A good condition Jeep is very rare, because men in the service like to drive them as much as you do. Consequently they keep them longer. It is not uncommon to see Jeeps that are 25–30 years old roving around army posts. A large percentage of these poor condition jobs are in the residue category, which means that only the body and frame are left. These would have to be completely rebuilt from the ground up. If you want to rebuild your own Jeep, this is the job for you. A residue Jeep also goes for the cheapest price, as low as $80.

To give some concrete figures, there are about 25–50 good condition Jeeps sold in the U.S. in a year. There are about 50–100 good condition utility trucks sold in a year, and about 500 pickups sold in the good condition category in any given year. That's why Jeeps are so high. They're in high demand and there are so few of them.

The ratio of poor and fair condition vehicles to good condition vehicles is about seven to one. But these ratios are distributed on a national basis, not within any given sale. One sale had almost every pickup offered listed in good condition, while most sales only list poor and fair condition trucks. So luck has to be on your side.

One note on these figures. They are never cut and dry. Your area may offer a great number of only a certain kind of unit. Then again they may decide to offer a large number of good condition vehicles to get rid of them. The market is about as predictable as the weather.

As for the prices, they're jacked up to the highest amount you would have to pay, not the lowest. Most often you would have to pay about two-thirds of the prices I have listed here. Remember that these prices are based on actual sales and are very accurate nationwide.

Advantages Vs. Disadvantages

Now that you know what's in store for you in the surplus market, you might want to compare the advantages and disadvantages of going surplus, compared to conventional 4WD vehicles.

After following the surplus sales program for some time, rebuilding my own 1966 Scout 800, talking to others who have bought Jeeps, pickups, vans, and other vehicles, I've compiled this list of pros and cons to give you an idea of how the surplus vehicles measure up compared to regular Detroit products:

ADVANTAGES
   1) relatively low cost
   2) heavier gauge body metal, more resistant to rust and corrosion
   3) vehicles are maintained well, necessary repairs are made over the life of the unit

4) good engines and gearing for off-road use

5) good off-roading equipment which often includes custom-made belly pans, tow hooks, and locking hubs.

6) built to stringent government standards, providing great durability

7) virtually indestructible bodies and interiors

8) long life expectancy (the body will last at least 20 years)

DISADVANTAGES

1) lack of any but nominal creature comforts: no air conditioning, no radio, stiff suspension, metal interior, little or no body chrome, olive drab color

2) difficulty in obtaining vehicle, long wait for sales, very uncertain market

3) parts very difficult to obtain on some models (24 volt electrical systems are common on military vehicles)

4) repairs or major rebuilding necessary on every vehicle

5) no high horsepower engines with the exception of recent Ford Broncos that have V8 engines.

You can expand your own advantages and disadvantages list after reading this buying guide, and particularly after seeing some vehicles at a sale. Military vehicles are in a different class from normal cars and even normal four wheelers. They are built strictly for economy and function. They do not perform as well in tough off-road situations as a fully-rigged pickup from the consumer market would, but their plus side is their extreme ruggedness and durability. For most people, surplus vehicles are a curiosity, but not something they would want to own as their only means of transportation.

THE LAND ROVER STORY

There are about as many misconceptions about the Land Rover as there are about the army surplus Jeep, though there isn't any fraud involved. These misconceptions range from the origin of the Land Rover, to why it is no longer available in North America.

The Land Rover, a very practical vehicle, was born of very practical necessities.

The British Land Rover. Shown here is the Series III, the last to be sold in the U.S. (Courtesy, British Leyland Motors, U.S.)

One of the original prototype Land Rovers under development at Solihull, England in 1947. This version had a centrally located steering wheel (Courtesy, British Leyland Motors, U.S.)

By the end of World War II, Great Britain's economy had been devastated. In order to bring growth back to basic industries it was necessary that England increase its exports, thereby bringing more money and jobs into its economy. As an encouragement to auto manufacturers in England, the government decided to ration sheet metal to automakers in proportion to the value of their exports. Rover was going to lose out because all of their vehicles were luxury vehicles and very few were exported. Too few to give Rover the sheet metal it needed.

In the spring of 1947 the Managing Director of the Rover Company, S. B. Wilks, and his brother, M. C. Wilks, met on the Isle of Anglesey to resolve this problem. They decided that the only way to increase their exports would be to produce a working vehicle that would suit the needs of tough jobs all over the world. In the autumn of 1947 they tested some prototypes and after overcoming some engineering and production difficulties introduced the first Land Rover model at the Amsterdam Motor Show on April 30, 1948. It attracted immediate and surprising attention. The orders for Land Rovers began pouring in from overseas countries and the British Army started ordering them for its use in 1949. Contrary to popular belief, the Land Rover was not developed strictly for the British Army's use.

Needless to say, the Land Rover was a great success, and demand continues to exceed the production capacity of the Rover plant in Solihull, Warwickshire, England.

The importer began phasing out the Land Rover in the U.S. in 1971, making only the shorter wheelbase version available. In 1974, Land Rover exports to the U.S. stopped completely. Why did Rover cease exports to the U.S.? It was not because they couldn't meet the energy absorbing bumper and emission control demands of the U.S., as most people believe. Rover fills contracts for police and military needs in over 120 countries all over the world. The options and requirements of these orders are so varied that few Land Rovers produced are identical, and it would be no problem for the Rover engineers to meet emission control requirements.

I wrote to British Leyland Motors, Inc., in Leonia, N.J., to ask them why Land Rovers are no longer marketed in the U.S. and received this answer:

"We stopped marketing the Land-Rover in the U.S. at the end of 1974. This decision was made because we were unable to get a large enough volume to en-

The British Leyland Range Rover, shown here, might become available in the U.S. if production could be increased enough. It is a sedan style full-time four wheel drive vehicle (Courtesy, British Leyland Motors, U.S.)

Shown here is the first Production Land Rover on the left, and the Series III 88-inch wheelbase model on the right (Courtesy, British Leyland Motors, U.S.)

able us to support a proper dealer organization. In order to support a proper marketing effort in this country, a minimum number of perhaps 5,000 units would be required. Land-Rover availability never exceeded 1,500."

Rover cannot supply and sell enough Land Rovers to support a proper dealership system in the U.S. And, unfortunately, there is no hint that Land Rovers will ever return. A few diehards still travel to England and buy one at the factory. At the present exchange rate, the British pound is at its lowest value in history, making the Land Rover a real bargain. Still, parts can be extremely difficult to come by, although one or two parts houses make them available by mail. Another major hurdle is that the vehicle must be adapted to meet U.S. emission and safety regulations before it can be used in the country. The greatest loss to the serious off roader is the non-availability of the Land Rover. It is the best made off-road vehicle in the world and one of the best vehicles ever made of any type.

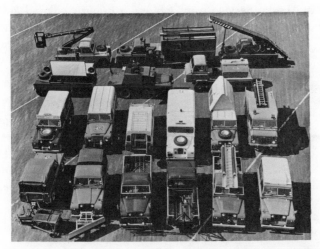

Some of the adaptations of the Land Rover, called "the world's most versatile vehicle". Shown are an ambulance, fire engine, portable audio-visual unit, compressor, armored vehicle, etc. The regular options include 27 body types and so many individual equipment options that each vehicle is uniquely adapted to the needs of the buyer (Courtesy, British Leyland Motors, U.S.)

There is one ray of hope. The Range Rover, the smaller sedan version of the Land Rover, is so popular in Europe that Rover has built a new plant for its production. If additional facilities open up for its production, the Range Rover would most likely be the model marketed here. Then those who want Land Rovers can buy them used or in England and hopefully be able to get parts more easily.

THOSE POSTAL SERVICE JEEPS

In the past few years the Postal Service has been selling its old delivery Jeeps. You may have seen some, they have a boxy body that overhangs the sides, with sliding doors on each side for quick entry and exit. On the whole they look like weaker versions of the army Jeeps.

You can find out if there are any sales in your area by contacting the manager of fleet operations, or by contacting the local Post Office Vehicle Maintenance Facility. In either case, it would be easiest to contact them by phone. They will quickly send you a mimeographed flyer announcing the sale, or give you the address so you can come in and see the vehicles for yourself. Inspection is allowed for a few days right before the sale so you have a chance to look over the merchandise before you buy.

The flyer will announce the time of the sale. The sale can be an auction or simply a sale where they have predetermined prices taped to the windshields. Unlike the army surplus Jeeps, the Postal Service Jeeps may be refurbished for the sale. Then again, they may only have the Postal Service emblem painted over and the stripes on the sides covered with spray paint. There is a great deal of variation in how each facility will handle the Jeeps put up for sale.

At one sale all the Jeeps were painted in bright colors, some two-toned, with a white top like the Postal Service paint job and a brightly colored lower half. The paint job was done with expertise, but I have to admit that they could have chosen a better set of colors. The colors ranged from purple (yecch!) to cocoa, red, light green, dark green, blue, yellow, and white. They look better than the Postal Service paint scheme, but not much better. Some of them looked pretty good, but I can't see anyone going nuts over the purple paint job.

Other visible parts of the exterior were fixed up as well. Glossy black paint was sprayed on the wheels, hubs, bumpers, and visible parts of the frame. Inside the cab nothing was done to improve the appearance of the vehicle. It looked dirty, dusty, rusty at places, and like it had never been cleaned. It wouldn't take much effort to clean it up inside and perhaps do some upholstering or painting, though. I was told that all the Jeeps at this sale were in "runnable" order. In other words, you should be able to drive them out of there.

Here is a typical description of a Jeep up for sale. (This description is for the one in the photo with the sale sign on it):

LOT # 1, 1970 Jeep, Model DJ-5A, ¼ ton, four cylinder, Auto-Trans. Mileage 28,496, Serial # 9944923, Chassis # 16738, Gold & White.

This is how Postal Service Jeeps look painted and reconditioned for sale

With stripes, bucket seats, new tires, wheels, and a tune-up you can have an inexpensive light-duty off roader. Four-wheel drive capability is hard to add on, but you may still be able to save money this way

They have four-cylinder engines, two-speed automatic transmissions, two-wheel drive, and no passenger seat. Very often they are right-hand drive. Next to the driver's seat, on the center of the floor where a stick shift would be, you have the transmission shifter. It is a metal tube mounted in a steel bracket, like an emergency brake handle on a truck. Behind it is the parking brake.

The engine looked like it was well taken care of to me, and had been recently tuned and received an oil change. I have to admit that for having 28,496 miles the engine looked pretty grimy. I'd say it was more like 128,496. I could easily imagine the Postal Service putting that many miles on it in eight years. The same went for the other vehicles, some had a mileage listing of 10,000 and others 24,000. They all fell between ten and thirty thousand, leaving me to believe that you could add a hundred thousand miles to that figure.

What did these babies go for? At the auction people paid from $900 to $2400 for them, and I was told that they go as high as $2600, depending on the audience at the auction. If this seems high to you compared to the army surplus prices, remember that all of these vehicles are in running order, with good recent paint jobs, and perfect bodies with no dents.

I've talked to some people who own them, and they say that the Jeeps are pretty beat when you get them. With a little work, nice tires and wheels, a good paint job, and some cleaning up and decorating inside, they can turn into a fairly decent vehicle.

As far as the legal requirements go, you receive a standard form so you can title the vehicle, and then license it. Payment must be made in full at the sale. I saw no provision for a bid deposit. So come prepared with the cash, cashier's check, certified check, or money order to pay for your Jeep. The Postal Service reserves the right to withdraw a vehicle from the sale if it doesn't feel that the highest bid is a fair price. This usually wouldn't happen.

The other Jeeps, those that are not reconditioned, go for lower prices. But these may not be in running order. You would have to bring a tow bar to get it home. There is no painting done except to cover up official Postal Service insignia, and no mechanical work. They're sold at a cheaper price, going from about $600 to $1500. They're not cheap, and don't expect to get a great bargain.

These vehicles are all 2WD. You could convert it to 4WD by picking up an army surplus Jeep and taking out the front axle and transfer case. You can't use the front axle from a stock AMC Jeep; they are much wider than the Postal Service version, and won't fit. Also, you'll have a problem fitting the transfer case onto the automatic transmission. I suggest you contact the makers of transmission and transfer case adapters I mentioned in the accessories chapter, give them the model and year of your Jeep, with specifications on the transmission. They will be able to give you advice and suggestions. In my opinion, the Postal Service Jeep is not a good idea for a capable four wheeler, and you'd be just as well off leaving it 2WD and taking it down trails. The extra off-road capability you would get with another driveshaft wouldn't make a great deal of difference with the engine and transmission these Jeeps have. In addition, by the time you go through all the trouble and expense of converting it, you could have had yourself a used AMC Jeep that would be an excellent off-road runner.

Quick Reference Specifications

For quick and easy reference, complete this page with the most commonly used specifications for your vehicle. The specifications can be found in Chilton, Repair & Tune-up Guides or on the tune-up decal under the hood of the vehicle.

TUNE-UP

Firing Order _____

Spark Plugs:

    Type _____

    Gap (in.) _____

Point Gap (in.) _____

Dwell Angle (°) _____

Ignition Timing (°) _____

    Vacuum (Connected/Disconnected) _____

Valve Clearance (in.)

    Intake _____   Exhaust _____

CAPACITIES

Engine Oil (qts)

    With Filter Change _____

    Without Filter Change _____

Cooling System (qts) _____

Manual Transmission (pts) _____

    Type _____

Automatic Transmission (pts) _____

    Type _____

Differential (pts) _____

    Type _____

COMMONLY FORGOTTEN PART NUMBERS

Use these spaces to record the part numbers of frequently replaced parts.

PCV VALVE	OIL FILTER	AIR FILTER
Manufacturer _____	Manufacturer _____	Manufacturer _____
Part No. _____	Part No. _____	Part No. _____

CHILTON REPAIR & TUNE-UP GUIDES FOR VANS, PICK-UPS, 4-WHEEL DRIVES AND RECREATIONAL VEHICLES

Blazer/Jimmy, 1969–1977
Covers Blazer, 1969 through 1977; Jimmy, 1970 through 1977; all 2-wheel and 4-wheel drive models.
260 pgs./illus. Part No. 6558
Paperback Code: 0-8019-6558-6
$7.95

Bronco, 1966–1977
Covers all models of the Ford Bronco, 1966 through 1977.
208 pgs./illus. Part No. 6701
Paperback Code: 0-8019-6701-5
$7.95

Chevrolet/GMC Vans, 1967–1978
All Chevrolet G-10, G-20, and G-30; All GMC G-1500, G-2500, and G-3500; both cargo vans and passenger vans; half, three-quarter, and one ton; 1967 through 1978.
228 pgs./illus. Part No. 6601
Paperback Code: 0-8019-6601-9
$7.95

Chevrolet LUV, 1972–1979
Covers all models, including 4X4, 1972 through 1979.
160 pgs./illus. Part No. 6815
Paperback Code: 0-8019-6815-8
$7.95

Chevrolet/GMC Pick-Ups, 1970–1978
Covers all Chevrolet and GMC pick-ups (2 and 4-wheel drive) up to and including ¾ ton models.
258 pgs./illus. Part No. 6700
Paperback Code: 0-8019-6700-7
$7.95

Datsun, 1961–1972
Covers Nissan Patrol, 1500-1600-2000 Sports Cars; 510, 1200, Pickups 410, 411 and 240Z, from 1961 through 1972.
244 pgs./illus. Part No. 5790
Paperback Code: 0-8019-5790-7
$7.95

Datsun Pick-Ups, 1970–1979
Covers all models 1970 through 1979.
180 pgs./illus. Part No. 6816
Paperback Code: 0-8019-6816-X
$7.95

Dodge/Plymouth Vans, 1967–1977
Covers Dodge models A-100, A-108, B-100, B-200, B-300, from 1967 through 1977; and Plymouth PB-100, PB-200, PB-300, 1974 through 1977.
216 pgs./illus. Part No. 6599
Paperback Code: 0-8019-6599-3
$7.95

Ford Courier, 1972–1978
Covers all models.
208 pgs./illus. Part No. 6723
Paperback Code: 0-8019-6723-6
$7.95

Ford Pick-Ups, 1970–1978
Covers all ½ and ¾ ton; 2 and 4-wheel drive pick-ups from 1970 through 1973.
236 pgs./illus. Part No. 6704
Paperback Code: 0-8019-6704-X
$7.95

Ford Vans, 1966–1977
Covers E-100, E-150, E-200, E-250, E-300, E-350, from 1966 through 1977.
294 pgs./illus. Part No. 6585
Paperback Code: 0-8019-6585-3
$7.95

International Scout, 1967–1973
Covers Scout 800, 800A, 800B, Scout II, from 1967 through 1973.
188 pgs./illus. Part No. 5912
Paperback Code: 0-8019-5912-8
$7.95

Jeep Universal, 1953–1979
Covers CJ-3B, CJ-5, CJ-6, and CJ-7 from 1953 through 1979.
260 pgs./illus. Part No. 6817
Paperback Code: 0-8019-6817-8
$7.95

Jeep Wagoneer, Commando, and Cherokee, 1966–1979
Covers Jeepster, Jeepster Commando, Commando, Wagoneer and Cherokee.
225 pgs./illus. Part No. 6739
Paperback Code: 0-8019-6739-2
$7.95

Mazda Pick-Ups, 1972–1975
Covers model B-1600, 1972 through 1975; Rotary Pick-ups, 1974 through 1975.
189 pgs./illus. Part No. 6274
Paperback Code: 0-8019-6274-9
$7.95

Ramcharger/Trail Duster, 1974–1975
Covers all models, 1974 and 1975.
217 pgs./illus. Part No. 6331
Paperback Code: 0-8019-6331-1
$7.95

Subaru, 1970–1978
Covers all models including 4-wheel drive station wagon from 1970 through 1978. Includes engine rebuilding section specifically designed for Subarus.
203 pgs./illus. Part No. 6693
Paperback Code: 0-8019-6693-0
$7.95

Toyota Land Cruiser, 1966–1974
Covers 1966 through 1974 Land Cruiser and Land Cruiser Station Wagon, F-Series engine.
151 pgs./illus. Part No. 6276
Paperback Code: 0-8019-6276-5
$7.95

Toyota Pick-Ups, 1970–1978
Covers all models, 1970 through 1978.
174 pgs./illus. Part No. 6692
Paperback Code: 0-8019-6692-2
$7.95

Winnebago Motor Homes, 1968–1974
Covers all Winnebago Motor Homes built on the Dodge chassis with 318, 413, or 440 cubic inch engines.
219 pgs./illus. Part No. 6014
Paperback Code: 0-8019-6014-2
$7.95

Chilton Repair & Tune-Up Guides are updated on a periodic basis. If you do not see your particular year or model listed, call or write:

Chilton Book Company
Chilton Way
Radnor, PA 19089

Attn: Automotive Advertising and Promotion Dept.